ADORNO AND HEIDEGGER

ADORNO AND HEIDEGGER

Philosophical Questions

Iain Macdonald and
Krzysztof Ziarek, Editors

STANFORD UNIVERSITY PRESS

STANFORD, CALIFORNIA

2008

Stanford University Press
Stanford, California

Assistance for the translation of Chapter 8 was
provided by the Université de Montréal.

Printed in the United States of America on acid-free, archival-quality paper

Library of Congress Cataloging-in-Publication Data

Adorno and Heidegger : philosophical questions / Iain Macdonald
    and Krzysztof Ziarek, Editors.
        p.   cm.
    Includes bibliographical references and index.
    ISBN 978-0-8047-5635-8 (cloth : alk. paper)
    ISBN 978-0-8047-5636-5 (pbk. : alk. paper)
        1. Heidegger, Martin, 1889–1976.   2. Adorno, Theodor W., 1903–1969.
I. Macdonald, Iain.   II. Ziarek, Krzysztof, 1961–
B3279.H49A33 2008
193—dc22

                                                                    2007001573

Contents

Acknowledgments

The editors would like to extend their thanks to a number of individuals and organizations for their help in making this publication possible. For their various and invaluable forms of financial support—including funding a three-day conference held at the Université de Montréal in 2004—we would first of all like to thank the Social Sciences and Humanities Research Council of Canada, the Fonds québécois de la recherche sur la société et la culture, the Canadian Centre for German and European Studies (Montréal branch), the Université de Montréal and its Département de philosophie, and the Department of Philosophy of McGill University. Additionally, we would like to thank Daniel Weinstock and Joseph Heath for their support. A number of other individuals have been of enormous help to us in a number of ways. In particular, we would like to express our gratitude to the following people (in alphabetical order): Alia Al-Saji, Suzanne Auger, Diane Bergeron, Jay Bernstein, Luce Botella, Brigitte Boulay, Frédérick Bruneault, Philip Buckley, Josée Carignan, Ian Chuprun, Karl Côté, Suzanne Dagenais, Philippe Despoix, Jocelyne Doyon, Maxime Doyon, Matthias Fritsch, Lucille Gendron, Jean Grondin, Susan-Judith Hoffmann, Dietmar Köveker, Philippe Langlois, Michel Ledoux, Claudine Lefort, Jessica Lim, R.T.M. McKnight, David Ouellette, Michael Palamarek, Claude Piché, Scott Prentice, Jamie Smith, Julien Théorêt, and Gregory Young. Special appreciation goes to Nicholas Walker, for translating Josef Früchtl's contribution, and to Philip Farah, for editorial assistance. Finally, the editors would like to thank their respective home institutions, the Université de Montréal and the State University of New York at Buffalo, for their diverse forms of support.

Abbreviations

The following standard abbreviations are in use in this volume.

GA   Heidegger, Martin. *Gesamtausgabe*. Edited by Friedrich-Wilhelm von Herrmann. Frankfurt am Main: Vittorio Klostermann, 1975ff.

GS   Adorno, Theodor W. *Gesammelte Schriften*. Edited by Rolf Tiedemann. Frankfurt am Main: Suhrkamp Verlag, 1970ff., 1997.

HUA   Husserl, Edmund. *Husserliana*. The Hague, Dordrecht, and New York: Martinus Nijhoff, Kluwer Academic Publishers, and Springer Verlag, 1950ff.

HUE   Husserl, Edmund. *Husserliana: Collected Works*. Dordrecht and New York: Kluwer Academic Publishers and Springer Verlag, 1980ff.

KSA   Nietzsche, Friedrich. *Kritische Studienausgabe*. Edited by Giorgio Colli and Mazzino Montinari. München/Berlin/New York: De Gruyter, 1980, 1988.

Contributors

Fred Dallmayr is Packey J. Dee Professor of Political Theory and teaches in the departments of philosophy and political science at the University of Notre Dame. He holds doctoral degrees from both the University of Munich and Duke University. Among his recent book publications are *Between Freiburg and Frankfurt* (Massachusetts, 1991); *The Other Heidegger* (Cornell, 1993); *Beyond Orientalism* (SUNY, 1996); *Alternative Visions* (Rowman & Littlefield, 1998); *Dialogue Among Civilizations* (Palgrave Macmillan, 2002); *Hegel: Modernity and Politics* (Rowman & Littlefield, revised ed., 2002); *Peace Talks—Who Will Listen?* (Notre Dame, 2004); and *Small Wonder: Global Power and Its Discontents* (Rowman & Littlefield, 2005).

Josef Früchtl is Professor in the Philosophy of Art and Culture Research Group at the University of Amsterdam. He has published numerous articles in the area of European philosophy and is the author of three books: *Das unverschämte Ich. Eine Heldengeschichte der Moderne* (Suhrkamp, 2004); *Ästhetische Erfahrung und moralisches Urteil. Eine Rehabilitierung* (Suhrkamp, 1996); and *Mimesis. Konstellation eines Zentralbegriffs bei Adorno* (Königshausen und Neumann, 1984). He is also the co-editor of a number of collections, including *Kunst und Demokratie. Positionen zu Beginn des 21. Jahrhunderts* (Meiner, 2003).

Matthew Grist is a research fellow with the Transcendental Philosophy and Naturalism project based at the University of Essex. His research interests center on Kant's transcendental conception of mental representation and related issues in the philosophy of mind, epistemology, and metaphysics.

Ute Guzzoni is Professor Emeritus of Philosophy at the University of Freiburg. She obtained her doctorate in 1961 with a thesis on Hegel's *Science of Logic*. Her 1969 habilitation thesis is on Aristotle's ontology. Recent monographs include *Über Natur. Zu einem anderen Naturverhältnis* (Alber, 1995); *Wohnen und Wandern* (Parerga, 1999); *Nichts. Bilder und Beispiele* (Parerga, 1999); *Sieben Stücke zu Adorno* (Alber, 2003); *Hegels Denken als Vollendung der Metaphysik. Eine Vorlesung* (Alber, 2005); *Wasser. Das Meer und die Brunnen, die Flüsse und der Regen* (Parerga, 2005).

Joanna Hodge is Professor of Philosophy at Manchester Metropolitan University. She has written *Heidegger and Ethics* (Routledge, 1995) and *Time in the Name of the Other: Reading Derrida* (forthcoming). She is currently working on the genealogy of transcendental aesthetics.

Iain Macdonald is professeur agrégé in the Department of Philosophy at the Université de Montréal and adjunct professor in the Department of Philosophy at McGill University. He has published in English and French on Hegel, Adorno, and Heidegger and is currently working on a book dealing with the Adorno-Heidegger question. His research focuses on the intersection of epistemology, metaphysics, and normativity.

Nicholas Walker has translated many essays and books in the field of continental philosophy, including writings by Heidegger, Gadamer, Adorno, and Habermas. In addition to translating the correspondence between Adorno and Walter Benjamin (Polity/Harvard, 1999), he has recently completed a translation of the correspondence between Adorno and Thomas Mann, to be published by Polity Press. He has also published articles on Hegel, Hölderlin, and Wagner.

Mario Wenning is a doctoral candidate at the New School for Social Research and the University of Frankfurt am Main. He also teaches philosophy at the New School and Seton Hall University and has published articles on narrative self-invention and Heidegger and Adorno. He is currently translating a collection of essays dealing with the Plato interpretation of the Tübingen School.

Krzysztof Ziarek is Professor of Comparative Literature at the University at Buffalo. He is the author of *Inflected Language: Toward a Hermeneutics of Nearness* (SUNY, 1994); *The Historicity of Experience: Modernity, the Avant-Garde, and the Event* (Northwestern, 2001); and *The Force of Art* (Stanford, 2004). He has also published numerous essays on Coolidge, Stein, Stevens, Heidegger, Benjamin, Irigaray, and Levinas, and co-edited a collection of essays entitled *Future Crossings: Literature Between Philosophy and Cultural Studies* (Northwestern, 2000). He is also the author of two books of poetry in Polish, *Zaimejlowane z Polski* and *Sąd dostateczny.*

Lambert Zuidervaart is Professor of Philosophy at the Institute for Christian Studies and an Associate Member of the Graduate Faculty in Philosophy at the University of Toronto. His primary research interests lie in philosophy of discourse, social philosophy, and continental philosophy, with an emphasis on German philosophy from Kant through Habermas. Zuidervaart is the author of *Social Philosophy After Adorno* (Cambridge, forthcoming), *Artistic Truth: Aesthetics, Discourse, and Imaginative Disclosure* (Cambridge, 2004), and *Adorno's Aesthetic Theory: The Redemption of Illusion* (MIT, 1991). He has co-edited three books, including *The Arts, Community and Cultural Democracy* (St. Martin's, 2000) and *The Semblance of Subjectivity: Essays in Adorno's Aesthetic Theory* (MIT, 1997).

ADORNO AND HEIDEGGER

Introduction

Iain Macdonald and Krzysztof Ziarek

In an exchange of letters dating from 1972, Max Horkheimer replied to Hermann Mörchen's request for background information on Adorno's critique of Heidegger by writing: "As I recall, Adorno's judgment related not least to Heidegger's style of thinking and expression, which was distant from ours. For that reason, it is with difficulty that I can imagine a productive debate taking place between the two schools. I cannot even give you the name of anyone today who would be competent in this regard."[1] He goes on to express polite regret that he himself is unable to take up this "highly important problem," though he says he would be interested in meeting someone who would be ready to defend the Heideggerian position in a debate. Of course, that no such debate ever took place only reflects the deeply entrenched view that Horkheimer expresses in his correspondence with Mörchen. This is the view that still prevails in many quarters today. Indeed, it is this view that informs the nearly universal "refusal of communication" that Mörchen laments in his central contribution to the literature on the Adorno-Heidegger dispute.[2]

And yet, there is more to this dispute than is obvious at first blush. For one thing, it is fairly well known that the first generation of Frankfurt School thinkers were not opposed *en bloc* to Heidegger's thought, at least not initially. Herbert Marcuse is the figure most often cited in this connection, because of his belief (in the late 1920s) that Heidegger's thought represented a necessary move toward a more concrete philosophy. Horkheimer himself seems to have held the same belief at one time; as a student of Heidegger's in the early 1920s, he too was clearly struck by Heidegger's emphasis on facticity.[3] Thus, while neither Marcuse nor Horkheimer was ever unambiguously in favor of Heidegger's approach, there was nevertheless something in his thought that fascinated them, something at once inspiring and dangerous.

Nowhere is this blend of fascination and critique more evident than in Adorno's sustained engagement with Heidegger. In 1931, Adorno, soon to become one of the leading intellectual lights of the Frankfurt School, launched a polemical attack on his philosophy;[4] Heidegger, for his part, never responded to Adorno's criticisms, claiming not to have read him. Over the decades, their respective philosophies followed quite different paths: on the one hand, Adorno strove to critique metaphysics and the distorted social relations of late capitalism; on the other hand, Heidegger concentrated on rethinking truth, history, and Being as part of an effort to turn away from metaphysics. In terms of their respective philosophical interests and especially their motivations (broadly construed: social emancipation vs. thinking an "other beginning" in the history of Being), they seem to be situated at opposite ends of the intellectual spectrum. Yet despite their differences, a preoccupation with Heidegger's thought remains in Adorno's writings and some pressing questions remain without satisfactory answers. Why should he have spent almost forty years on Heidegger if his intention were simply to dismiss him? What is it about Heidegger's approach that merits this prolonged treatment? Or, conversely, what is it in Adorno's own thought that makes the critique of Heidegger so persistent and continually pertinent?

The answer to these questions may not be the one that is most often given, namely, that it is simply Adorno's total opposition to Heidegger's philosophy that informs the polemic. Critical examination of the material leads in a rather different direction, suggesting that the terms of the critique sharpen because there are undeniable points of proximity between Adorno and Heidegger. There are certainly intersecting concerns in their critiques of technology, positivism, and the vapidity of contemporary social existence—not to mention the difficulties they each saw in developing an ethics suited to the condition of modern humanity. But such resemblances, often superficial, rest on a deeper commonality: the imperative that philosophy should serve history and experience, that it should be concerned with "relevant things."⁵ This was precisely what Heidegger's thought promised, and what initially appealed to Horkheimer, Marcuse, and Adorno himself: it set out to deal with facticity and history, with concrete existence. Could it be then that Adorno took Heidegger so severely to task because of what he saw as a broken promise? Adorno provides us with several reasons for posing the question in this way, not the least of which is the "ontological need" (*ontologische Bedürfnis*) for concrete content. As Adorno puts it, the success of Heidegger's thought "would be unintelligible if it did not meet an emphatic need, a sign of something missed, a longing that Kant's verdict regarding knowledge of the Absolute should not be the end of the matter."⁶ If the terms of Adorno's critique are so harsh, then, it is first and foremost because Adorno thinks that Heidegger recognizes this need but fails to meet it adequately, because the "treatment of relevant things relapsed into abstraction."⁷ Insofar as the need for content relapses into abstraction, it is false.⁸ So while Adorno accepts the ontological need understood as a desire for content, he ruthlessly attacks the ways in which it is betrayed by forms of thought that only purport to meet it. It is the betrayal of this need for content that largely explain both the virulence and the scope of Adorno's critique: Heidegger promises us bread, but gives us stones.⁹ Nevertheless, his critique finds its starting point in a desire for content, which they both share.

This proximity is marked in other ways in Adorno's corpus, and not always in the virulent form that we most often associate with the polemic. For both Heidegger and Adorno, philosophical experience consists in probing, provisional gestures that cut 'occasional' paths into the landscape of experience. It is in part in this way that thought attempts to do justice to the content that it works and transforms. Thus, shortly after Heidegger's *Holzwege* was published, Adorno wrote to Horkheimer saying that Heidegger was "*in favour* of occasional paths [*Holzwege*] in a way that's not very different from our own."¹⁰ Once again, it is precisely such self-avowed points of contact that need to be taken up and interpreted if we are to understand what is at stake in the Adorno-Heidegger dispute.

Much more could be said, but this short introduction is not the place to reply to the questions posed to us by the debate. Until relatively recently, however, the problem has been that few researchers have questioned the decades-long standoff between the two thinkers and their supporters, or explored the details of Adorno's polemic in order to understand why it was so sustained. This volume of essays hopes to contribute to reorienting the terms of the debate by bringing together essays that evidence an (often qualified or cautious) openness to dialogue between these two thinkers' works and their respective philosophical traditions. Thus, the aim in assembling this collection was not to dismiss as unfounded the oppositional character of the dispute. Rather, more modestly, the aim was simply to inquire into the validity of, and the real justifications for, the barriers that kept Adorno and Heidegger separate from the early 1930s on. Within the purview of this aim, we target the main areas of tension: aesthetics, ethics, epistemology, metaphysics, nature, and modernity. By choosing to focus on these topics, the contributors have been able to explore specific points of contact and conflict between the traditions of Adornian critical theory and Heideggerian thinking, while at the same time leaving room for more general reflections on how this dispute is to be understood in the history of philosophy and in terms of broader critiques of modernity.

In our view, there is much to be gained from working through and reassessing the differences that have kept these two thinkers' works quarantined from each other for more than seven decades. At this juncture, it seems more than a little outmoded to continue to keep them apart, for the reasons already mentioned and for others that come out in the essays in this volume—but also because it seems clear now just how rich this terrain is. Adorno's research in the 1930s into phenomenological method remains largely unexplored, as does Heidegger's struggle with the Hegelian-Marxian tradition that was so important to the critical theorists. Moreover, the need for renewed reflection on the framework and aims of the dispute, which we hope will open up new avenues of thought, has become even more evident with the recent publication of many previously unknown works by Heidegger. These manuscripts, especially those dating from the late 1930s and early 1940s, manifest the extent to which Heidegger, not unlike Adorno, was centrally preoccupied with rethinking the technological determination of human relations and experience in modernity and with preparing for the possibility of a decisive transformation in these determinations.[11] These texts repay careful study and help to refine certain resemblances and differences that commentators have remarked upon. They also contribute a great deal to understanding Heidegger's relation to dialectical reason. Similarly, Adorno's recently published lecture course on *Ontology and Dialectics,* the still-untranslated *Philosophical Terminology,* and other lecture courses require us to reconsider the ways in which the Adorno-Heidegger dispute has generally been characterized.[12] More specifically, much of this material prompts us to consider the parallels that exist between their respective approaches—*parallels,* that is, not necessarily or always convergences or divergences.

Building upon these parallels involves going beyond both the dismissively critical tenor of (post-) Adornian dialectics and the customary silence on the side of (post-) Heideggerian thinking. At the same time, of course, these explorations point beyond the confines of the Adorno-Heidegger debate precisely because of the pivotal role that these thinkers play in contemporary European thought. In this context, we hope that this volume will not only help advance the state of research about Adorno and Heidegger, but also highlight the significance of the debate for the direction of future reflections on the predicament of modernity.

Ethics and Authenticity: Conscience and Non-Identity in Heidegger and Adorno, with a Glance at Hegel

Iain Macdonald

Adorno's Critique of Heidegger: The Suppression of Non-Identity

In *Negative Dialectics*, Adorno makes the following possibly astonishing concession: "Heidegger gets as far as the borderline of dialectical insight into the non-identity within identity." Granted, it is a meager concession, especially since it is followed up by the usual invective:

But he does not carry over the contradiction into the concept of Being. He suppresses it. Whatever can be thought of under the concept of Being mocks the identity of a concept and the object 'meant' by it; but Heidegger treats it as identity, as pure Being itself, devoid of its otherness. He hushes up the non-identity in absolute identity like a skeleton in the family closet.[1]

The aim of this chapter is to discuss what Adorno might be aiming at when he says that Heidegger gets "as far as the borderline of dialectical insight into the non-identity within identity," and what he thinks are the principal reasons why he can go no further. Doing so will also require an assessment of Adorno's critique and the stakes of his own thought. The result, with any luck, will be insight into why the struggle between Adorno and Adorno's Heidegger is not one that can be settled by siding with either Adorno or Heidegger.

What seems obvious for starters is that the left-handed nature of the concession allows Adorno to come at Heidegger from a familiar angle: to say that he has got as far as the borderline of dialectical insight into non-identity amounts to saying that he is totally undialectical, as Adorno already says of Heidegger in his 1931 inaugural address:

If philosophical interpretation can in fact only thrive dialectically, then its first dialectical target is given by a philosophy that cultivates precisely those problems whose removal seems more urgently necessary than the addition of a new answer to so many old ones. Only an essentially undialectical philosophy, which aims at ahistorical truth, could imagine that the old problems could simply be removed by forgetting them and starting fresh from the beginning. In fact, the deception of the beginning [*der Trug des Beginnes*] is precisely that which in Heidegger's philosophy comes under criticism first of all.[2]

This passage is, for a number of reasons, key to understanding how to read Adorno on Heidegger. I will quickly mention a few points to bear in mind, simply in order to recall some of the salient features of Adorno's critique of Heidegger.

First, the charge of being undialectical needs to be understood in connection with two related charges: (1) what Adorno here calls "the deception of the beginning" and what he elsewhere calls Heidegger's archaism, his insistence on the primordiality of Being, and (2) Heidegger's alleged ahistoricality, or his indifference to historical contingency, suffering, and adversity. Heidegger, he says, commits himself to a concept of Being that in its very primordiality sacrifices the material, historical dimension of thought to an *arche* that is indeed always historical but only indeterminately so, through the formal, universal structures of Being. Thus, historicality (*Geschichtlichkeit*) is primordial, for Heidegger, whereas determinate history is merely factual. In this sense, says Adorno, Heidegger forgoes the comprehension of "*historical Being in its most historical determinateness.*"[3] And so he claims that the categories of Being elaborated by Heidegger fail to do justice to historical reality; or in other words, they do not look outward toward the "concrete inner-historical determinateness [of beings, *das Seiende*]."[4] Consequently, the problems posed by history cannot be addressed by Heidegger's ontological strategy, which restricts itself to investigating formal structures of Being.[5]

This historical objection leads to the further charge of dressing up what is basically a tautology and serving it up as philosophy. Concerning this tautological spinning in the archaic void, Adorno says that "the so-called question of Being condenses into a zero-dimensional point, into what it admits as the only legitimate [*echtbürtig*] meaning of Being. It turns into a ban on any step beyond this, and finally into any step beyond the tautology whose manifestation in Heidegger's prose is that time and again self-unconcealing Being says nothing else but 'Being.'"[6] What Adorno has in mind here is the fact that Heidegger's approach, at least in *Being and Time*, involves the interpretation of Being in terms of a being, Dasein, for whom, "in its very Being, that Being is an *issue* for it."[7] In other words, for Adorno, the way Heidegger lays Being bare involves nothing more than explaining Being in terms of Being.

Finally, by way of this tautology, we come to the question of identity. "Tautology," he says in the essay "The Idea of Natural History," "appears to me to be less a self-grounding of the mythical depths of language than a new way of covering over the old classical thesis about the identity of subject and object."[8] More explicitly, he also says that the "tautological tendency can only be clarified through the old idealist theme of identity. It [the tendency] has its origin in the subsumption of historical Being by the subjective category of historicality. The historical Being that has been subsumed by the subjective category of historicality is supposed to be identical with history. Being has to conform to the categories with which historicality stamps it."[9] According to Adorno's reading, then, *what is* is for Heidegger adequately conceivable by categorial comprehension; nothing essential falls outside the web of interpretive existentiales. There is no non-identity in Heidegger, and no impetus to dialectical movement and engagement with history; there is only the claim that Being can be understood—and in fact is always already understood, if only implicitly.

These charges regarding ahistoricality, archaism, tautological thinking, and identitarian thinking are the real cornerstones of Adorno's critique of Heidegger, and are therefore more serious than some of the other, more satirical accusations leveled against Heidegger in various places—accusations such as bureaucratism, agrarianism, arty-craftiness, and homely murmuring. The question that needs to be asked at this juncture, however, is whether Heidegger, in arriving at the borderline of the dialectical insight into the non-identity within identity, has anything at all to offer us on the subject of the non-identical; or does he rather (as Adorno would claim) fall into the camp of ahistorical, identitarian busybodies? As a starting point, though it may seem obvious to some, there is more to what Heidegger says in *Being and Time* than Adorno is letting on. However, at the end of the day the aim here is not to defend Heidegger against Adorno. Instead, I will simply try to put one aspect of Heidegger's thought into dialogue with Adorno's historical and ultimately ethical concerns.

Heidegger's Critique of Adorno: Non-Identity in the Phenomena of Conscience and Guilt

One reason for focusing on the sections of *Being and Time* on conscience and guilt is that it is in these passages that Heidegger deals with the question of Dasein's self-identity in connection with normativity and the existential basis for historical, ethical action. Interestingly, it is also a section of the book where Adorno's assault on Kierkegaardian or existential pathos might seem most germane—wrongly, but more on that in a moment. For now, suffice it to say that it is here that we find the most convincing evidence for what Adorno says is suppressed in Heidegger's thought.

In this chapter of *Being and Time,* Heidegger is seeking an "attestation" or demonstration (*Bezeugung*) of Dasein's capacity for authenticity. Ultimately, the search for this authentic Being-one's-Self will culminate in the concept of resoluteness (*Entschlossenheit*), whereby Dasein tears itself away from its lostness in the 'they' and "brings itself back to itself"[10] as authentic potentiality-for-Being. But it is only the phenomena of conscience and guilt that provide Heidegger with the means to articulate resoluteness. For this reason, it is not resoluteness as such that interests me here; to understand resoluteness we have, at any rate, to pass through conscience and guilt. Moreover, it is conscience and guilt themselves as distinctive moments of articulation between inauthentic and authentic individual Dasein that really provide us with Heidegger's ontological understanding of normativity. Thus, to be clear about what is at stake here: in this chapter of *Being and Time*, we are presented with an understanding of normativity rooted in non-identity.

Up to this point in the book, we have not as yet come across an analysis that lays out the way in which Dasein apprises itself of what it must do, of what it ought to do, nor (what will amount to the same thing) an analysis of how norm-based action is possible. Conscience as a "*primordial* phenomenon of Dasein"[11] is what, according to Heidegger, provides the key to understanding authentic potentiality-for-Being-a-Self; and it is conscience that will therefore attest Dasein's authenticity. Obviously, Heidegger does not have in mind the everyday concept of moral conscience, which he shows up as being inconsistent and derivative. He does, however, take everyday interpretations of the 'voice of conscience' into account, precisely because, through the variety of ways in which conscience is ordinarily understood (e.g., good, bad, or guilty conscience), he sees their generic possibility as rooted in a necessary structure of Dasein.

Thus Heidegger accepts that conscience "gives us 'something' to understand," that it "calls" us in a certain way, in the sense that I am interpellated by conscience and 'pushed' by it, as it were, in a certain direction, called *to* something. But these more or less usual ways of understanding the call of conscience are to be taken absolutely generally, as the necessary moments of concrete instances of conscience 'telling me something,' whereby it is unequivocal to me who the 'me' is (it is always *me*), as well as what the 'something' is, even if this 'something' is at first only the sense that things are 'out of joint.' In its generality, then, freed from everyday conceptions, conscience is an interpellation of the self that consists in a self-appraisal aimed at realizing something. Or, as Heidegger puts it, in acting on conscience I enact a "choosing to choose [*Wählen der Wahl*] a kind of Being-one's-Self,"[12] which in turn is what will define resoluteness.

However, this call of conscience, as formal as it is, is nevertheless always rooted in individual Dasein's concrete situation: "Dasein exists as a potentiality-for-Being," says Heidegger, "which has, in each case, already (*je schon*) given itself over to definite possibilities. . . . Dasein 'knows' what it is capable of, inasmuch as it has either projected itself upon possibilities of its own or has been so absorbed in the 'they' that it has let such possibilities be presented to it by the way in which the 'they' has publicly interpreted things."[13] The 'call' of conscience is therefore both a calling *away*, as it were, whereby the individual Dasein breaks away from its fascination with the hubbub of idle talk, and a calling *back* of this Dasein to itself and its essential, individual role in the determination of possibility. This call is non-vocal, but it is still a mode of discourse, by which he means only that the call of conscience is a kind of *articulation of intelligibility*. Discourse "articulates intelligibility" (*sie gliedert die Verständlichkeit*), as Heidegger puts it.[14] This is a way of saying that in the call of conscience, something takes shape for Dasein in terms of its potentiality-for-Being, or, in other words, conscience calls Dasein to understand its possibilities, and to give them substance in action—instead of simply going along with what the 'they' inclines it to do. Heidegger speaks of this aspect of the call of conscience as "the momentum of a push—of a disconcerting awakening."[15] This is still rather vague, of course, and so the coherence of Heidegger's account of conscience will depend on how he explains the particular articulation of intelligibility that constitutes the call of conscience.

But what does Heidegger mean when he says that the call of conscience, as a non-vocal mode of discourse, "articulates" intelligibility? To articulate intelligibility means laying out or interpreting (in the sense of *auslegen*) the concrete possibilities that engage Dasein at any given moment; it means making these possibilities manifest as possibilities. Heidegger goes into some detail in chapter 5 of Division I about how this is a necessary aspect of Dasein's Being-in-the-world. Here, it is enough to say that in the call of conscience Dasein engages in a specific form of this discursive articulation by apprising itself of some actual tension or conflict, such that I find myself interpellated and summoned to my ownmost potentiality-for-Being; I am summoned to my own Self.[16] Put more plainly, I am compelled to 'take stock' and act by whatever hitch or tension it is that roused me from my usual tendency of floating along with whatever everyone else is doing. Again, we are on a level of phenomenological generality that precludes specific prescriptions; all that Heidegger is pointing out is that such a self-relation, in which I find myself individuated and in tension with possibility, is absolutely necessary for us to understand moral action, as opposed to mere animal behavior. The call of conscience in its existential generality, then, "asserts nothing, gives no information about world-events, has nothing to tell."[17] It is merely the self-relation by which I become aware of a tension (a contradiction, a conflict) in the concrete *existentiell* possibilities in which I am involved.

In the call of conscience, then, Dasein calls *itself*. Adorno's accusations of tautological, identitarian thinking may seem justifiable, in view of this circular self-relation, in which Dasein seemingly reacts only to itself;

but in fact, on closer analysis, this is far from what Heidegger is claiming. As Heidegger himself puts it: "it is not enough to answer that Dasein is *at the same time* both the caller and the one to whom the appeal is made."[18] This is because there is something unfamiliar and uncanny about the call of conscience in that the call "comes *from* me and yet *from beyond me.*" He even uses the impersonal form, "'it' calls" ('*es' ruft*), to stress this point; when Dasein calls itself it is, in a special sense, *not itself.* What this means, and how Heidegger avoids the tautology of a pure self-relation, is made clearer in the concept of guilt.

In laying the ground for introducing the concept of guilt, Heidegger returns to the concept of anxiety in saying that the call of conscience is "attuned" by anxiety.[19] Without going into too much detail on anxiety as such, one could say that Dasein's anxiety is focused on its potentiality-for-Being, in the sense that Dasein "exists as an entity which has to be *as it is* and as *it can be.*"[20] If Dasein is anxious, then, it is anxious as regards the difference between its 'as it is' and its 'as it can be' and indeed, ontologically speaking, this difference is what constitutes Dasein's essence, its existence. But more concretely, what this means is that Dasein's anxiety involves the realization that it is always abandoned to itself and that, faced with *its own* concrete existentiell possibilities, it can have no alibi.[21] Following up on this claim, Heidegger proposes a phenomenological interpretation of guilt that fills out what he has in mind.

Guilt is central to responding to Adorno, because it is in this context that Heidegger says explicitly that it is the existential concept of Being-guilty (*Schuldigsein*) that can provide us with a coherent way of approaching issues of responsibility, moral guilt, law-breaking, or in short normative, inner-historical questions.[22] Again, however, this is a formal concept that relates back to Dasein's existential structure, and so any of our usual associations (original sin, law-breaking, moral blameworthiness, etc.) are to be seen as stemming from existential guilt. What characterizes guilt, then, is not failing to meet a standard or to respect a pre-existing norm, but rather a 'lack'—not in terms of a concrete lack of respect or what have you, but rather in terms of the inelimineable difference between what Dasein is *as it is* and *as it can be.* The lack in question lies in the difference between these two dimensions of Dasein's existence. For this reason, Heidegger will say that "Dasein constantly lags behind its possibilities."[23]

Heidegger fleshes this thought out by saying that guilt is to be understood according to two equiprimordial aspects of Dasein's constitution: first, that it is a "thrown basis" or ground (*ein geworfener Grund*) in relation to its existence and possibilities; and second, that Dasein is essentially a "nullity" of itself (*eine Nichtigkeit seiner selbst*). As regards the first aspect, Being-a-thrown-basis, Heidegger brings Dasein's thrownness back into play: the idea that I am not in charge of all my possibilities—that it is not up to me that I was born here rather than there, that in this day and age certain things are possible that were not possible a hundred years ago, and so on; I am also not in control of whatever is lurking around the corner or lying in wait for me; some possibilities just arise or are imposed by circumstance. And yet I am at the center of how I deal with this thrownness, insofar as it is incumbent on me (and no one else) to engage with these possibilities that arise or that are given, to construe and 'arrange' them, to transform them, and to actualize some of them. It is in this sense that Being-a-basis "means *never* to have power over one's ownmost Being from the ground up,"[24] as he says. But this Being-a-basis therefore implies a certain negativity, insofar as thrownness means that there is always a gap between what I am and what I can be, since what I can be is not entirely up to me, is not entirely in my power. Moreover, any actualization of possibility entails the foreclosure of other possibilities. Dasein, says Heidegger, "always stands in one possibility or another: it constantly is *not* other possibilities, and has waived these in its existentiell projection."[25] It is in this sense that Dasein is a "nullity of itself": it is what it is only by relating itself to what it is not, that is, to what it can be (or can no longer be)—or even to what is not, and ought *not* to be. Taken together, these two dimensions of Dasein's existence allow Heidegger to explain guilt as "Being-the-basis of a nullity."[26]

Why does Heidegger choose to call this guilt? Because it is only as this combination of factors (not having power over all possibility and yet its nevertheless being incumbent on me to actualize one possibility rather than another) that *responsibility* is conceivable, where responsibility is understood as being individually answerable or accountable for having understood things in a certain way and choosing one interpretation or course of action over another. In short, if I were not guilty in this specific sense, if I were not the thrown-basis of a nullity, then I could not be responsible.

There is no argument here for a particular set of norms, but there is one for individuated responsibility based on the way in which the particular Dasein exists as the nexus of possibilities that it realizes, of those that it has forgone and of those that it still holds open, with the understanding that it is not the origin of possibility in general, but merely an *agent of possibility.* Being-guilty means being an individuated, responsible agent of possibility.

It is important to point out here how the self-relation of the call of conscience avoids simple self-identity. The self-relation that characterizes the call is not strictly one of self-identity, because the Dasein who calls is *not* the Dasein who hears the call; rather, the Dasein who calls is a Dasein who is *not,* or rather *not yet.* Certainly, this 'not' that is at the heart of the concept of guilt, or the gap between Dasein *as it is* and *as it can be,* is the inevitable condition of existence in general (by Heidegger's definition of existence); but more specifically, it is also the inevitable condition of responsibility. To exist is to be responsible for the nexus of possibility that I am. I can of course disclaim responsibility (this is inauthenticity) but I cannot renounce it, because to do so would be tantamount to renouncing the distinction between action and mere behavior, or between being *in* a world and being poor-in-the-world (*weltarm*), as Heidegger thinks is the case with animals. In any case, the self-relation of conscience is not a simple relation of identity, since Dasein's distance from itself in conscience relies precisely *on the lack of identity* between who I am and who I can be. Conscience and guilt therefore express the general possibility of positing a norm in the concrete act of taking responsibility. The norm will always be more or less concrete or existentielly replete, but that there can be any normativity *at all* depends on the possibility of individual Dasein drawing a distinction between what *is*, on the one hand, and what *can be*, or, perhaps more directly: what *ought to be,* on the other.

Now, it seems clear enough that this distinction needs to be understood *normatively,* as one between what *is* and what *ought to be,* even though this is not quite how Heidegger puts it, because for existing Dasein what it merely *can be* may not concern it at all (in the sense of being merely logically or metaphysically possible, e.g., it is possible for me to become the king of France). To say that Dasein is the being for whom, "in its very Being, that Being is an *issue* for it," is just to say that it is not primarily concerned with indifferent possibilities (mere possibility), but with *its* possibilities, those which it chooses or accepts as imposed, with the understanding that it has not got power over all possibility. The possibilities it seizes on are therefore precisely those which for it *ought to be,* and so the call of conscience, or the *self-apprisal* of something being needful, is also the impetus to actualize what ought to be. Conscience makes explicit the fact that Dasein sets its own norms for action and is responsible for doing so in both the authorial and the moral senses of the word. The irreducible and necessary distinction that is at the core of the call of conscience, then, between what *is* and what *is not* but *ought to be,* is of a piece with both existence in the Heideggerian sense and normativity in general.[27] This is what Heidegger means when he says, using transcendental language, that in his interpretation of conscience, it is not a question of delimiting "any concrete possibility of existence . . . but rather [of delimiting] what *belongs* to the *existential condition for the possibility* of [the particular Dasein's] factical-existentiell potentiality-for-Being."[28]

    This existential condition for the possibility of factical existentiell potentiality-for-Being will of course be the battleground for Adorno's challenge to Heidegger. On the one hand, conscience and guilt make explicit a formal, absolutely necessary structure of experience. But on the other hand, the Self of Dasein is not a pure, point-like, self-identical Self; it is rather a self divided, pitted against itself (its they-self) as it sorts through its existentiell possibilities. In other words, Dasein's self-identity contains an irreducible moment of negativity, of non-identity, in the form of this gap between what Dasein is and what it can or ought to be. The gap is neither bridgeable nor fillable, and the difference it makes essential to existence always remains, no matter how Dasein pursues its projects.

    The claim, then, is that the moment of non-identity in the call of conscience and guilt is an acknowledgment of non-identity, which Adorno accuses Heidegger of undialectically suppressing. In fact, I think that the non-identity in play in conscience and guilt is fully compatible with Adorno's dialectical understanding of non-identity. But in order to clarify this claim, it may be worthwhile to take a brief detour onto the dialectical terrain of Hegel's thought, because Heidegger's concepts of conscience and guilt find startling parallels in Hegel—parallels that may help to situate Adorno's criticisms of Heidegger.[29]

Interestingly, Heidegger seems to recognize that what he is saying resonates with Hegel's description of the bifurcation (*Entzweiung*) of consciousness, but he categorically refuses to admit any influence; astonishingly, he even refuses to consider that Hegel could have *anything* of interest to say on the matter. At the heart of his discussion of guilt, Heidegger has this to say:

> Why does all dialectic take refuge in negation, though it cannot provide dialectical grounds for this sort of thing *itself*, or even just establish it *as a problem*? Has anyone ever made a problem of the *ontological source* of notness, or, *prior to that*, even sought the mere *conditions* on the basis of which the problem of the 'not' and its notness and the possibility of that notness be raised?[30]

Reading this passage, one might well think that Heidegger in 1927 had not yet fully come to grips with the *Phenomenology of Spirit*, which, it seems to me, is a four-hundred-and-some-odd–page answer to precisely the sorts of questions posed here by Heidegger. But instead of berating Heidegger for not giving Hegel his due (in spite of having read him extensively—which he had), the following question should be considered: does the specific form of non-identity discussed by Heidegger in connection with conscience and guilt help in responding to Adorno's charge of suppression of the non-identical? A quick look at Hegel on guilt and the bifurcation of consciousness may be useful in relating Heidegger to Adorno on this point.

Excursus on Hegel

Hardcore Adornians may be rolling their eyes at this point. Is Heidegger not merely proving Adorno's point in these passages on conscience and guilt? That is, is he not simply demonstrating that what he is after is an ahistorical, transcendental, categorial comprehension of experience that only pays lip service to the historically individuated Dasein? Well, it all depends on how we understand the Adornian alternative of non-identity. But before coming to Adorno on this issue, it is important to stress that, in spite of what he says, Heidegger is really far closer to Hegel in the passages on conscience and guilt than to Kierkegaard, for example, though the concept of guilt itself, as well as the theme of individuation from the 'they,' may seem at first to have a Kierkegaardian tenor. What I have in mind is first of all the reflection on guilt and crime from chapter VI of the *Phenomenology of Spirit,* but more generally the definition of consciousness that makes this guilt possible, as this definition is given in the introduction to the *Phenomenology.* In chapter VI, in the context of analyzing the tensions between conflicting normative orders, Hegel says that action, the "ownmost essence" (*sein eigenstes Wesen*) of self-consciousness, leads necessarily to guilt.[31] Hegel makes it clear in this passage what the nature of this necessity is: "Guilt," he says,

> is not an indifferent, ambiguous affair, as if the deed, seen as it *actually* is in the light of day, could, or perhaps could not, be the action of the self, as though action were bound up with something external and accidental that did not belong to it, from the perspective of which it [the action] could be seen as innocent. Rather, action is itself a bifurcation [*Entzweiung*] that consists in the self positing [1] itself for itself and [2], opposed to this self, an alien external actuality; that there is such an alien, external reality stems from the action itself, through which the actuality is what it is. For this reason, *only non-action is innocent,* like the being of a stone, not even that of a child.[32]

It should be clear from this passage that guilt, for Hegel as for Heidegger, is not a psychological state that depends upon failing to live up to some pre-established standard; it is, rather, constitutive of self-consciousness in the sense that my action is what it is *only* through the deed, which is a positing; there is no external standard by which it can be measured, nor is there some accidental outcome that could result in automatic exculpation—*I* am responsible for saying what is or is not right, for establishing or reacting to what I take to be alien to me. Action as actualization necessarily involves assuming this responsibility, this guilt, because construing something as alien and external is an immanent act that consciousness has to be able to justify.

Now, this construal and the action stemming from it are possible only for a being that can recognize a certain deficiency in actuality, in short, for a self-conscious being structured by an immanent split between 'the way things are' and 'the way they could or should be.'[33] Hegel is, then, making two related points in this passage on guilt: first, that the difference between 'the way things are' and 'the way they should be' is immanent to consciousness and therefore, second, that consciousness itself is responsible (guilty) for how it negotiates this difference. And ultimately, for Hegel, this rift is just a specific form of the general bifurcation of consciousness discussed in the introduction to the *Phenomenology*, where he says that "the essential point to bear in mind throughout the whole investigation is that these two moments, 'concept' and 'object,' 'being-for-another' and 'being-in-itself,' both fall *within* the knowledge being investigated."[34]

In other words, for Hegel, as for Heidegger, without such a bifurcation or split, norm-based action would be *impossible*; again, it is only such a self-relation that can explain the difference between moral action (involving responsibility and guilt) and animal behavior. This point needs to be stressed, for two reasons: because Heidegger claims to get nothing from Hegel, whereas his debt is clearly greater than he admits, but also because the reference to Hegel helps in understanding how we can begin to relate Heidegger's ontological approach to Adorno's dialectical approach.

Adorno, Non-Identity, and Guilt

On some level, Adorno too must recognize the bifurcation of consciousness as fundamental—as the moment in which the constitutive role of non-identity is tacitly admitted even as it is brought under the yoke of identity. In fact, Adorno's reading of Hegel centers on just this point. For example, Adorno writes that "at central points Hegel fails to do justice to his own insight. The insight says that even though the non-identical is identical—as self-mediated—it is nonetheless non-identical: other to all its identifications. Hegel does not carry the dialectic of non-identity through to the end. . . . "[35] First of all, it is interesting just to note that what Adorno says here about Hegel greatly resembles what he says about Heidegger's suppression of non-identity. But in the present context, what is crucial about this passage is rather that Adorno reveals the truth moment in Hegel's thought, what has to be rescued from Hegel: the fundamental, insurmountable distinction between conceptual identity and non-identity.[36]

This is why Adorno must on some level accept Hegel's account of guilt and the bifurcation of consciousness; but *for the very same reason*, he should likewise accept Heidegger's similar claim about guilt and Dasein's non-identical self-relation in the call of conscience. The reason he should accept these claims is just that *without* such a non-identical self-relation, non-identity simply would not matter, it would not 'register' as a demand, and norm-based action would not be possible (we would simply "fall to and consume"[37] things, as Hegel says of animals). But if the moment of non-identity is essential to knowledge as what Adorno calls "the secret *telos* of identification, and what has to be rescued from it,"[38] then it is clear that he believes that cognition, rationality, knowledge, and normativity all depend for their possibility on a capacity to recognize non-identity at the heart of identity. In other words, Adorno has to accept a version of Heidegger's and Hegel's claims regarding the condition of possibility for normativity; otherwise, he risks ending up in a crassly materialistic historicism or relativistic pragmatism.

Now, an anti-transcendental objection could perhaps be raised here (perhaps in favor of strongly materialist or pragmatist alternatives), based on passages where Adorno lashes out at transcendental ahistoricality, or where he links transcendental subjectivity to the principle of self-preservation and Darwin's survival of the fittest.[39] But if put too strongly, this would lead directly to divesting Adorno's thought of its principle of coherence. Ultimately, as I suggested at the outset, the point of tension between Heidegger and Adorno centers on the following question: *to what extent can Adorno object to Heidegger's alleged identitarian ahistoricality by invoking non-identity, without making the immanent construal of non-identity a necessary moment of rationality, knowledge, and normativity?* For it is one thing to say that reason and morality are offshoots of the principle of self-preservation, which may well be true insofar as we are natural beings, but it is quite another to claim that for that reason, thought and normative claims have no necessary structure, that their parameters and architecture are utterly contingent (whether naturally or socially or both). Were Adorno to believe the latter claim, he would be committing himself to a kind of non-identity that manifests itself to the subject only mysteriously or arbitrarily, like fate: the subject either would be passive in the face of it or could ignore it with impunity because it is not an immanent moment of human self-constitution and survival. Ironically, Adorno would thereby admit the legitimacy of the very idealism he rails against (the pure ego struggling heroically against nature, or, alternatively, asserting itself in sovereign fashion, unconstrained by 'reality'). But quite to the contrary, it should be clear that Adorno accepts the stronger idea, that non-identity is a necessary and universal condition of possibility for thought and identification, while still falling short of full-fledged categorial status—because the moment of non-identity can be fleshed out only historically, in concrete situations of suffering and conflict; in thought, it is a mere placeholder, a bifurcation.

As regards his critique of Heidegger, then, we should weigh carefully what Adorno himself says about guilt, because it may contain the key to his polemic and its consequences: "Dialectics is the consistent [*konsequent*] consciousness of non-identity," he says. "It does not begin by taking a standpoint. Thought's inevitable insufficiency, its guilt in relation to what is thought, drives it toward dialectics."[40] This "inevitable insufficiency" or "guilt" are precisely markers for Adorno's own history-neutral condition of possibility, what must be for him a necessary moment of cognition (with the qualification: at this point in the evolution of the species). In short, Adorno's negative dialectic requires guilt and, more particularly, guilt of the sort described by Heidegger—understood as the point of articulation between what is necessary for human action (the gap between *what is* and *what can be* as *my* responsibility) and what is necessarily historical, the concrete action undertaken by individuals who either respect or disrespect non-identity on the basis of having in any case presupposed it. In fact, Adorno makes this history-neutral claim quite plainly when he is not otherwise occupied with deflating transcendental subjectivity with the pinprick of self-preservation: "In truth," as he puts it, "there is *no* identity without non-identity."[41] If we take him to mean, for example, that there are no pure categories without the history that simultaneously vitiates them, then we must also take him to mean that knowledge is possible only for a being whose cognitive capacities include the ability to relate identity to non-identity, or what amounts to the same: knowledge and responsibility are possible only for a being structured by the immanent bifurcation of identity and non-identity. What we are left with is then not a category, strictly speaking, but a universal and necessary—though perhaps asymmetrical and natural—relationship between identity and non-identity. This is Adorno's history-neutral moment, borrowed from Hegel, but shared with Heidegger.

What this comes down to is that we are caught between the Scylla and Charybdis of no longer allowing ourselves to hope for a philosophy that adequately translates history into categorial knowledge, because on the one hand non-identity is more than a formal placeholder—it is the ineliminable surplus of historical experience—but on the other hand, to avoid arbitrariness, we cannot put our hopes in historical non-identity either, unless we first admit the necessity (for history, knowledge, and responsibility) of consciousness being so structured as to recognize the claim of the non-identical. The Adorno-Heidegger debate plays itself out along these lines, with Heidegger emphasizing non-identity as a formal condition for action and Adorno insisting on non-identity as the surplus that historically surges up to condemn thought for its identitarian arrogance. On the one hand, without the sort of necessary structures described by Heidegger, construing history would be impossible (it would just be "one damn thing after another"); but on the other, without the sort of materiality that Adorno defends, thought would inevitably turn its back on historical suffering and convict itself of prioritizing identity over the non-identity at its heart. Between the two, I hope, stands the non-partisan thinker interested in pursuing the work of correcting the abstraction of concepts with the only tool available: the abstraction of concepts.

CHAPTER TWO

Truth and Authentication:
Heidegger and Adorno in Reverse

Lambert Zuidervaart

The dialectical extremes of twentieth-century German philosophy touch in their conceptions of truth. More specifically, they touch in their conceptions of how truth is authenticated. Whereas Heidegger says this occurs in the 'authenticity' of Dasein, Adorno locates the authentication of truth in 'emphatic experience.' I wish to explore this dialectic, using Martin Heidegger's *Being and Time*[1] and Theodor W. Adorno's *Negative Dialectics*[2] as my primary sources. Like Heidegger and Adorno, I consider truth to be a comprehensive idea that cannot be reduced to notions of propositional correctness or empirical accuracy. But I also regard correctness and accuracy as indispensable dimensions of truth. Similarly, I take authentication to be a comprehensive attestation of truth that cannot be reduced to discursive justification or verification. Yet justification and verification are inescapable ingredients of authentication.

My exploration has three stages. First I summarize and criticize Heidegger's account of authenticity. Next I examine Adorno's appeal to emphatic experience. Portraying 'authenticity' and 'emphatic experience' as each other's reverse image, I claim that neither one suffices to authenticate truth. Then I conclude with an alternative account of authentication that draws out the significance of these dialectical extremes.

1. Truth and Authenticity

In *Being and Time*, Heidegger argues that the disclosedness (*Erschlossenheit*) of Dasein is the primary locus of truth. This means that propositional truth, or the truth of assertions, is not the primary locus. Rather, whatever truth accrues to assertions and to the practice of making assertions stems from the fundamental openness that characterizes human relationships to other entities, to fellow human beings, and to one's self. Moreover, the empirical accuracy of our statements and claims stems from the "discoveredness" (*Entdecktheit*) that characterizes entities in relation to the disclosedness of the world Dasein inhabits. Accordingly, "only with the disclosedness of Dasein is the *most primordial* phenomenon of truth attained. . . . In that Dasein essentially *is* its disclosedness, and, as disclosed, discloses and discovers, it is essentially 'true.' Dasein *is 'in the truth.'*"[3]

For philosophers who maintain the primacy of propositional truth, Heidegger's emphasis on the disclosedness of Dasein has unsettling consequences. Ernst Tugendhat, for example, claims that Heidegger surrenders the concept of truth, even though he continues to use the word.[4] This occurs because Heidegger equates truth and disclosedness without asking what distinguishes truth from untruth in various modes of disclosedness: "Heidegger has given the word truth another meaning. The broadening of the concept of truth, from truth as assertion to all disclosedness, becomes trivial if all that one sees in truth as assertion is the fact that it discloses in general."[5] As a result, Tugendhat claims, Heidegger also surrenders the idea of critical consciousness. Yet Tugendhat recognizes the appeal of a conception "that, without denying the relativity and lack of transparency of our historical world, . . . once again made possible an immediate and positive relation to truth: an alleged relation to truth that no longer stakes a claim to certainty, yet which also no longer poses a threat to uncertainty."[6]

There is something to Tugendhat's criticism. As I have tried to show in my book *Artistic Truth,* however, Heidegger's conception has resources not only to counter this criticism but also to provide a more satisfactory account of propositional truth or assertoric correctness than the one Tugendhat assumes.[7] Without rehearsing my arguments here, let me point out that Heidegger's discussion of truth has greater nuance than Tugendhat recognizes. At a minimum, Heidegger introduces five different ways in which truth can be distinguished from untruth.[8] (1) The discoveredness of entities can be distinguished from their being covered up. (2) The disclosedness of the world and of Dasein can be distinguished from their lack of disclosedness. (3) The authenticity of Dasein's disclosedness can be distinguished from the inauthenticity of Dasein's disclosedness. (4) Dasein's falling prey within its disclosedness can be distinguished from Dasein's reclaiming itself from falling prey. (5) The illusion (*Schein*) and distortion (*Verstellung*) into which discovered entities sink (relatively to Dasein's falling prey) can be distinguished from their having been wrested from concealment. Provided such distinctions and their recognition need not have the same apparent rigor and certainty as the difference between the correctness and incorrectness of a simple assertion, Tugendhat's complaint is too crude. Whereas Tugendhat seems intent on deriving any broader conception of truth from an account of assertoric correctness, Heidegger aims to demonstrate the derivation of assertoric correctness from a more comprehensive ontology of truth.[9]

1.1 Authentic Disclosedness

Contra Tugendhat, Heidegger does not so much surrender the idea of critical consciousness as transpose it into the demand for authenticity. That is where the fulcrum of his ontology of truth lies. On the one hand, the discoveredness of entities and the disclosedness of Dasein are conditioned, at least in part, by the authenticity with which Dasein seizes upon Dasein's "potentiality-for-being-in-the-world."[10] On the other hand, Dasein can reclaim itself from falling prey and can wrest entities from illusion and distortion only to the extent that Dasein's own disclosedness is authentic. Heidegger signals the pivotal role of authenticity when he describes the possibility of authentic disclosedness:

This possibility means that Dasein discloses itself to itself in and as its ownmost potentiality-of-being. This *authentic* disclosedness shows the phenomenon of the most primordial truth in the mode of authenticity. The most primordial and authentic disclosedness in which Dasein can be as a potentiality-of-being is the *truth of existence*. Only in the context of an analysis of the authenticity of Dasein does it [the truth of existence] receive its existential, ontological definiteness.[11]

The significance of the concept of authenticity is borne out by Heidegger's subsequent discussion of Dasein's "authentic potentiality-for-be-ing-a-whole" (*das eigentliche Ganzseinkönnen*) in Division Two ("Dasein and Temporality").[12] There he states that his discussion results in a more complete grasp of that truth of Dasein which is "most primordial" be-cause "it is *authentic*."[13] Tugendhat, with his phenomenological notion of 'evidence,' gives too little attention to Heidegger's emphasis on authen-tication.

Without detailing Heidegger's elaborate 'primordial existential in-terpretation' of Dasein in Division Two, let me briefly summarize his ac-count of authenticity (*Eigentlichkeit*). His account calls attention to three topics, namely, (1) the ontological status of authenticity, (2) the existential conditions of authenticity, and (3) the primary characteristics of authentic disclosedness.

(1) To begin with, Heidegger regards authenticity as ontological. The concept of authenticity pertains primarily to Dasein in its modes of exis-tence, in its potentiality-of-being or ability-to-be (*Seinkönnen*), and not to actual attitudes, behaviors, accomplishments, or beliefs. Earlier, Heidegger had distinguished three equiprimordial modes of Dasein's existence: un-derstanding, attunement, and talk. Of these three, understanding provides the primary (but not sole) locus of authenticity and inauthenticity. This implies that authenticity has a projective character and is future-oriented. In its projective orientation to the future, authentic understanding aims at Dasein itself. Authenticity has to do with Dasein's understanding it-self in terms of its ownmost (*eigenste*) possibility or potential rather than in terms of the world and others. When Dasein understands itself in this way, Dasein anticipates death. It anticipates death as that ownmost possi-bility which would render Dasein's existence impossible. This anticipated possibility is private, individualizing, unavoidable, certain, and indefinite. Authentic existence amounts to Dasein's being-its-self in an impassioned "freedom toward death."[14]

(2) This sheds light on the existential conditions that make authen-ticity possible. Since, to be authentic, Dasein must understand itself in terms of its ownmost possibility, nothing outside Dasein can make au-thentic existence possible. Rather, authentic existence is made possible by Dasein's own choice. It is made possible by Dasein's choosing to choose Dasein's ownmost potentiality-for-being-its-self rather than choosing to remain lost in the 'they.'[15] This potentiality-for-being-its-self is attested by

conscience.[16] Indeed, such choosing to choose amounts to our wanting to have a conscience. Wanting to have a conscience is itself an understanding of Dasein's being directly called "to its ownmost potentiality-of-being-a-self."[17] Moreover, the call of conscience is the call of care, a call Dasein gives to itself in its alienation from the public world.[18] The self-given call of conscience summons Dasein to understand its own being-guilty as the null basis of its own potentiality-of-being.[19] Choosing to choose Dasein's ownmost possibility and hearing Dasein's own conscience are the existential conditions of authenticity.

(3) This leads Heidegger to characterize authentic disclosedness (*Erschlossenheit*) as "resoluteness" (*Entschlossenheit*). He assigns three primary characteristics to Dasein's authentic potentiality-of-being (*eigentliches Seinkönnen*). These characteristics link back to the three equiprimordial modes of Dasein's disclosedness, to understanding, attunement, and talk. Authentic potentiality-of-being consists in (a) wanting to have a conscience (that is, authentic self-understanding), (b) readiness for anxiety (*Angst*) as an attunement, and (c) reticence (*Verschwiegenheit*) or keeping silent (*Schweigen*) as a mode of talk. Taken together, these characteristic manners of understanding, attunement, and talk make up "resoluteness" as the "distinctive and authentic disclosedness" of Dasein.[20]

Perhaps we can say that resoluteness is what authenticates truth in Heidegger's conception. He puts it this way: "Now, in resoluteness the most primordial truth of Dasein has been reached, because it is *authentic*."[21] As the authenticating of Dasein's truth, resoluteness modifies the discoveredness of entities, the disclosedness of the world, and the concern of Dasein's being-with others.[22] Resoluteness even "appropriates untruth authentically."[23] It reveals the authentic truth of existence. To this truth there corresponds an "equiprimordial being-certain" (*Gewisssein*), whereby Dasein unflinchingly and flexibly maintains itself in the actual factical situation disclosed by resoluteness.[24]

Such certainty has little to do with having the present under control or the past in our grasp, for resoluteness "is authentically and completely what it can be only as *anticipatory resoluteness*."[25] Moreover, authentication does not stop at the level of ontological structures. Just as anticipation (of death) is not simply an existential structure but an "existentiell potentiality-of-being,"[26] so too anticipatory resoluteness is not simply existential (that is, an ontological structure) but also existentiell (that is, an ontic way of life that a particular Dasein can embrace). As a way of life, anticipatory resoluteness disperses "every fugitive self-covering-over." It leads one to take action 'without illusions,' for it springs from a 'sober understanding' of one's factical possibilities. "Together with the sober *Angst* that brings us before our individualized potentiality-of-being, goes an unshakable joy in this possibility."[27]

Hence the orientation with which Dasein inhabits its own disclosedness becomes decisive for Heidegger's conception of truth. Only the readiness and willingness and ability to face Dasein's own finitude and fallibility—not just once, and not simply upon occasion, but always again and anew—allows Dasein to be true and, in being true, to let other entities truly be. Dasein's truth can only be true insofar as it is authenticated.

1.2 Self-Denial

As I have said elsewhere, "there is something fundamentally right . . . about Heidegger's refusal to reduce truth to the correctness of assertions or the discoveredness of entities. He is correct not to exclude the ontological stance of those beings for whom truth itself, like Being, is a question and can never not be a question. Heidegger has successfully removed this question from the realms of Platonic perfection and Cartesian certainty. He has relocated it in those regions of human striving and disillusionment where getting things right often involves also getting them wrong, and where genuine discoveries seldom occur without difficult self-sacrifice."[28]

Even so, Heidegger's account of authenticity is problematic in three respects. First, it turns a substantial concept pertaining to actual merits into a formal state of being self-related. Second, it transfigures a historically conditioned and destructive rupture in the fabric of modern society (that is, 'alienation') into an ontological and authenticating encounter with one's own finitude. Third, it turns a mediated process of disclosure into a denial of mediation. Let me take up each problem in turn.

1. In ordinary usage, people describe something as authentic when it proves itself unique, or is particularly trustworthy (e.g., 'the real thing'), or meets high expectations (e.g., 'genuine'). To use the term in this way, one must already have sufficient dealings with the entity in question both to

detect its characteristic tendencies and to discriminate whether, in comparison with other entities or with other pathways open to this particular entity, its characteristic tendencies are particularly praiseworthy. Hence, whether in German ('*eigentlich*') or English ('authentic'), ordinary usage serves the making of substantial judgments about the merits of an entity or its accomplishments.

Heidegger's account of authenticity exploits the nimbus of discrimination surrounding 'authentic,' as ordinarily used, to commend what is little more than a formal state of being self-related.[29] The formality of this state emerges in the ease with which Heidegger's account equates self-*understanding* with *deciding* ('choosing to choose'), *desiring* ('wanting to have a conscience'), and *adopting* modes of comportment (anticipation and resoluteness). Moreover, that which distinguishes such authenticity from inauthenticity is neither available for intersubjective judgment nor susceptible to 'verification' by way of personal self-criticism. At best, the constituents of resoluteness (that is, wanting to have a conscience, readiness for anxiety, and reticence) are predispositional states of consciousness or states of preconsciousness. As such, they need have no intrinsic connection with the self's characteristic understandings, dispositions, and linguistic practices. Presumably one could want to have a conscience, be ready for anxiety, and be reticent in conversation without characteristically having a conscience, being anxious, or exercising conversational restraint. Indeed, the self to which one 'relates' in resoluteness is little more than the possibility of a possibility—one relates to the possibility that one's own existence could be impossible. To call such a state of self-relation 'authentic' is to forestall any assessments of the actual merits of that self and of its accomplishments, whether these assessments occur as self-criticism or as intersubjective judgment.

It is so, of course, that Heidegger does not intend his account of authenticity to provide criteria for self-criticism or intersubjective judgment. Yet his notions of self-understanding, anticipation, choosing to choose, and keeping silent make little sense apart from the notion of an individualized self that finds itself (and, according to Heidegger, reclaims itself) among other selves in a public world. Heidegger admits as much when he describes anticipatory resoluteness as not only *existential* but also *existentiell*.

But what does it mean for a self to find itself among other selves in a public world? Heidegger's own answer turns on the notion of letting others be themselves by wresting one's own self from falling prey to public talk. I quote: "[R]esoluteness toward itself first brings Dasein to the possibility of letting the others who are with it 'be' in their ownmost potentiality-of-being, and also discloses that potentiality in concern which leaps ahead and frees. . . . It is from the authentic being a self of resoluteness that authentic being-with-one-another first arises, not from ambiguous and jealous stipulations and talkative fraternizing in the they and in what [the] they wants to undertake."[30] Accordingly, *inauthentic* existence is characterized by irresoluteness, by subservience to public understandings and interpretations, by "being at the mercy of the dominant interpretedness of the they. As the they-self, Dasein is 'lived' by the commonsense ambiguity of publicness in which no one resolves, but which has always already made its decision. Resoluteness means letting oneself be summoned out of one's lostness in the they."[31] For Heidegger, then, to find one's self among other selves in a public world is to remove one's self from that world and, in this removal, to endorse a similar removal on the part of others. But this amounts to *not* finding one's self among others as they are in public but rather finding others in relation to what one could be in one's own anti-public stance.

The problem, as I see it, is that Heidegger's formalism leaves little room for the self's authenticity to be either constituted or tested in public. Because the self's authenticity is neither constituted nor tested in public, it cannot authenticate truth in a public way. Insofar as the self's authenticity is Heidegger's primary and perhaps exclusive path for authentication, truth itself becomes a privilege of non-public existence. It is only a small step from this position to the even more problematic position that participation in an exclusive community is the proper path to authenticating truth.[32] To that extent, Adorno had good reason to attack the 'jargon of authenticity' as a 'German ideology.'

Michael Zimmerman and other commentators have attempted to ameliorate this problem by tracing it back to a 'voluntarism' that Heidegger did not fully embrace in *Being and Time*, and that he later abandoned when he transposed the notion of authenticity into that of "releasement" (*Gelassenheit*).[33] Such commentators might dismiss my criticisms as overemphasizing the voluntaristic elements in Heidegger's account of authenticity. But my criticisms do not revolve around the question of voluntarism. Even if Heideggerian authenticity were construed as a posture of acceptance, of 'letting-be,' rather than of resoluteness, of 'choosing to choose,' the self that either accepts or resolves would remain a nonpublic or anti-public self. And this, I submit, undermines the public authentication of truth.

2. Another way to say this is to claim that Heidegger's account of authenticity transfigures alienation. This is the second problem I mentioned earlier. The alienation of which Heidegger speaks occurs between Dasein and the public world. Discussing conscience as "the call of care," he writes:

[The caller] is Dasein in its uncanniness, primordially thrown being-in-the-world, as not-at-home, the naked 'that' in the nothingness of the world. The caller is unfamiliar to the everyday they-self, it is something like an *alien* voice. What could be more alien to the they, lost in the manifold 'world' of its heedfulness, than the self individualized to itself in uncanniness thrown into nothingness?[34]

At the core of authenticity, and voicing itself as Heideggerian conscience, is Dasein's alienation from its own everyday concerns, from the public world in which these concerns have their place, and from the public communications, perceptions, and interpretations that give these concerns their shape.[35] To be authentic, Dasein must be triply alienated, alienated from everyday concerns, from the public world, and from public interpretations of everyday concerns. For Heidegger, this 'must' reflects not a historical condition but an ontological necessity.

Accordingly, when Heidegger elaborates his notion of conscience and contrasts this with other conceptions, he insists on a state of 'being-guilty' prior to any responsibility or obligation. His is essentially an amoral conception of guilt. Dasein is guilty just by virtue of being Dasein and never gaining "power over one's ownmost being from the ground up"[36]:

The summons [of conscience] calls back by calling forth: *forth* to the possibility of taking over in existence the thrown being that it is, *back* to thrownness in order to understand it as the null ground that it has to take up into existence. This calling-back in which conscience calls forth gives Dasein to understand that Dasein itself—as the null ground for its null project, standing in the possibility of its being—must bring itself back to itself from its lostness in the they, and this means that it is *guilty*.[37]

Hence, the call of conscience is neither related to any specific deed nor critical with respect to specific courses of action.

Unfortunately this account turns a sociohistorical problem into an existential virtue. The very notion of an interior self whose authenticity resides in public withdrawal and perennial impotence is itself the philosophical expression of a modern cultural tendency whose societal matrix lies in the development of a market economy, privatized family life, and a depoliticized middle class.[38] It would not be difficult to find in Heidegger's characterization of authenticity the forms of alienation identified in Karl Marx's *Economic and Philosophical Manuscripts* and explained in Marx's subsequent writings. What Marx criticizes as social ruptures—the alienation of workers from their labor, products, and fellow workers—Heidegger celebrates as ontological clues to the most primordial truth of Dasein. The result is the picture of a sober and anxious self whose inner authenticity renders it immune from both praise and blame for decisions and actions that are inescapably public. Not only does this self not find itself among others in public but also it secures itself against any challenge they might bring to the truth it claims and to the authentication it supposedly supplies.

For this reason, I remain skeptical of attempts to find a basis for ethics in Heidegger's account of conscience. In an illuminating paper, Iain Macdonald argues that Heidegger's account offers us "an understanding of normativity rooted in non-identity."[39] The non-identity lies in the difference between Dasein as it is and Dasein as it can be. Because of this difference, Dasein is always already "guilty."[40] Macdonald interprets such guilt to mean that individual Dasein exists in the gap between what it *is* and what it *ought to be*: "Dasein's self-identity contains an irreducible moment of negativity, of non-identity, in the form of this gap between what Dasein is and what it can and ought to be. The gap is neither bridgeable nor fillable, and the difference it makes essential to existence always remains, no matter how Dasein pursues its projects." Because of this difference, Macdonald thinks Heidegger cannot be accused, à la Adorno, of "undialectically suppressing non-identity."[41]

I am not convinced by this attempt to rescue Heidegger, for three reasons. First, Heidegger's self-constituting 'difference' does not lie between 'is' and 'ought' but between 'is' and 'can be.' Nothing in his account of conscience, guilt, and resoluteness would turn a possibility into an obligation. Perhaps Heidegger thinks individual Dasein has an 'obligation' to pursue what it can be rather than staying stuck in what it is. But such an 'obligation' would be completely formal and open-ended, since my possibilities, while not infinite, are so varied that choosing any one of them, no matter how trivial and misguided, could count as my discharging the 'obligation.'

In the second place, to the extent that an 'ought,' an 'obligation,' surfaces in Heidegger's account, it is completely individual and self-related. Individual Dasein is called—indeed, calls itself—to be what it can be. Although this may seem to make me "responsible for saying what is or is not right," as Macdonald puts it,[42] it does not make me responsible for *doing* either what *is* right or what *others* say is right. This is a strange sort of 'responsibility,' for it strips the self of any shared vocation, social ethics, or moral duty. Nor is it clear that an individual has a *responsibility* to pursue what 'ought-to-be-for-me.'

My third objection concerns the relation between guilt and responsibility. On Macdonald's construal, individual Dasein is responsible by virtue of being guilty, where guilt is understood as the unavoidable condition of the self's never being what it can be. Yet this gets matters precisely backward. If I am not already responsible for who I am and who I am becoming, then the gap between who I am and who I can be would not be a condition of guilt. It would simply be a gap between actuality and possibility, and deciding on one possibility over another would simply be an arbitrary choice. Nor would I be "answerable or accountable"[43] for such a choice, whether to myself or to others, unless I were already responsible, in some sense, for who I am and who I am becoming.

At bottom, all three of my objections to Macdonald come to this: because Heidegger's non-identity is a purely formal difference between the actual and the possible, it cannot be a source of normativity. In Kantian terms, to make individual Dasein the source of its only genuine norms is to reduce moral obligation to one's pursuing idiosyncratic maxims without asking whether those maxims are right.

(3) Yet it is precisely this alienated self, in its predispositional state of self-relation, that provides the authentication for truth in Heidegger's account. As I noted earlier, he regards the discoveredness of entities and the

disclosedness of Dasein as conditioned by Dasein's authenticity. Only to the extent that Dasein's disclosedness is authentic can Dasein wrest entities from illusion and distortion and reclaim itself from falling prey to them. This means, however, that Heidegger's "most primordial" truth[44] is precisely the opposite of that complex mediation which his own critique of correspondence theories might lead one to expect. The most primordial truth is not a process in which various individuals and communities criticize, correct, and confirm each other's insights and dealings. Nor is it a process in which such insights and dealings are generated, tested, and revised by way of the entities to which they pertain. Rather, the most primordial truth is an anticipatory resoluteness whereby Dasein secures its own 'freedom toward death' in disentanglement from the entities, including others, to which Dasein necessarily stands in relation. Hence Heidegger's ontological key to truth is not mediation. Instead, it is Dasein's self-disentanglement from the mediations whereby it is itself constituted. And because the only orientation for such self-disentanglement is the possibility of Dasein's own death, the most primordial truth amounts not only to a denial of all that helps constitute the self but also to a self-denial.

It is because of this displacement from mediation to self-denial that Heidegger can consider Dasein to be "equiprimordially in truth and untruth"[45] and can claim that Dasein's resoluteness "appropriates untruth authentically."[46] In both of these formulations, untruth has to do with Dasein's unavoidable entanglement with entities and others that would divert Dasein from its "ownmost possibility." To think of these relations along the lines of entanglement and diversion, however, is to refuse those mediations without which, in my view, no self could be authentic and no truth could occur.

Lest this criticism of Heidegger seem hasty or unfair, let me quote at length from the pages that explain what the authentic appropriation of untruth comes to:

As the they-self, Dasein is 'lived' by the commonsense ambiguity of publicness in which no one resolves, but which has always already made its decision. Resoluteness means letting oneself be summoned out of one's lostness in the they. The irresoluteness of the they nevertheless remains in dominance, but it cannot attack resolute existence. . . .

For the they, however, [the] situation is essentially closed off. The they knows only the *'general situation,'* loses itself in the nearest 'opportunities,' and settles its Dasein by calculating the 'accidents' which it fails to recognize, deems its own achievement and passes off as such.

Resoluteness brings the being of the there to the existence of its situation. . . . [T]he call of conscience does not dangle an empty ideal of existence before us when it summons us to our potentiality-for-being, but *calls forth to the situation.*[47]

It might seem at first as if Heidegger here acknowledges the mediations with entities and others that help constitute the self. Yet it is only Dasein as a 'they-self,' not as a resolute and authentic self, that is so constituted: "Resoluteness means letting oneself be summoned out of one's lostness in the they." Again, it might seem as if such resoluteness is mediated with the public world on which resolutions depend. Yet the content of resoluteness does not arise from the situation upon which resolution seizes, but rather from a conscience that calls one forth into the situation and allows Dasein to make its own "factical existence possible for itself."[48] The relation between Heidegger's resolute self and the public world is not one of mediation but rather one of self-disentanglement.

Hence, I cannot fully endorse Taylor Carman's ingenious attempt to combine the two sides to Heidegger's account of selfhood. Taking a middle road between Charles Guignon's "metaphysically optimistic" and Hubert Dreyfus's "pessimistic" construals of Heideggerian selfhood,[49] Carman reads Heidegger as both a "social externalist" (Carman's term) and an "ontological personalist" (my term). On the one hand, Heidegger's account of "the they" or "the one" (*das Man*) makes anonymous social normativity constitutive for all of Dasein's hermeneutic practices, including those of authentic self-interpretation. Although Dasein has "a structural tendency . . . to lapse into banal, inauthentic interpretations of itself," established social practices have a "positive role" to play "in normatively structuring our practices and thereby constituting the intentionality of our everyday understanding."[50] Consequently, according to Carman's interpretation of Heidegger, "existing authentically does not consist simply in freeing oneself from all entanglements with the one, but rather in taking up a new, distinctive relation to the social norms always already governing one's concrete possibilities."[51] On the other hand, Heidegger's non-expressivist and non-holistic account of authenticity emphasizes both the ontological irreducibility of a first-person perspective and "a profound asymmetry between first-person and second- and third-person modes of interpretation."[52] This first-person emphasis is so strong that Heidegger omits the social character of being a self and neglects the "other-oriented dimension of selfhood, indeed authentic selfhood."[53]

While I agree with the main lines of Carman's double reading, I wonder whether he recognizes sufficiently how the gap between social externalism and ontological personalism vitiates Heidegger's account of authenticity. For the problem is not simply, as Carman puts it, that Heidegger's account remains silent about the hermeneutic conditions for bringing first- and other-person perspectives together "in an overarching interpretation of human beings as selves." The problem is not simply to say how it is possible "to come to understand myself, if only partially, as another" and thereby to engage "in empathy and imagination that is arguably essential to our mundane ethical self-understanding."[54] Rather, the problem is that Heidegger does not recognize—indeed, he explicitly rejects—the constitutive role that others play in the emergence of a first-person perspective.

As Carman himself correctly observes, Heideggerian conscience "expresses and communicates . . . an explicit recognition of the distinction between the everyday self of the one . . . and the *proper* self, or one's *own* self, which is an ontological structure formally distinct from any of its own self-interpretations. . . . Conscience calls Dasein away from all its ordinary self-interpretations back . . . to the bare fact of its existence in all its concrete particularity."[55] But this presupposes, problematically, it seems to me, that there can *be* a 'proper self' in its 'concrete particularity' that is not always already, in its very 'mineness,' constituted by the relationships it sustains with other selves. It presupposes that one can have the perspective of 'I' without always already having the perspectives of 'myself' and 'me,' perspectives that do not emerge unless the 'I' stands in relation to others and internalizes those relationships into its own 'I-ness.' From a Hegelian perspective, Heideggerian authenticity should be considered 'abstract' rather than 'concrete': social normativity must always remain *external* to this self and can never play a positive *normative* role in structuring the authentic self's existence. A Heideggerian authentic self can neither learn from social normativity nor contribute to it. This self is fundamentally asocial and therefore also ontologically impossible.

Let me summarize my three criticisms of Heidegger's account of authenticity. I have argued that his account reduces authenticity to a formal state of self-relation, transfigures historical ruptures in modern society into an ontological state of alienation, and turns the truth of Dasein into a denial of mediation. Because of the pivotal role 'authenticity' plays in Heidegger's general conception, his idea of truth becomes internally untenable: despite the emphases on interdependence and intersubjectivity in his notions of "being-in-the-world" and "being-with," the most primordial truth of Dasein, whose own disclosedness is itself truth in the most primordial sense, lacks interdependence and intersubjectivity. Or rather, authenticity displays interdependence and intersubjectivity only in a privative way, as that from which Dasein must take distance in order to be authentic.

In other words, the possibilities opened up by Heidegger's expansive idea of truth as disclosedness get slammed shut by his account of authentication. For if the authentication of truth depends upon Dasein's authenticity, and if Dasein can be authentic only in anti-public self-relation, then truth itself can no longer be attested in public. I would submit that, even on the most comprehensive conception of truth, what cannot be publicly authenticated is not truth at all.

2. Critique and Experience

It should be apparent that my criticisms of Heidegger resemble and indeed draw on Adorno's. Nevertheless, if one asks what account of authentication Adorno himself would offer instead of Heidegger's, one discovers a remarkable point of contact. This connection does not show up in the part of *Negative Dialectics* on Heidegger's ontology.[56] Nor does it surface in the closely related ideology critique titled *The Jargon of Authenticity*. Rather, the point of contact appears at the beginning and end of *Negative Dialectics*, in the introduction and in the concluding "Meditations on Metaphysics," where Adorno takes on the issues to which Heidegger's account of authenticity responds. I shall concentrate on a passage from the introduction where Adorno explicates the concept of philosophical experience.[57]

2.1 Philosophical Experience

In general, Adorno's negative dialectic is a philosophical attempt to conceptualize the nonconceptual without subsuming the nonconceptual under a system of concepts. As such, negative dialectical philosophy must rely on experience that provides access to the nonconceptual and is neither conceptually prescribed nor incompatible with conceptuality. The experience on which philosophy must rely can be called "emphatic experience." Following J. M. Bernstein, I use the term "emphatic experience" (*Erfahrung*) to refer to something the subject undergoes in relation to a particular object in its nonconceptualized particularity. Emphatic experience is characterized by novelty and by the object's directing the subject's response. It involves "a transformation of the individual [subject] and the emergence of a new object domain."[58] Adorno sees modern societies as having diminished the possibility and authority of such experience. That is why what he calls "philosophical experience" is crucial. Philosophical experience would reconnect rationality with emphatic experience while making palpable its modern demise. Adorno's concept of 'philosophical experience' points to the complex ways in which the mediation of conceptualization and the nonconceptual occurs.[59]

Inevitably the question arises whether Adorno's appeal to experience is arbitrary. He takes up this question in the section titled "Privilege of Experience."[60] The section begins by claiming that "the objectivity of dialectical knowledge" requires more from the epistemic subject rather than less. The standard 'positivist' objection to this requirement would be that the requirement is 'elitist and undemocratic.' It is elitist and undemocratic, says the objector, because the 'experience' on which dialectical objectivity supposedly depends is itself the prerogative of individuals who have a particular ability and biography. How can 'philosophical experience' be a condition of knowledge if not everyone is capable of such experience?

Adorno immediately concedes that not everyone is capable of philosophical experience. But he says the standard objection ignores a fundamental reason for this incapacity, namely, how "the administered world" intellectually cripples the inhabitants of its iron cage. Only those who resist the pressure to fit in can challenge such a society, and their number is limited. In fact, the 'privilege' of having experiences from which to critique an undemocratic society is created by that very society: "Critique of privilege has become a privilege: that's how dialectical the course of the world is."[61] Conversely, to expect that everyone in this society could understand everything worth noticing would be to orient knowledge to 'pathological traits' of people whose capacity to have experience (*Erfahrungen zu machen*) has been destroyed "by the law of perpetual identity [*Immergleichheit*]."[62] Although seemingly democratic, this expectation of public intelligibility would actually undermine the critique needed to counter anti-democratic tendencies.

The privilege of experience is not really elitist, Adorno suggests, because it comes with a moral obligation. Those who, despite the constraints of prevailing norms, are capable of experience that gives rise to social critique have a moral obligation to express what most people cannot see. Expressing this is a "representative" (*stellvertretend*) effort in which some speak on behalf of many. Nor would 'elitist pride' befit philosophical experience, since the capacity for such experience is largely an accident of history and results from the way class-based society is structured.[63]

Still, one could ask whether philosophical experience suffices. Should not the critique to which philosophical experience gives rise be subject to public discussion? And what about the experience itself? Should not it be subject to intersubjective testing? Adorno suggests two responses to this line of questioning. The first is simply to say, Let's not confuse truth with public intelligibility: "The criterion of what is true is not its direct communicability to everyone. . . . Truth is objective and not plausible."[64] Adorno's second response is that truth mediated through experience loses its supposedly privileged character by becoming publicly discussable. This occurs when philosophical truth claims do not make special pleas for the experiences that give rise to them, but instead enter "configurations and contexts of justification" (*Begründungszusammenhänge*) that either bear them out or establish their inadequacies.[65] So philosophical experience gives rise to claims whose truth can be debated, even though what makes them true is not their public intelligibility.

Even so, Adorno glosses 'philosophical experience' in a way that raises the worry of elitism he has just tried to allay. I quote: "Within philosophical experience chances that the universal randomly grants individuals turn against the universal that sabotages the universality of such experi-

ence. Were this universality achieved [*hergestellt*], the experience of all individuals would change accordingly and would lose much of the contingency that meanwhile continues fatally to disfigure their experience. . . . "[66]
In other words, thanks to the way society is structured, certain individuals
are capable of an experience that challenges this structure and its distorting
of other people's experience. To the extent that other people's experience is
distorted, not accidentally but necessarily, by virtue of society's structure, it
would appear that the experience that challenges this structure is itself immune from intersubjective testing. Would not intersubjective testing itself
be suspect, insofar as this occurs under distorting societal conditions?

2.2 Restricted Truth

This looks to me like a reverse image to Heidegger's account of authenticity, including its attendant problems. Like authenticity in Heidegger's ontology, philosophical experience is supposed to authenticate
truth in Adorno's negative dialectic. But just as Heidegger's concept of authenticity renders truth immune from public authentication, so Adorno's
idea of truth cordons truth-authenticating experience off from intersubjective testing. Each of the three problems already noted in Heidegger's
account of authenticity has a reverse image in Adorno's account of philosophical experience. Whereas Heidegger turns a substantial concept into a
formal state of self-relation, Adorno derives a substantial experience of the
nonconceptual from a formal concept of societal structure. Whereas Heidegger transfigures sociohistorical ruptures into an ontological structure,
Adorno transforms particular experiences of such ruptures into universal
sources of critical insight. Whereas Heidegger turns a mediated process of
disclosure into a denial of the self's mediation, Adorno turns an affirmation of the self's mediation into a restriction on the process of disclosure.
Let me indicate how each of these problematic reverse images shows up in
Adorno's text.

(1) The first problem in Adorno's account of philosophical experience pertains to the relation between societal structure and substantial experience. Adorno regards the structure of late capitalism as highly abstract
and as one that operates through universal abstraction. In permeating everyday life, such abstraction "sabotages the universality" of philosophical

experience. Yet at the same time this very same structure "randomly grants individuals" chances that "turn against" universal abstraction. And from this random bestowal an experience somehow emerges that resists universal abstraction. Adorno considers this experience sufficiently substantial to secure access to the nonconceptual that must be conceptualized but not systematized.

I find Adorno's own account of this relation highly abstract, quite unlike the very specific comments he makes about the ideological positioning of Heidegger's 'jargon of authenticity.' Adorno refrains from identifying the sociological roles and cultural traits that would be prerequisites for having philosophical experience. Although he waves his hand at the class structure that remains in effect, he makes no effort to acknowledge the differential insights various class positions could afford. The transition from universal societal structure to particular experience has a nearly magical quality. His claim that the experience of certain unnamed individuals is an exception, an exception made possible by the universal rule of abstraction, threatens to become a mere assertion.

(2) Nevertheless, Adorno repeatedly claims that philosophical experience, of which many people have been made incapable, is a crucial source of critical insight into the society that incapacitates them. Not only is it a crucial source, but also it is a universal source, in two respects. First, it puts the one who has philosophical experience in a position to speak on behalf of all others. It entitles, indeed, morally obligates, the critical theorist to make this 'representative' effort. Second, philosophical experience comes with the presumption that the insight it generates is universally true. In fact, there would likely be no moral obligation to express what most people cannot see if philosophical experience were not presumed to generate universally true insight.

Unfortunately, to turn particular experiences of sociohistorical ruptures into universal sources of critical insight is to cordon these experiences off from intersubjective testing. The problem, as I have said elsewhere, is that Adorno has made philosophical experience self-authenticating: "His account of the 'privilege of experience' makes philosophical experience speak for itself and entirely on its own authority. So no matter how much the articulation of such experience enters contexts of justification, the experience being articulated cannot really be challenged."[67] The 'elitist' element in Adorno's account of philosophical experience is not that it puts some people in a position to speak on behalf of everyone else. The elitist element is that the representative is both self-nominated and self-elected. This is not simply a matter of careless formulation on Adorno's part. By describing others as incapacitated by the societal system, he has effectively disqualified them as participants in the critical process. Or, rather, he has acceded to the disqualification purportedly carried out by society itself. Such disqualification comes back to haunt the position that declares others disqualified. For if *they* are disqualified, then the 'representative' effort also loses its point, and the quality of the critical theorist's experience no longer matters. Experience that is self-authenticating in this way cannot be a universal source of critical insight.

(3) Compared with Heidegger's account of authenticity, Adorno's account of philosophical experience has the advantage that it affirms rather than denies the objective mediation of the self. Adorno rightly criticizes Heidegger's account for ignoring such mediation. According to Adorno, it is because society mediates the self that truth requires subjective mediation. When he develops this emphasis on the self's mediation in his account of philosophical experience, however, he does so at the expense of truth's public intelligibility. A dramatic instance occurs when Adorno declares: "Today every step toward communication sells out the truth and makes it false."[68] One wonders how this rather jaundiced view of public intelligibility jibes with Adorno's subsequent acknowledgment that truth claims arising from philosophical experience need to be justified. Presumably the 'contexts of justification' are ones where public intelligibility is required. Yet Adorno makes it seem that the public intelligibility of a philosophical truth claim has no direct bearing on the truth of the claim or on the truth of the experience from which the claim arises.

To the extent that this is indeed Adorno's position, his idea of truth becomes untenable. It is made untenable by his regarding self-authenticating experience as the way to authenticate truth. Adorno tries to forestall this consequence by saying that the interwoven texture (*Geflecht*) of truth is "the index of itself."[69] In saying this he subscribes to a holistic idea of truth, as Heidegger does with his insistence on disclosedness. But just as Heidegger undermines his ontological idea of truth by seeking authentication in anti-public resoluteness, so Adorno weakens his negative dialectical idea of truth by seeking authentication in publicly unintelligible experience. For if the strands that supposedly make up the texture of truth cannot be contributed or checked by those on behalf of whom the dialectical thinker weaves or unfolds this texture, then truth will be an index that few will consult. We shall be left with what Habermas and Wellmer describe as an esoteric idea of truth.

The problem with an esoteric idea of truth is not that it is 'elitist and undemocratic,' charges that people too easily trot out when they understand a critique but wish to ignore it. Rather, the problem is that an esoteric idea of truth cannot do justice to truth itself as a mediated process in which everyone has a stake and outside which no one in contemporary society can flourish. Nor can truth be authenticated by publicly unintelligible experience that an abstract societal structure randomly grants, even though this experience claims to be a universal source of critical insight. While correcting Heidegger's account of authenticity, Adorno shares his failure to provide for the public authentication of truth.

3. Authentication of Truth

Earlier I distinguished truth from the authentication of truth. But that distinction is not transparent. Although one can speak of truth that has not been authenticated, it is difficult to imagine authentication that does not already claim to be true. So the distinction between truth and authentication cannot assign equal weight to each side. Rather, authentication must be regarded as an extension of truth. Although the unfolding of truth relies on this extension, the direction of truth's unfolding does not derive from authentication. Hence, to work out a viable conception of authentication, one must begin with a sufficiently comprehensive idea of truth.

Elsewhere I have characterized truth as an indissoluble and dynamic correlation between human fidelity and societal disclosure.[70] I have qualified the disclosure of society as "life-giving disclosure." By this I mean a societal process in which human beings and other creatures come to flourish in their interconnections. I have also specified human fidelity as faithfulness to societal principles such as justice and solidarity that commonly hold for people and that people hold in common. The correlation between disclosure and fidelity is indissoluble: creaturely flourishing depends in part on how human beings pursue fidelity to the commonly holding/held, and the telos of their fidelity is to promote the interconnected flourishing of human beings and other creatures. The correlation is also dynamic: it is a continually unfolding process, not a static structure. So, too, the principles in question are historical horizons, not timeless absolutes: they emerge from social struggles in which such principles are always already at stake.

Regarded in this way, truth can be authenticated if cultural practices and social institutions enable people to bear witness to a correlation between societal disclosure and their fidelity to societal principles. But what people attest cannot simply be the general process of correlation. It must be specific correlations that occur as people engage in cultural practices and participate in social institutions. In that sense, as Heidegger claimed about authenticity, authentication is both existential and existentiell. Because authentication is supported by cultural practices and social institutions, however, and because it occurs through involvement with these practices and institutions, authentication is intrinsically intersubjective, unlike Heideggerian authenticity. At the same time, one must recognize that society as a whole can be so distorted that specific correlations between societal disclosure and principial fidelity are the exception rather than the rule. In that sense, Adorno's appeal to 'emphatic experience' is not misplaced. Yet, because the possibility and occurrence of these correlations depends upon practices and institutions sustained by that same society, the 'exceptions' cannot be attributed to a 'privilege of experience.' They are made possible by the very principles and disclosive process that a distorted society occludes. In other words, authentication depends on truth. As both Heidegger and Adorno acknowledge, truth cannot be exceptional.

What does it mean to bear witness to correlations between disclosure and fidelity? It does not mean simply to articulate concerns in language and to raise and defend certain validity claims, even though linguistic and discursive practices are indispensable ingredients. Rather, to bear witness is to participate in such correlations in a manner that invites both oneself and others to do the same. If, for example, the correlation of contemporary justice and human flourishing requires the elimination of systemic racism, one bears witness to this correlation by doing what one can, with others, to transform the racist practices and institutions to which one belongs, whether through gestures, policies, or public protests. To bear witness to the truth means to do what truth requires in a social context and with respect to others who co-inhabit that context. Bearing witness involves the full range of human activities, not only linguistic and discursive but also aesthetic, ethical, political, economic, and the like.

Whereas truth is the processual correlation between fidelity to principles and life-giving disclosure, the authentication of truth is an invitational enactment of specific correlations in particular circumstances. It is the invitational quality of this enactment that makes authentication public and not privileged. For an invitation always welcomes a response from those invited, including the one who invites. And to be an open invitation rather than a demand or statement or idiosyncratic gesture, it must invite uncoerced acceptance or rejection or inattention.

Describing authentication in this manner casts a different hue on those modes of authentication which Western philosophy has valorized. I think here of a standard emphasis on discursive justification and verification. Earlier I claimed that justification and verification are inescapable elements of authentication to which authentication cannot be reduced. Now I wish to add that, as elements of authentication, justification and verification themselves are at bottom invitational enactments of correlations in context. What distinguishes them from other modes of authentication is their peculiar structure, which singles out the purported universality and necessity of enacted correlations. Such discursive practices try to bear out the purported universality of the validity claims raised in other linguistic practices. They try to do this with an appeal to their own inherent validity. Their inherent validity is not a matter of other societal principles such as solidarity and justice but rather a matter of logic and rhetoric. Hence the appearance arises that justification and verification are not modes of authentication and that what gets justified or verified has little to do with the comprehensive idea of truth. Moreover, given a pervasive "logical prejudice" (Dahlstrom) in Western philosophy, which both Heidegger and Adorno challenge, it also appears that the comprehensive idea of truth has little to do with truth 'properly speaking'—that is, with truth as correctness or accuracy.

Such appearances get things precisely backwards. What drives discursive practices and makes them important is their role within multidimensional processes of authentication. Part of invitationally enacting correlations of fidelity and disclosure is to test the reach of the principles at stake and to establish the extent of the circumstances in which correlations are enacted. It makes a difference for the enactment itself whether justice is only for 'just us' or is also for 'others,' whether the flourishing of some comes at the expense of others. It also matters that we have discursive practices and discursively attuned institutions within which deliberation about such differences can occur. For this, neither prelinguistic intuitions nor postdiscursive decisions suffice.

Yet it would be a mistake to think that discursive practices have the final word or that they transcend the contexts of authentication. Discursive practices occur within multidimensional processes of authentication; other modes of authentication provide their context. This implies that conflicts can occur between discursive and nondiscursive modes of authentication, and that such conflicts cannot always be resolved in a discursive fashion. What is logically true can be contextually false: a 'good argument' can support unjust and destructive arrangements. Conversely, what is 'true in practice' may receive articulations and defenses that are logically invalid.

Nevertheless, the normative role of justification and verification as modes of authentication is to test the universality of societal principles and the necessity of specific correlations between principial fidelity and societal disclosure. Is the contemporary principle of justice such that systemic racism must be eliminated? And are particular gestures, policies, or protests necessary in that regard? Although one does not need well-articulated answers to such questions in order to challenge systemic racism, resistance would falter if the questions never arose.

The structurally peculiar focus on validity, combined with Western philosophy's 'logical prejudice,' has led many philosophers to link the public character of authentication with the 'rationality' of discursive practices. Both Heidegger and Adorno question that linkage. They do so, however, at the expense of authentication's public character. I have proposed, in a preliminary fashion, to retain their concern for the comprehensive authentication of truth without either surrendering the public character of authentication or reducing authentication to discursive practices. Truth as such may not be democratic, but its invitational enactment must be public. A public invitation will be open to free recognition and acceptance on the part of those invited. To that extent, and to the extent that public freedom, recognition, and participation are the hallmarks of democracy, the authentication of truth must be not only public but democratic.

It is precisely because Heidegger and Adorno emphasize nondiscursive authentication that their contributions are important and their hidden point of contact deserves further attention. Both Heidegger and Adorno recognize that philosophical conceptions of truth have far-reaching implications for the kind of society we inhabit and the sorts of people we become. They make compelling cases for the claim that traditional Western conceptions of truth, whether classical and metaphysical or modern and epistemological, have supported destructive tendencies in society, while also opening up potentially fruitful paths. Neither one thinks that 'truth' can be left to the logicians and the technicians of philosophy. Each has attempted in his own way to reconnect the idea of truth with the cultural issues and social crises from which overly professionalized and hyper-specialized philosophies take distance. Their assessments may be dramatically opposed, but together Heidegger and Adorno have placed such matters at the center of philosophical attention.

The concern Heidegger and Adorno share for the authentication of truth needs to be understood in this societal context. Both of them recognize that truth is not simply a theoretical concern, that truth must be borne out in contemporary lives and practices and institutions. Both of them claim that the historical trajectory of modern Western society makes this requirement increasingly difficult to sustain. Both of them seek a site from which that trajectory can be resisted and perhaps redirected, whether the site be the authenticity of Dasein or the occurrence of emphatic experience.

But these sites are oppositional rather than transformative, and their access is restricted rather than open to a broader public. As I have tried to suggest, oppositional and restricted sites of authentication are inadequate for the comprehensive process of truth that both Heidegger and Adorno endorse. Their philosophies leave us with an exceptional challenge: to discover how truth can be borne out in ways that are authentic, emphatic, and thoroughly democratic. In such modes of public authentication, and in a society that sustains them, the dialectical extremes of Heidegger and Adorno's philosophies would not only touch but be true.

CHAPTER THREE

Transcendental Realism and Post-Metaphysical Thinking

Matthew Grist

Introduction

Transcendental realism is a philosophical perspective from within which philosophers are seen as being charged with the task of uncovering and codifying the One True Structure of Reality.[1] Such detective work is thought by transcendental realists to bestow on philosophy the dignity that separates it from other theoretical disciplines. Traditional metaphysics as practiced by Plato, Aristotle, Descartes, Leibniz, Spinoza, and Locke is distinguished by its transcendental realist credentials. Some contemporary scientistic philosophy has inherited these credentials and sees itself as continuing the detective work of traditional metaphysics.

In contrast to the scientism of some 'analytic' philosophy, there is a common perception that the 'Continental' philosophical tradition has freed itself from the presuppositions of transcendental realism. By examining Heidegger's and Adorno's attempts to think 'post-metaphysically,' I want to challenge this perception. I think Heidegger's and Adorno's criticisms of traditional metaphysics are cogent, but that they both, in different ways, allow transcendental realist prejudices to color their positive philosophical pictures. Thus my concern in this paper is to assess whether their post-metaphysical thinking indulges in the sort of transcendental realism, which they both reject. If it turns out that it does, I will take that to be a *reductio* of their claims to be post-metaphysical thinkers.

Before moving to Heidegger and Adorno I will first lay out Kant's criticism of transcendental realism. I will argue that avoiding transcendental realism is simply learning to do philosophy after Kant.

Kant

Kant was the first philosopher to see that *any* approach that employed the transcendental realist model would find itself caught up in the 'bloodless wars' of metaphysical speculation. What allowed Kant to come to such a conclusion was his realization that the general argument structure that transcendental realists employ leads to paradox. I formulate the argument that leads to Kant's insight as follows:

1. The universe is real in the sense that it has a determinate structure at any given time, which is how it is independently of our epistemic access to it.

2. To *know* whether one of our terms for a part of the universe uniquely identified it as the part it is, we would have to be able to be certain there was no discrepancy between how we take the part to be, and how it is.

3. But the universe is how it is independently of our knowledge of it (by the definition of it in 1), so it would be impossible to reach a point where we *knew* our term for any part of it uniquely identified that part.

To make this paradox vivid, imagine a physicist trying to ascertain the correct referent for the singular term 'smallest particle in the universe.' How would the physicist ever know that the particles she identified as the referent of the term did not simply exhaust the limits of her perceptual abilities and her methods of measurement, rather than the objectively real limits of the universe?[2]

It was Kant's great insight, then, that traditional metaphysics, because of its transcendental realism, was committed to the paradox that philosophy could know what it is impossible to know. But we need to be careful here. Kant's insight does not show realism to be incoherent; that is, it does not show that it is unintelligible to think of the universe as having a determinate structure that is mind-independent. All it shows to be paradoxical is the thesis of transcendental realism, which is the *epistemic* thesis that we can *know* that our beliefs limn an independent reality as it is in itself. I will call the anti-metaphysical import of Kant's insight into the epistemic futility of transcendental realism his 'restriction thesis.'

Heidegger

What unifies traditional (European) metaphysics according to Heidegger is its representation of reality as the embodiment of the *forms* or *ideas* of human thinking.[3] This makes the metaphysical tradition in Heidegger's eyes one that consistently thinks of reality as nothing more than a reflection of its own conceptual scheme, yet hides this fact from itself by dogmatically assuming that such a scheme limns the One True Structure of Reality. This leads, for Heidegger, to a forgetting of the question*able* nature of Being, that is, to a covering over of the original question which philosophy must consistently ask: How is it that things are intelligible at all?

Now, avoiding transcendental realism *just is* seeing Being as questionable in Heidegger's sense: we are forced, on pain of paradox, to refrain from the dogmatic identification of our central concepts and theories with the One True Structure of Reality. Such metaphysical restraint means *any* understanding of Being will be seen as conditional on its basic conceptual presuppositions and thus intrinsically questionable, because such presuppositions cannot, in principle, be shown unconditionally to be the right ones. So this is my claim with regard to Heidegger: if avoiding 'onto-theology' is the task set for a thinking that wants to overcome traditional metaphysics, then that task is equivalent to carrying on doing philosophy within the bounds of the Kantian restriction thesis outlined above.

Being and Time

In Division One of *Being and Time* Heidegger's aim is to bring to light through phenomenological analysis, the transcendental features of human existence (*Dasein*).[4] What is revolutionary here is that Heidegger shows our existence to be articulated by an interdependent network of *abilities* (which he terms *existentialia*), rather than a set of static properties ascribed to human beings in the same way that properties are ascribed to the objects of the natural sciences. What Heidegger calls 'fundamental ontology,' then, is an investigation into the *existentialia* which circumscribe the framework of possibilities that any particular set of human practices concretely actualizes. This makes Heidegger's phenomenological descriptions in *Being and Time* similar to Wittgenstein's descriptions of language games in his *Philosophical Investigations*. The difference between the two approaches, however, lies in the fact that Wittgenstein accepts that our language games are contingent, shying away from giving a 'transcendental' account of their necessary conditions. Heidegger, on the other hand, *is* concerned to give a transcendental account of the underlying 'meta-practices' that structure the contingently ordered practices of any given culture.[5]

To get his analysis going, Heidegger points to the fact that human beings are not 'in' the world in the same way that objects are in the world, and thus any ontology that determines human existence through the categories appropriate to the latter is 'vulgar'—that is, incapable of describing anything fundamental about human life. Marking this 'ontological difference' between objective categories and existential categories enables Heidegger to discern that in its 'everydayness,' *Dasein* does not relate to objects in a univocal way. In fact, *Dasein* is structured in its 'everydayness' by a historically specific interpretation of its *existentialia*. Such an interpretation circumscribes a world of tasks and projects in which objects function as various species of *Zeug* (equipment or stuff), that is, as invested with meaning relative to the practices they function within. Heidegger calls this practice-relative space in which objects are determined the "in-order-to" structure (*das Um-zu*) of "Being-in-the-world" (*In-der-Welt-Sein*).[6] This structure is constitutively teleological, in the sense that all the dealings *Dasein* has with objects are aimed at some end or set of ends (what Heidegger calls the "for-the-sake-of-which"—*das Worumwillen*).

Once we have the practice-relative teleology of *Dasein's* 'Being-in-the-world' in view, we can see that Heidegger's talk of "authentic" and "inauthentic" (*eigentlich* and *uneigeintlich*) *Dasein* is not talk that is intended to prescribe some particular form of activity aimed at some particular end. It is talk, rather, that aims to show that the possibility of acting 'authentically' or 'inauthentically' arises only because there is no way that *Dasein* can adduce what *definitive form* its actual activities must take. That is, because the normative statuses of human activities are determined by practices, and because such practices are always inherited as part of a continuing hermeneutical process, there can be no grounding for our present practices that is not merely contingent on such a process. This latter fact means we are capable of realizing that our present practices could have been otherwise if the hermeneutical choices taken before us, and those we take ourselves, happened to be different. Once this realization is in place, we can either continue along with the practices we have, or consider formulating new ones. To do the former is to act inauthentically, and to do the latter is to act authentically. The normative distinction between the two modes of acting lies only in the formal achievement of making or not making a hermeneutic choice. If one chooses to make an interpretative choice (even if the choice is to stick with the status quo), one is actualizing a potential for self-determination that is specific to *Dasein* (what Heidegger calls *Dasein*'s "ownmost possibility").

The radicalness of Heidegger's existential analysis lies in its identification of the fact that *Dasein* could never ground its practices in a way which was not open to questioning. This is so because the limits of what is actual in such practices are set by the limits that the practices themselves set on what is possible. No inference can therefore legitimately be made from what is actual to what the right ordering of our practices should be, because what is actual is simply the result of some previous contingent ordering. Thus, reformulating our practices will always be just more such ordering. This means that the meaning people and objects are invested with is not grounded in some ultimate source exterior to *Dasein*, but in the contextualizing and projective activities of *Dasein* itself. Hence, the metathesis of *Being and Time* is that *Dasein* is the being for whom Being itself is always an issue.

The fact that *Dasein* can become aware not only of how to distinguish particular objects but also of the *process through which* objects come to be determined in the first place means that *Dasein* has a privileged kind of knowledge. This second-order knowledge is what an "understanding of Being" amounts to for Heidegger. It is, for the Heidegger of *Being and Time* anyway, knowledge of the *existentialia* that make practice possible. To use a metaphor that Heidegger borrows from Plato at the end of *The Basic Problems of Phenomenology*,[7] fundamental ontology gives an understanding not of the objects that appear 'lit up' by the light that allows intelligibility, but of the 'light itself,' that is, the existential categories that articulate all human experience.[8]

Heidegger makes the further point that any 'understanding of Being' will be temporalized, that is, will be a projection of future possibilities based on a selection of past ones. And temporality, Heidegger insists, is the answer to the question of 'Being in general.' I take this to mean that the framework of temporally articulated *existentialia* that fundamental ontology describes constitutes a transcendental structure within which *any* particular understanding of Being must be formed.

The Later Heidegger

It is clear, however, that answering the question of the meaning of Being 'in general' is not a satisfactory philosophical resting place for Heidegger. For he expresses a desire to move to the question of the meaning of Being 'as such' once the 'preparatory analyses' of *Being and Time* have been completed. It is not immediately clear what this question could be asking after. It seems at first blush to be nothing more than Heidegger's stated intention to "de-structure" (*abbauen*) the history of metaphysics through an analysis of how each metaphysical system shapes the transcendental framework that *Being and Time* uncovers. One can imagine that such a 'de-structuring' might serve the purpose of providing counterexamples to our contemporary 'understanding of Being,' and of allowing us to understand past cultures through analyses of the presuppositions of their metaphysical systems. But Heidegger is not satisfied with this clarificatory philosophical work. He wants to push his questioning a stage further, beyond the subjective structure of *Dasein* to *the source of intelligibility itself,* which is what the question of Being 'as such' asks after.

Is there really a substantive philosophical question here? Heidegger certainly thinks there is. For it is his dissatisfaction with the philosophical emptiness of the process of 'de-structuring' that leads to his 'turn' (*Kehre*) away from the 'subjectivistic' approach of *Being and Time*. This means that Heidegger thinks the special second-order knowledge *Dasein* has access to is not restricted to the transcendental framework of *existentialia* described in *Being and Time*, but extends to some kind of knowledge of the non-human origin *of* that framework. To use the light metaphor again, understanding Being 'as such' is not merely articulating the lighting-up process of intelligibility from within the human standpoint, it also extends to knowledge of the source of the light itself. For the rest of this section of the chapter I want to examine to what Heidegger's further question about Being might amount. I will argue that there is no question hereabouts that philosophy could answer, because any answer would require us to violate Kant's restriction thesis. And, as answering the question of Being 'as such' just is the task of overcoming metaphysics for the later Heidegger, any answer that indulges in transcendental realism will not be an answer that overcomes metaphysics at all.

After *Being and Time,* Heidegger continues to explore a fundamental experience as grounding the questioning of Being. That experience is anxiety, or the experience of the 'Nothing.' What we experience in anxiety, the post-*Kehre* Heidegger thinks, is not simply the fact that nothing could ground our projecting of possibilities (as in Division One of *Being and Time*). Anxiety also reveals our inability to think 'Being as Being'—to think Being as the 'light' of intelligibility itself without reducing it to categories that are suited only for distinguishing between individual beings (entities). The history of metaphysics for Heidegger is the result of such reductive thinking; it is the history of a process of constantly covering over the thought of 'Being as Being' in the very act of trying to express that thought. Heidegger thinks it the task of post-metaphysical philosophy to somehow 'think' Being in a way that does not reduce it to a category of our thought but does justice to it *as* Being.

In texts like *Contributions to Philosophy, The Question Concerning Technology*, and *Time and Being*, Heidegger tries to develop a line of thought which has it that philosophy must somehow think 'Being as Being' as part of a world-historical shift in perspective—a shift often referred to in *Contributions to Philosophy* as "the other beginning." This shift in thinking is necessary if we are to bring about a genuine grounding of thinking in Being itself, rather than a metaphysical dissimulation of it.[9] One innovation in cognitive method that Heidegger initiates, in order to bring about such a shift in thinking, is his assertion that something can be known not only by its presence, but by its absence too. Being 'as such' is known by such a lack of presence, that is, by the fact that it is (in Heidegger's philosophical jargon) 'self-concealing.' This is how Heidegger puts the point in the late short essay *Time and Being*: "The sending in the destiny of Being has been characterized as a giving in which the sending source keeps itself back and, thus, withdraws from unconcealment."[10] Now, Heidegger uses, to great effect, philosophical arguments in *Being and Time* that rely on interpreting privative attitudes positively. For example, in the context of social interaction or *Mitsein*, Heidegger sees that *not* speaking or acknowledging one's fellows is more than a simple inert absence of discourse. Rather, it is a meaningful absence—a snub, an expression of indifference, a mark of thoughtfulness. He is thus able to show that various philosophical presumptions about solipsism are false once subjectivity is viewed phenomenologically rather than naturalistically. His argument works by reminding us of an implicit social context that not-speaking takes place within, a context that has been missed by naturalistic analyses. However, identifying the role played in Heidegger's discussion of silence by this implicit context should make us wary of generalizing such 'negative as positive' arguments. For inferring the presence of something (a social attitude) from the absence of something else (speech), works as an explicatory strategy only if *it is reasonable to assume* the implied context (that is, if the implied context is itself acknowledged by the readers of the explication). Being *not* being known by the categories of metaphysical thinking—or, as Heidegger sometimes puts it, Being's 'refusal' to be known by such thinking—does not necessarily mean we can infer that there is something substantive—Being 'as such'—to be known. This is because it is not particularly reasonable to assume the implicit context that metaphysical thinking is said to occlude. In fact, the assumption seems to rest on a philosophical expectation that is unwarranted yet inveterate, to wit, the expectation of a first philosophy that deduces the 'ground' of all subsequent knowing, the source of all intelligibility. Just to be clear; I am not saying there *definitely is not* such a ground, I am saying that there *is no reasonable expectation that there should be.*

But perhaps this just shows a philosophical timidity in the face of what Heidegger would call "essential thinking." However, I want to insist that the inference to Being's presence from its felt absence is in contravention of Kant's restriction thesis and is thus a form of transcendental realism. This means that Heidegger is overcoming metaphysics by doing more traditional metaphysics. Why so? Well, Heidegger's moves hereabouts are paradox inducing, because any 'new form of thinking' that claims to think 'Being as Being' turns out, on examination, simply to be more of the old form of thinking. Consider the following quote from *The End of Philosophy*: "Only what *aletheia* as opening *grants* is experienced and thought, not what it is as such. . . . Does this happen by chance? . . . Or does it happen because self-concealing, concealment, *lethe* belongs to *a-letheia*, not just as an addition . . . but as the heart of *aletheia*?"[11] This quote is asking us to think about the fact that only what Being *grants* is 'experienced and thought,' not 'what it is as such'—that is, what it is as grant*ing*. What could such granting be? It cannot be the transcendental framework of *existentialia* explicated in *Being and Time,* because that *can* be 'experienced and thought' via fundamental ontology. But if not that, what? Let us reflect for a moment on what would be involved in a thinking that could think the 'granting of Being as such.'

Heidegger glosses Being as that which conceals itself in the process of granting intelligibility, which is why its presence can be detected through its absence. The signal that we would still be 'stuck' within the paradigm of metaphysical thinking would presumably be that we would continue to know Being by its absence. But now imagine if we *did* succeed in thinking 'Being as Being'; how would we *know* we had succeeded? We can no longer rely on the recognition of Being's absence as our epistemic criterion, because our 'new way of thinking' would not cause that absence. What would we rely on? As our only present criterion for identifying the presence of Being 'as such' is its absence, we are left bereft of a criterion for thinking Being as presence in the new context. Another way of putting this is to say that trusting the criterion that our 'new way of thinking' would employ to identify Being would be a complete leap in the dark. We could not, from within our 'old way of thinking,' distinguish between any number of speculative claims that declared themselves exemplifications of our 'new way of thinking.'

Now, two points follow from this difficulty over a criterion for thinking Being as presence. First, it is the mark of transcendental realism that it presumes we can know what is knowledge-transcendent. Plumping for any one of the 'new' speculative claims about Being from within our 'old way of thinking' would just be to claim to know what is knowledge-transcendent from our present context, and thus would be a species of transcendental realism. So that can hardly be called an overcoming of metaphysics. Second, imagine (*per impossible*) that we are suddenly in the context of our 'new way of thinking.' If we are in the business of making claims about Being 'as such' from within that new context, how would we ever *know* that we were not just mistakenly believing we had left our 'old way of thinking'? Perhaps we would *in fact* still be employing the latter form of thinking, and thus be falsely inferring that our presentation of how Being 'as such' appears is how Being 'as such' actually is (that is, speculatively identifying our thinking with the independent objects it thinks about, as transcendental realists are wont to do). Either way, any 'new form of thinking' would turn out to be a species of transcendental realism, and thus not new at all.

As I have said, I cannot prove there is no substantive question of Being 'as such.' But I hope to have shown that the very idea of philosophical thinking 'going beyond' metaphysics by thinking 'Being as Being' is paradox inducing. So Heidegger faces a dilemma. On the first horn is a position that stays within the bounds of Kant's restriction thesis and accepts that one cannot indulge in the paradox of transcendental realism. If Heidegger plumps for that position, he avoids paradox but must forget about asking after Being 'as such.' On the second horn is a position that ignores the paradox of transcendental realism and presses on with the questioning of Being 'as such.' But if Heidegger takes this position, he is not now overcoming metaphysics, because he is going in for the kind of metaphysical speculation that Kant's restriction thesis forbids. The conclusion is that one can either think post-metaphysically—that is, within Kant's restriction thesis—or ask after Being 'as such.' One cannot do both.

Adorno

For present purposes, I will be interpreting Adorno through the lens of J. M. Bernstein's reading of him.[12] Bernstein's claim is that Adorno's 'negative dialectics' is aimed at freeing up the suppressed material contents of concepts in order to bring us to see the inadequacy (and hence reductive nature) of 'semantic idealism.' The latter is a paradigm of thinking in which the possible range of material objects is reduced to the possible object domains that the cognitive structure of the thinking that individuates them operates with. As Bernstein sees it, showing that the processes of conceptualization depend on the material contents of concepts is showing that they depend on contextually sensitive networks of material inferences such as 'this tomato is red, therefore it is ripe for eating.'[13] Such networks of material inferences partly constitute what Bernstein calls 'anthropomorphic nature.' Adorno's critique of semantic idealism, according to Bernstein, is aimed at bringing the latter to light, and thus aimed at elucidating 'constellations of material inferential practices' obscured by the dominance of closed systems of conceptualization.

Bernstein makes the further claim that elucidating material inferential practices will lead us to a kind of moral realism by grounding our processes of conceptualization in an anthropomorphic nature that is free from suffering, cruelty, and domination. Thus according to Bernstein, we are to ground our moral practices in our 'natural' affective responses to the material manifestations of suffering in others and nature in general. I do not want to deny that many of our moral practices are grounded in such affectivity. What I want to deny is that such affectivity could ground a robust form of moral realism.

Dialectic of Enlightenment

Bernstein traces the impetus for Adorno's critique of conceptualization to his work with Horkheimer in the *Dialectic of Enlightenment*. The question being asked there is: how is it "possible that the rational process of enlightenment which was intended to secure freedom from fear and human sovereignty could turn into forms of political, social, and cultural domination in which humans are deprived of their individuality and society is generally emptied of human meaning."[14] The answer is that Enlightenment reason, in seeking to become independent from the impulses and desires of (what the Enlightenment construes to be) our irrational natural embodied selves, transforms the domination of nature it seeks to escape into the domination of both the natural and human worlds through a reduction to rationalized forms. The representation of nature (including our own bodies) by Descartes as pure extension to be sliced at will by algebraic geometry, and thus as bereft of any intrinsic meaning on which *we*, as cognitive subjects, might be dependent, is the paradigm here. Adorno and Horkheimer attribute the source of the paradigm to the general epistemic procedure of conceptualization as abstraction: "Abstraction, the tool of enlightenment, treats its objects as did fate . . . : it liquidates them. . . . [T]he levelling domination of abstraction . . . makes everything in nature repeatable."[15] Once abstractive processes become reified as what is real, objects are reduced to nothing more than what reason "*determines* them to be, hence as *merely* a token or case or example or specimen of what is already known."[16] So transcendental realism in Adorno's hands faces dialectical reversal and becomes semantic idealism. For the real material features of objects that traditional metaphysical knowledge is supposed to capture are presumed to be identical with the forms of thought that individuate them; but this claimed sufficiency is actually the undoing of transcendental realism, because by idealistically identifying thought with things, it 'liquidates' the objects of its knowledge and knows nothing but itself.[17]

The question I want to push is not whether Adorno's analysis of the dialectical reversal of transcendental realism is right—I take it that it is—but rather whether Adorno's conception of post-metaphysical thinking, as construed by Bernstein, implicitly appeals to transcendental realist premises. This is obviously a massive topic, so I must restrict myself here to an analysis of Bernstein's thesis that a class of ethical material inferences could act as the shared basis for moral realism about our affective responses to suffering.

The Critique of the 'Simple Concept'

Adorno's critique of 'identity thinking' goes through his critique of the process of conceptualization. The latter reduces all conceptual contents to what Bernstein calls the contents of 'simple concepts.' The concept 'prime number' would be a paradigm example of a simple concept because its content is nothing more than the algorithmic application of the definition 'A natural number divisible by no other natural number than itself and 1' to the domain of natural numbers. Although we may not have an answer to the question 'What is the largest prime number?' we have exhaustively defined the truth condition that any possible answer would have to satisfy. Simple concepts are distinguished by having such determinate and context-independent truth conditions.

To view concepts per se as simple concepts would be to deny what Bernstein calls our conception of the 'complex concept.'[18] The latter conception allows not only for simple concepts, but for concepts that do not have determinate context-independent truth conditions because they are tied to the material circumstances in which the propriety of their application to objects is grounded. Bernstein uses as an example of a concept that is intrinsically indexed to material circumstances the predicate 'is living.' To know how to use this predicate someone must be familiar with the material qualities living and non-living objects display, the object-involving states of the world with which the predicate is indexed such as 'wriggling,' 'inanimate,' and 'dead.' Here, Bernstein is taking his cue from a series of thoughts from Wittgenstein's *Philosophical Investigations*:

Look at a stone and imagine it having sensations.—One says to oneself: How could one so much as get the idea of ascribing a *sensation* to a *thing*? One might as well ascribe it to a number!—And now look at a wriggling fly and at once these difficulties vanish and pain seems able to get a foothold here, where before everything was, so to speak, too smooth for it.

  And so, too, a corpse seems to us quite inaccessible to pain—Our attitude to what is alive and to what is dead, is not the same. All our reactions are different. . . . [19]

To think of nature purely in terms of the simple concepts of mathematical physics would be to miss the orienting role that states of affairs such as a wriggling fly play in ordering our reactions to the world around us. Thus to reduce our thinking to simple concepts is to deny that "all our reactions are different" because they are normatively oriented by being indexed to material states of affairs.

  Very roughly, Bernstein interprets Adorno as arguing that the rationalization of life typical of Enlightenment thinking consists in the denial or forgetting of the orienting role of material inferences like the one from 'the fly is wriggling' to 'it is living.' Such a forgetting takes place because the descriptive premise of the inference is indexical and so not reducible to a closed deductive system of simple concepts. The drive to communicate conceptual contents by presenting them as reducible to all the true inferences that follow from them in a deductive system (the central tenet of semantic idealism), leads to an impoverishment of the 'naming' axis of the concept[20] that indexing to material contexts exemplifies. This conceptual impoverishment leads to the withering of our awareness of the anthropomorphic nature upon which the shared 'forms of life' that constitute our conception of an objective world are based. In Bernstein's terms, then, to forget the material orientation that the indexical moment in concept formation and application instantiates is to view ourselves as independent from our embodied nature. Thus the attempt to deliver an objective world through unchecked conceptual abstraction is self-defeating, because the very objective aspect of experience—the determination of conceptual content by the indexing of our perceptual reactions to objects in the world—is 'liquidated.'

A world stripped of object-dependent normative boundaries, such as the boundaries indexically demarcated between inanimate and animate objects, is a disenchanted world. According to Bernstein, Adorno's response to such a disenchanted world comes in two stages: a preparatory stage of 'negative dialectics,' and a positive stage of 'ethical modernism' where we try to establish or re-establish the material inferences necessary for ethical practices. The concrete utopian hope of Adornian philosophy is thus actualized in the (re)constructed material inferential practices that express the intrinsically morally compelling features of the injurious fragility of living beings.

Re-enchanting the World

Negative dialectics is Adorno's version of Heidegger's 'negative as positive' argument. According to Adorno, from within our disenchanted world we have a sense of guilt over the reduction of other people and nature to the simple concept. The pervasiveness of identity thinking means 'non-identity' is felt by its absence. This inference of presence from absence is perfectly legitimate if we remember that even identity thinking is normatively oriented toward truthful representation. If I claim to know person X and the normative force of my claim is directly correlated to its degree of representational truthfulness, then my first-personal experience of X may jar against any reductive account I have given of her. In other words, my own experience—despite being mediated by the concepts that structure the disenchanted world I inhabit—is not so deadened as to forbid my at least recognizing where the simple concepts I routinely employ may have come up short. Tracking the insufficiencies of the simple concept in this way is the task of negative dialectics.

The next stage in the cognitive re-enchantment of the world is to bring to language, in a non-reductive way, the material elements of my experience that have escaped the simple concept. The paradigm for Bernstein here is the identification of states of affairs in which the suffering of living beings is expressed. Such states of affairs, because only indexically identifiable, fall outside the remit of the closed world of semantic idealism. In a re-enchanted world such states of affairs would intrinsically demand cognizance as the descriptive premises of material inferences like "there is suffering, therefore I should help abate that suffering."[21]

So Adorno's "cognitive utopia"[22] in Bernstein's hands amounts to re-inflating the material elements in the processes of conceptualization. This is to be achieved through heightening our sensitivity to the myriad constellations of material inferences that constitute our (now) withered anthropomorphic nature. Such re-inflation would demand that individuals institute or re-institute ethical practices by careful, qualitative discrimination of their 'emphatic'—that is, undiminished by reduction to the simple concept—experience of the suffering of other living beings.

Emphatic experience is our guide to re-enchanting the world because it tracks states of affairs that are *intrinsically* morally compelling. Taking our cue from such experience, the material inference from 'there is suffering' to 'therefore I should help abate that suffering' is not an enthymemetic expression of a general moral rule, it is rather the expression of an indexical ability to find objects themselves normatively constraining. Thus emphatic experience on the one hand reveals the insufficiencies of the simple concept and on the other locates the origin of ethically 'thick' concepts in states of affairs themselves. This grounding of ethical practice in intrinsically morally compelling states of affairs is what I referred to earlier as Bernstein's interpretation of Adorno's utopian view of cognition as moral realism. In the disenchanted world of the simple concept, our subjective reactions to objects are viewed as projective propensities to be distrusted; in the re-enchanted world of emphatic experience, they are viewed as the most objective experiences we possess, constituting the paradigm of truthful representation. Emphatic experience thus achieves for Bernstein what Adorno calls the 'axial turn toward the object'; that is, it makes our conception of truth object-dependent in contrast to the indifference to objects that semantic idealism displays.

Problems with Bernstein's Moral Realism
as 'Cognitive Utopia'

In non-ethical material inferences such as 'this fly is wriggling, therefore it is living,' the inferential import of the descriptive premise of the inference is more or less analytic. Barring outlandish suspicions that the wriggling fly is a mechanical stooge, there can be little dispute over the goodness of the inference. However, for moral realism to be based in emphatic experience, people would have to agree on the descriptive portion of the relevant material inference, and also on the correct inferential response to it. This might be plausible in a few extreme cases, such as Bernstein's paradigmatic ethical material inference from 'this person is bleeding badly,' to 'therefore I should apply a tourniquet.'[23] But it is not plausible in many less extreme cases. Take the case of children's suffering expressed in their crying. Some people might feel that every case of a child crying yields the material inference from 'there is suffering' to 'I shall nurture and comfort.' But many others would interpret a substantial portion of such material inferences differently, as they happen to view many instances of children's crying as triggering the material inference 'there is attention-seeking, therefore I shall ignore it.' Perhaps yet another group of people would hold that there is indeed suffering, but that because they think 'good' people are somewhat Spartan (and less self-centered for it), for the sake of the child's overall well-being in the long term, they will ignore her suffering. A moral realist of Bernstein's stripe could not allow this divergence of views over whether a child's crying always expresses suffering; nor could he allow there to be such divergence over what material inference follows from a child's crying once it is seen as an expression of suffering. But how would it be possible to choose the correct 'morally real' response to the child's crying from among the differing responses of the various parties? Such a choice would require an interpretation of what the correct moral response is. And how would such an interpretation be made that was not itself contingent on a myriad of background beliefs about what is 'good' for a child?

Material inferences such as 'this child is suffering, therefore she deserves attention' depend for their validity on how we understand the material content of the concept 'suffering' (that is, what inferences it licenses in what situations). And our recognition of such behavior as suffering in the first place depends on what we take the extension of the predicate 'is suffering' to be. So Bernstein's picture is too one-sided: states of affairs may well be intrinsically morally compelling, but their individuation as the states of affairs they are—*as* morally compelling—is itself *relative to* a background body of beliefs.

Is this to deny the existentially orienting role predicates such as 'is living' play? Not at all. My orientation in the world may rely on a host of such indexical predicates that I apply in concert with my fellow human beings. But even where there is general agreement over the content of the descriptive portion of a material inference (and there may not even be agreement over this in some cases), I cannot see how states of affairs can uniformly command the same material inferences across different agents in different cultures, apart from when they trigger a more or less analytic judgment such as 'this fly is wriggling, therefore it is living.' In many more cases, including most that are morally relevant, *agreement over what to infer from descriptive contents will not be 'analytically' guaranteed by the content itself, but will depend on how such content is interpreted.*

So Bernstein's rendition of Adorno's 'cognitive utopia' in a morally realistic register seems to share the same vain epistemological hopes of transcendental realism. According to that rendition, Adorno's understanding of genuine ethical experience is similar to traditional metaphysics not only because it shares a 'transcending impulse,' but also because its epistemological realization is equally impossible.[24]

Conclusion

I have identified the general requirement on any post-metaphysical thinking that it refrain from indulging in transcendental realism lest it contradict itself. While 'Continental philosophy' is often taken to gain its philosophical head of steam from rejecting transcendental realism, I have shown that Heidegger and Bernstein's Adorno slip back into it. I am sure there are a good many philosophers who consider themselves part of the 'Continental' tradition who have not made the same mistake. But there is a problem over this issue, and it is time that everyone in that tradition faced up to it.

CHAPTER FOUR

Poietic Epistemology: Reading Husserl Through Adorno and Heidegger

Joanna Hodge

In this sense phenomenology sets about breaking out of a fetishism of
concepts. It shakes up the ornaments, which take on in the domain
of abstract conceptuality a mask-like, pernicious articulation of mere
surface appearance, as the architecture and the music of the same period
did with respect to sensuous ornamentations.[1]

Introduction

These remarks fall into four brief sections after this introduction: a
section on framing, a section on style, a section on some differences between three stages in Adorno's responses to Husserl, and a short, inconclu-
sive excursus on Kant. Adorno's diagnosis of Husserl's phenomenology is
well enough known: that it is an idealism driven to the point of subvert-
ing idealism. Less clear is what, in Adorno's considered view, is to take the
place of such an outmoded idealism; nor is it clear that Adorno's subsequent return to a version of Kant's critical philosophy is to be preferred to
the program launched by Husserl.[2] The point of this chapter is to suggest
a reassessment of Husserl's phenomenology, via a re-reading of Adorno's
critique, which I shall explicitly discuss, and in the light of Heidegger's appropriation of Husserl, which will have to remain less to the fore. The aim
is to assess Adorno's critique of Husserl, and to suggest an odd collaboration between Heidegger and Adorno, which obscures the genuine inno-

vation at work in the notions of categorial intuition and of passive synthesis. I suggest that neither the appropriation of Husserlian themes, by Heidegger, nor the rejection of Husserl's phenomenology, by Adorno, does justice to the distinctiveness of Husserl's work. This can be shown to provide an account of a new formalism, as pure grammar, which is no longer held in place by Aristotelian or Hegelian distinctions between form and matter, concept and nature, cause and effect. This formalism can then be shown to be resistant both to any dialectical operation or modification and to the standard critiques of, for example, Kantian formalisms with respect to thinking of space and time and with respect to ethics.[3] This resistance results from Husserl shifting the frame of inquiry from a theory of cognition to a theory of meaning, and from a correspondence theory of truth to one of ideal fulfillments. Adorno's emphasis on reading Husserl as a theorist of cognition shows up what is wrong in the diagnosis and paradoxically reveals the radical innovation of thinking questions of cognition through questions of meaningfulness.

Adorno and Heidegger are perhaps understandably over-impressed by the systematic presentations of phenomenology made by Husserl in the *Logical Investigations* of 1900/1901 and in *Ideas: General Introduction to Pure Phenomenology* of 1913. They are thus less attuned to the intellectual struggle and the philosophical work to be found stretched out across Husserl's writings, in the preparatory drafts and lecture cycles.[4] A reading of Husserl's work, by contrast, across the published writings, rather than reading each as a separate event, leads to a less distorting, more open-ended notion of what Husserl's phenomenology consists in. It permits a consideration of what remains constant and what evolves in the course of a fifty-year struggle to formulate a philosophical breakthrough. This kind of transverse reading leads into the notion of a poietic epistemology, as given in my title, one which constructs itself in the practices of thinking, undertaken by each bearer of thought, for themselves, and it leads up to a notion of phenomenology, as that which is in process of formation. There is then an important difference to be marked between the temporal conditions for knowledge claims based on cognition, which have a certain universality and non-localizability in terms of time and historical context, and the temporal conditions for the fulfillment of meaning intentions, which are simultaneously universal and temporally neutral with respect to meaning content, and temporally singular to the occasion of each fulfillment. I shall show that these temporal differences have not received the attention they deserve. This connects to a difference between the notions of time and space deployed in relation to Kant's notion of intuition and the determinations of time under development in Husserl's notion of intuition. In conclusion to these remarks, I shall draw attention to a gap between Husserl's thought and that of Kantian idealism, not noticed by Adorno, by attending to a complication of the notion of intuition in the famous 'Principle of all Principles' from section 24 of Husserl's *Ideas I.*

Framing the Discussion

I shall make one remark about this notion of transverse reading, one about the notion of the poietic, and one about Adorno's mode of reading Husserl and Heidegger as conjoined, before proceeding further. One implication of the notion of transverse reading is that phenomenology is not to be understood as completed system or doctrine, and does not propose itself as attempting to provide either of these. This renders suspect Adorno's mode of reading Husserl as subscribing to what he calls, in 1924, a transcendental systematics, a term that drops out of the later readings. The 1924 text, under the title "Die Transzendenz des Dinglichen und Noematischen in Husserls Phänomenologie" ("The Transcendence of Thingliness and the Noematic in Husserl's Phenomenology") presents a markedly different reading of Husserl from that proposed in the later text from 1956.[5] Thus Adorno's reading of Husserl, too, is marked by an evolution in time, and by shifts of perspective, which may not be as internally consistent as the shifts identifiable in Husserl's writings. Husserl's writings can be seen to propose a system as a series of temporal relays, whereas those of Adorno appear to wander from a neo-Kantianism in the 1920s, to a Hegelianism in the 1930s and 1940s, and back to a different version of neo-Kantianism in the 1950s and 1960s. One distinctive feature of twentieth-century philosophy is that, in place of completed systems or delimited position statements, philosophy has tended to be written under the sign of incompleteness, and thus has the open-ended form of a practice which requires the active participation of its inheritors. This is filled out by Husserl's account of the necessary reactivation of meanings and the fulfillments of meaning intuitions, in sense-giving acts, to secure sense. Nor is there any such definitive separation of philosophical domains of inquiry, which Adorno's notion of a critique of a theory of cognition seems to presuppose. I will, however, attribute an epistemology in formation to each of these three thinkers, Husserl, Heidegger, Adorno, for they write in the form of a practice requiring the active participation of its inheritors. However, none of them proposes an epistemology as free standing with respect to other dimensions of philosophical enquiry.

For Adorno, epistemology cuts off analysis of knowledge from its actual historical and political conditions, thus attempting to take meaning as a given, rather than as historically constituted. For Heidegger, there is a different sense in which epistemology cuts theorizing off from consideration of the sources of meaningfulness for the terms in which it is analyzed. In *Being and Time* this is done in terms of a priority for the notion of being-in-the-world, which later drops out in favour of the notion of the sendings of being, and their historical determinations (*Geschick/Geschichte des Seins*). The dispute between Adorno and Heidegger on how to understand these connections between knowledge, meaning, and history must regretfully be left to one side.[6] For Husserl, unlike, for example, Kant and Hume, the enterprises of epistemology and ontology do not separate off from one another, and one result of Adorno's emphasis on the limitations of epistemology as *Erkenntniskritik* is to draw attention to this. A poietic epistemology, then, is one which is by no means neutral with respect to ontological commitments, nor yet to the efforts of individual inquirers to make sense of transmitted and invented meanings. The two main aims of this chapter, then, are to propose a re-reading of Husserl; making out a case for considering the term 'poietic epistemology' as capturing what is distinctive about Husserl's work.

'Poietic' is then intended as a reprise of the Greek notion of innovative making, each time for the first time, as opposed to a notion of collectively constituted praxis, of repeatable actions. The emphasis is on a difference between an activity, *poiesis*, for which the rules are not pre-formed and are coextensive with the activity itself, and a practice, *praxis,* for which there are externally valorized criteria of what counts as well formed within the practice. In this sense of *poiesis,* there is no problem with distinctive modes of formulation, for example the register of Hölderlin's writing, or indeed that of Samuel Beckett. Indeed, the point at issue is that which resists interpretation and appropriation, whereas, when both are subordinated under some more general term such as 'poetic writing,' there is a loss of the distinctive point of either, in an analysis of the rules of formation of some such generic practice. My thought then is that knowledge and meaning are more fully revealed for what they are in such practices of writing, where the commonalities between writers are less important than their distinctiveness, than in practices like rowing a boat, where isomorphism of movement is normative for the practice.

While Adorno emphasizes Husserl's alignment to *Erkenntniskritik*, he is also in the habit of running a reading of Husserl and of Heidegger together, and while this too might be contested, it does have the virtue of preventing a split between an ontological and an epistemological phenomenology setting in. He treats the ontological emphasis of the phenomenology of Heidegger and the epistemological emphasis in that of Husserl as complementary, intertwined, and equally unsatisfactory. My view is, rather, that Husserl is no less concerned with ontology than Heidegger is, and that Heidegger is as concerned with the modes of presentation to awareness as Husserl is. Indeed, the analyses in *Being and Time* of the modes of everydayness, of indifference, and of ecstatic exteriorization are nothing less than diagnoses of such different presentational modes.[7] Neither Heidegger nor Husserl, of course, is a classical metaphysician in the style of Leibniz, nor yet a theorist of knowledge in the style of Hume, or indeed in the mode of any of the twentieth-century positivists. Thus Adorno's attempt to read Husserl as an exponent of epistemology is significantly distorting, all the more so if, instead of 'epistemology' or 'theory of knowledge,' *'Erkenntnistheorie'* is translated more restrictedly as 'theory of cognition.' For this elides the role of the methodology of reduction, in guaranteeing evidence, and that of imaginary variation and of fantasy presentation in the articulation of Husserl's analyses of meaning.[8] The attempt to foreclose Husserl's writings under such a rubric is significant, and is to be explored and transformed in the following remarks. It is undermined by Adorno's own insistence on the continuity between Husserl and Heidegger. Thus I shall attempt, in part, to mobilize one part of Adorno's critique of Husserl against another, and, in part, to give Husserl the right of reply to Adorno's critique. This is legitimated by the posthumous publication of lecture notes, to some although not all of which Adorno could not have had access. My thought is that Husserl's phenomenology is less caught up in the constraints of his historical moment than Adorno supposes.

Adorno has one line of argument with Husserl, and another with Hegel, about how to think dialectically. By contrast to the notion of suspended dialectics, explored by Adorno in *Negative Dialectics* (1966), Husserl has a rather different proposal to make concerning a movement from thinking to thought, and back, which, although not strictly speaking dialectical, captures some of the force of what Adorno seeks to retrieve from Hegelian dialectic while avoiding more effectively the absolutist tendency of any attempted appropriation of Hegelian dialectic, as a completed accomplishment.[9] Adorno disputes the notion of a Hegelian dialectic as a historically completed accomplishment in the labyrinthine complexities of *Negative Dialectics,* under the slogan "Philosophie, die einmal überholt schien, erhält sich am Leben, weil der Moment ihrer Verwirklichung versäumt ward." ("Philosophy, which once seemed overcome, remains alive since its moment of actualisation was missed.")[10] Husserl would, of course, dispute both parts of this remark: he would dispute that philosophy could ever have been overcome, and he would also dispute that its moment of accomplishment could be thought to be unique, and could therefore have been missed. The attempt to use Hegel's notion of dialectic against Husserl, when Husserl is in dispute with Adorno about how to reinterpret it, is thus illegitimate.

Adorno fails to appreciate the nuance in Husserl's writings with respect to differences between natural and transcendental meaning, which recalls the better-known parallel between empirical and reduced pure consciousness. Natural meanings are given in historically specific contexts, and are subject to erosion and to what Husserl comes to call sedimentation; ideal transcendental meaning is given as limit condition for any such historical meaning, as its unspoken condition of possibility. Adorno also misses Husserl's nuance with respect to the accomplishments of thinking in relation to time, temporal process, and the constitution of a pure time, which does not, as Adorno supposes, deny a specificity of historical circumstance nor yet the workings of duration. For these are irreducible in the invention, preservation, and indeed distortion of meaning, which takes place in sedimentation. I shall argue that Adorno's challenge to Husserl is worthy of close attention, but mainly in order to dispute various common misrepresentations of Husserl's phenomenology. It is spread out over three phases: in the 1920s, with his doctoral work; in the 1930s, when he reads the *Cartesian Meditations* (1931) in French, and wrongly deduces from it that Husserl was simply endorsing a return to a Cartesian dualism; and in the 1950s, when he publishes his *Zur Metakritik der Erkenntnistheorie*, taking Husserl as exemplary of a certain historical foreclosure in theorizing knowledge.

Oddly, Adorno does not foreground the historical constraints within which each of these phases of his engagement with Husserl are to be placed, and he does not modify the critique in the light of the different aspects of Husserl's phenomenology, available to him in, respectively, the 1920s, the 1930s, and the 1950s. Born in 1903, Adorno could have, but appears not to have, attended Husserl's *Lectures on Passive Synthesis* from 1920–21, repeated in 1923, and in the winter semester, 1925–26.[11] He could also have attended the lectures of 1923–24, *First Philosophy*, parts one and two, on the Critical History of Ideas, and on the Phenomenological Reduction.[12] He is thus precluded from grasping what Iso Kern calls the threefold route into Husserl's phenomenology—that of a historical retrieval of the Cartesian intervention, that of descriptive intentional psychology, and that of reduction—all of which are designed to arrive at the same result: a retrieval of the task of philosophy.[13] Adorno rather seems to shift between the descriptive phenomenology of *Logical Investigations* and the Cartesian moves of the later texts, precisely failing to grasp their systematic intent. Nor does he mark the impact of Eugen Fink's publication in 1939, in the first issue of the *Revue internationale de philosophie,* of Husserl's now-famous essay "On the Origin of Geometry," in which he begins to elaborate publicly the notions of genesis and of history, toward which he was still working at the time of his death in 1938.[14] After the defeat of Nazism, Eugen Fink returned to teach in Freiburg im Breisgau, from 1946 on, and Adorno returned to Frankfurt am Main from exile in the United States.[15] I shall attempt to draw attention to the manner in which the changing historical and political conditions from the 1920s to the 1930s to the 1950s might have changed the manner in which Adorno approaches Husserl.

Stylistic Specificities: Introducing
Poietic Epistemology

The remark from Adorno with which I began seeks, as might be expected, to pick out something philosophically distinctive about Husserl's prose style. It is not, however, entirely clear which of the various artistic movements of the early twentieth-century Adorno is identifying Husserl with. The intended comparison is probably with the Bauhaus School of architecture and with the Second Vienna School of composition. In these, there is to be found a reduction of the components of composition to a minimum, along with the development of a rigorous set of rules for the use and arrangement of those components. This undoubtedly captures a feature of Husserl's inquiries. I take the suggestion to be that there is in Husserl's writings a bare economy of style, with the form of a modernist minimalism, which indeed contrasts strikingly with the baroque flourishes of Adorno's struggles with language, and contrasts both to a *fausse naïveté* of Heidegger's later style and to the neo-scholastic tone, in the earlier writings, in evidence both in the Marburg lectures and in *Being and Time*. For Husserl, form follows function, and function is determined by a commitment to analyzing how meaning works. It would then be necessary on another occasion to show how latter-day phenomenology has complemented, or supplemented, this with attention to an unworking of meaning, where the uncertainty and indeterminacy of notions of world and horizon disrupt the terms regionalized within the wider context, with Samuel Beckett, Maurice Blanchot, and Jean-Luc Nancy to the fore. In the interests of concision and focus, I shall have to leave this now to one side.

In terms of style, then, Husserl is a philosopher who manages to arrive in the twentieth century, for good or ill, whereas Adorno and Heidegger, in my view, are locked in struggle with their respective debts to German idealism and Marxian terminology, to Christian dogmatics and Greek thought, and with what has to be an ever-present sense of inferiority in relation to Nietzsche's way with words. Husserl, by contrast, is intimidated neither by Greek thought nor by a Christian inheritance, and, while perhaps a reader of Nietzsche, he is sufficiently a man of his own world not to be robbed by Nietzsche of the capacity to write. Reading Husserl, in the various redrafting of his texts, and in their various degrees of incompleteness, reveals a craftsman of great skill, with respect to both words and concepts, with respect to both syntax and the articulation of argument. He arrives at an expression of thought of the highest order and the utmost rigor, saying neither more nor less than is licensed by his own protocols, in the twisting together of words and concepts, syntax, and line of argument. A diagnosis of a supervenience of mind, of intellectual processes, on physiological electrical brain states is a well-known conceit; an analysis of a supervenience of ideal concepts on the words of natural language, and of rigorous argument on arbitrary syntactical sequence is philosophically more telling, and is made available by Husserl's writings from *Logical Investigations* on. Pure logical grammar supervenes on the grammar of natural languages but is not identical to that of any one natural language.

As indicated, poietic epistemology imposes on each postulant bearer of knowledge the task and effort of forming apparently inchoate streams of sensory material into patterns and configurations, which can then be deployed to make a claim on conceptual status. In Husserl's case this then retrospectively reveals that there are transcendental structures implicit in those streams, given in advance of analysis, and holding these classificatory possibilities in place, in accordance with a logic of parts and wholes and a practice of imaginative variation. These structures play an irreducible role in permitting these patterns and configurations to come into form and to be held in place, for the attention of natural consciousness. Indeed, they ground the orderliness both of natural consciousness and of its contents, as presentations of what there is. These structures are then expressed and transmitted in natural languages, but those languages become alienated and alienating forms of transmission of meaning when the activity of forming meaning and identifying patterns is surrendered to the mechanisms of stabilizing meaning in definitive, not provisional, determinations of meaning. An open-ended process of writing concepts and rigorous orderliness into existence is what the term 'poietic' in my title is intended to capture, and it seems especially apposite to attend to this process, in its rather different guises, in the writings of Husserl, of Heidegger, and of Adorno. For each is in process of generating a distinctive philosophical intervention, by a refinement and transformation of the available resources for linguistic expression.

The word 'generation,' here, is to be preferred to a word such as 'production,' for all the usual reasons: that production suggests working in accordance with a pre-given schema. By contrast I seek here to draw attention to these various attempts at invention of new possibilities of schematization, in response to reconfigurations of spatio-temporal relations, in relation to the kinds of entities that are identified within them, and in response to corresponding intensifications and distentions of sensibility. Roughly speaking, these developments call for a recasting of the account of transcendental aesthetics, as first set out by Kant, in the first *Critique,* to which I read Husserl as making a major contribution, but that would be a topic for another, much longer paper.[16] I already have here then three unfulfillable promissory notes: on an unworking of meaning, to be thematized with the help of Beckett, Blanchot, and Nancy; on supervenience, a notion borrowed from analytical philosophy, for an account of a logic of sense, in relation to natural language; and on a reconfiguration of transcendental aesthetics, to be explored as a reception of, and reworking of, the meanings bequeathed to philosophy by Kant's transcendental innovations. These three mark the as-yet-unclaimed strengths of a Husserlian inheritance, and they provide the three main strands of a proposed defense of Husserl's phenomenology, from the combined critiques, and random combinations of themes, in which such critiques often consist, from Adorno and Bergson; from Heidegger and Sartre.

There is of course an irony in the fact that it is Heidegger who draws attention to the proximity between such *poiesis* and thinking, in his reflections in the later writings on the word *Dichtung*, and on the poetry of Hölderlin; and that Adorno analyzes the possibilities and restrictions imposed by stylistic difference, while also engaging in polemics against Heidegger about Hölderlin. I suggest, however, that, between them, Adorno and Heidegger split word from flow of thought, concept from its embedding in syntax; they are, in short, caught in the toils of an all-too-Kantian set of antinomies, which Husserl—by starting again from the beginning, and by rethinking imagination, intuition, synthesis, transcendentalism, apriorism—can turn around. Husserl, then, is the thinker with whom these antinomies of a philosophical inheritance are to be resolved. This, of course, again, has its comic edge against Adorno's critique of Husserl, as developed in the 1930s, which is predicated on the presumption that the antagonisms of the real cannot be registered in the unmediated insights postulated by Husserlian intuition.[17] I shall, however, deploy the notion of antinomy in support of Husserl and as a defense against Adorno's critique. Nevertheless, Adorno does have a serious reading of Husserl, which is not simply to be put to one side, even if it is somewhat selective in its choice of texts to read, and overburdened by an uncritical commitment to the rightness of certain Hegelian notions: the concept, dialectics, and mediation, just for example. Adorno's reading repays careful scrutiny, not simply because of the scope of its influence, and only a sketch of this can be attempted here.

Three Stages in Adorno's Reading of Husserl, Three Points of Contestation

The three stages of Adorno's reading of Husserl are made up of the work going into the doctoral dissertation of 1924, already mentioned; the papers written in Oxford in the 1930s; and his *Zur Metakritik der Erkenntnistheorie*, from 1956. The pieces from the 1930s—one written in 1937, which forms the basis of part four of *Zur Metakritik*, and another published in 1940, in, of all places, the *Journal of Philosophy*—are extensively commented on in Adorno's exchange of letters with Walter Benjamin, making clear the degree of Adorno's investment in his critique.[18] The texts read by Adorno are principally *Logical Investigations* and *Cartesian Meditations*, to which he had access in the French translation by Emmanuel Levinas, from 1931. To a lesser extent, he draws on the 1913 first volume of *Ideas*. In 1955, he could but appears not to have consulted the recently published volumes of the complete Husserl edition, *The Idea of Phenomenology* (*HUA* II), the second and third books of *Ideas* (*HUA* IV and V) and the critical edition of *The Crisis of the European Sciences* (*HUA* VI).[19] Striking is the layered nature of Adorno's *Zur Metakritik der Erkenntnistheorie*, and the manner in which the focus for critique shifts. The emphasis is on a theory of cognition and of transcendental systematics early on; the notion of antinomy and the use of the Hegelian concept of mediation comes to the fore in the 1930s; and a refusal to distinguish between Kantian and Husserlian apriorism, and transcendentalism, comes out most clearly in the reframing of the analysis in the 1950s. The doctoral dissertation of 1924 was prepared under the direction of Hans Cornelius, who had famously found Benjamin's *Origin of German Tragic Drama* to be "an incomprehensible morass." It is then legitimate to wonder what sense he may have made of Husserl, and what degree of agreement with his own position he expected of his doctoral students. It would be instructive to read Cornelius's critique of Husserl, to discover how much of Adorno's reading is determined by the moves made in it.[20] While in the 1930s Adorno reads Husserl's *Cartesian Meditations* in Emmanuel Levinas's French translation, when it comes to publication in 1956, he makes use of the German edition, which has in the meantime appeared, for some but not all of his citations. It is just one of those ironies of intellectual history that Levinas here gives comfort to the Hegelian onslaught against Husserl; it also raises the question what Levinas might have made of the welding together of Husserl and Hegel by Eugen Fink. The fraught relation between Husserl and Heidegger must also remain to one side, since their various mutual accusations of anthropologism lead into difficulties and complexities well beyond the compass of this chapter.[21]

There are two problems with Adorno's reading, one concerning his notion of logic and another concerning his notion of consciousness. Adorno refuses the notion of a transcendental logic, and reads Husserl's notion of logic as if it were a discursive logic and a logic of argumentation. However, both Husserl and Kant have a richer notion of logic, to which Adorno is reluctant to do justice, since it competes more strongly than a discursive logic of argumentation with the residual notion of dialectical logic that he, Adorno, extracts from the remnants of Hegel's system. Here it would be necessary to interpolate a reading of Husserl's *Formal and Transcendental Logic,* and of the sections published as appendices to that in the German edition in 1974, now translated into English as the introduction to the 1920–21 lectures, *Analyses Concerning Passive and Active Syntheses: Lectures on Transcendental Logic*, by Anthony Steinbock.[22] Similarly, Adorno's commitment to a kind of philosophy of consciousness, which is refracted through the trickery of false consciousness, leads him to miss the manner in which Husserl has a thinking of consciousness as giving access to the structure of reality itself. Where, for Adorno predication and objectivity can come apart, for Husserl the conditions of meaningfulness just are the conditions for the constitution of objectivities in their ontological independence. What distinguishes Husserl from the naïveté of ordinary language philosophy is that he distinguishes between empirical and transcendental meaning, between *Bedeutung* and *Sinn*; thus his conception of meaning is not mortgaged to the constraints of any particular natural language. Husserl has a theory of meaning, not a theory of cognition, and is thus not restricted to the limits set out by a theory of knowledge nor to those of any particular natural language. Adorno identifies this Kantian moment in Husserl's thinking, but rather than also identifying the differences between Husserl and Kant, especially on the question of the status of a thinking of time and space, in relation to the constitution of what there is, Adorno seems to presume that since Hegel is an improvement on Kant, so Hegel must also be an improvement on Husserl. One of the aims of this reading then is to reopen the question of the connection between Husserl and Hegel, who, for Adorno of course, are entirely distinct, whereas, as noted, for Eugen Fink, they are oddly close. The distance between Frankfurt and Freiburg is undoubtedly greater after the World War II than before.

For Husserl, by contrast to the Hegelian enmeshing of consciousness in an account of freedom and history, consciousness is articulated along the lines of a transcendental logic, which simultaneously maps the contours of consciousness, and the contours of what there is. In so far as any empirical thinking fails to measure up to the structure of reality, and fails to attend to the things themselves, it has remained anchored in natural prejudice, and failed to attend to the intimations of this rigorously given logic of possible meanings. Thus for Husserl there can be no split between thinking what there is, and analyzing the contents of consciousness, whereas of course, for Adorno, it is these gaps between thinking and what there is that generate antinomy, political delusions, and social catastrophes, the genesis of which he seeks to trace out. These differences point up the importance of a properly conceived transcendental logic, and point up the gap not just between what Husserl intends with 'consciousness' and what it means for Adorno, but also between Kant and Husserl on the notion of the transcendental. On this topic Husserl is loquacious from *Logical Investigations* onwards, so it is, to put it mildly, odd that Adorno refuses to distinguish sharply between them, and then, perversely, prefers Kant.

Adorno thus misses the point of Husserl's innovations and fails to understand the importance of the stylistic specificity of Husserl's thinking, even while pointing it out. He also manages to be quite alarmingly offensive, in his deployment of sexual innuendo and political diatribe, in ways that on reflection are rather more comically apposite against their author, sheltering in Oxford during the dark days of Nazism, rather than against Husserl, who seems to me to be one of those rare figures who are as admirable as they are self-absorbed. Writing for publication in 1956, Adorno claims in part four of *Zur Metakritik der Erkenntnistheorie* that Husserl was "already surpassed before the arrival of Hitler," thus oddly agreeing with Martin Heidegger, whose views on the inadequacies of Husserl's phenomenology are a matter of ungracious record. Adorno is skeptical with respect to Husserl's attempt to re-establish philosophy as a systematic, organized discipline, and to align it as rigorous *Wissenschaft*, in the phrase of the 1911 *Logos* article. Adorno reads this attempt as a failure to grasp the historical conditions for philosophical work and as a failure to take up the inheritance of dialectical thinking, a discussion of which forms the third part of his meta-critique of Husserl's philosophy.

There are then connections between these three aspects of Husserl's thinking, as contested by Adorno: the identification of Husserl as concerned with *Erkenntnistheorie*, already opened up for discussion; the scope of the concept of rigorous science; and a problem concerning the interpretation of Husserl's commitment to idealism, which, as noted, is overswiftly identified with a certain view of Kant's idealism. The contestation concerning what it means to claim philosophy to be *Wissenschaftlich* also turns on a question of translation, for it can mean 'scientific' and it can mean 'systematic' but perhaps in this context it is best translated as 'having the form of rigorous disciplinarity.' The point is most swiftly made by noting that mathematics is the standard appealed to by Husserl most often, and that mathematics is no more a natural science than historical inquiry is. The appeal to mathematics gives access to a notion of transcendental meaning, neutral between natural languages, with no ontological regionalization. Adorno seems to assume that the commitment to a rigorous disciplinarity must mean that there is no room for a role for, and understanding of, historical difference, and this Husserl contests, even and especially in relation to geometry. This indicates Adorno's commitment to a misguided notion of scientificity, affirming some neo-Kantian dualism concerning natural and historical science. It also secures as unchallenged Hegel's no-

tion of rigorous disciplinarity, as in a *"System der Wissenschaften."* One of
the various disservices rendered by Eugen Fink is a covering over of this
contestation between Husserl and Hegel on the topics of the status of both
logic and *Wissenschaftlichkeit.*

Adorno's critique of Husserl in the 1920s takes as its focus the supposedly undecided status of the inquiries between idealism and realism. This
criticism highlights Adorno's impatience with Husserl's project of developing an idealism, compatible with a materialism, about the nature of what
there is, and with a realism, of some kind, about the contents of knowledge
claims. Adorno focuses attention on the supposition of an interdependen-
cy of immediately given contents, as the first presumption of transcendental method, and seeks to put pressure on the notion of immediacy. He
remarks that this emphasis leads to a relative neglect of the notion of an insight into essences (*Wesensschau*) and of the theory of abstraction through
which Husserl seeks to explain how, from the empirical definiteness of particular experiences, it is all the same possible to form general ideas, under
which such particulars may be subsumed. Unlike Heidegger in the introduction to the lectures *The Phenomenology of Religion*, Adorno does not
identify as a strength Husserl's distinction between the processes of a generalization of ideas from particulars, and of a formalization of ideas, each
on the basis of their givenness, in concrete meaning contexts. This distinction is implicit in *Logical Investigations* and is made explicit in section 13
of *Ideas I*, through the development of the phenomenological reduction,
prior to demonstrating, in a second reduction, their transcendental and,
for Husserl, ontologically determinate status.[23] Adorno also queries the
distinction in the formulation of the 'Principle of all Principles' from *Ideas
I,* between the phenomenal givenness of original perceivings, and the supposition that nevertheless access is thereby given to 'things.' This I think
shows a misapprehension concerning the purpose and function of phenomenological reduction, which does not so much deny the existence of
things in the world as deny their relevance in the process of explaining how
there comes to be access to and knowledge of things, without simply pre-
supposing knowledge of what there is to be accessed. Husserl not unrea-
sonably supposes that it is a mistake to presume knowledge of things in the
world by which to measure the adequacy of the knowledge supposedly to
be derived. The phenomenological reduction then is to be understood as

eliminating assumptions about that which is to be known rather than denying its status as independent of empirical consciousness. The next stage of the argument proceeds to a reduction of these phenomenally and phenomenologically given contents of consciousness, to reveal their transcendental conditions, given as the orderliness of what there is.

Adorno's reading of Husserl in the 1920s focuses on the status of the 'thing,' a theme for Kant but not for Husserl, and it generates a series of perplexities connected to the distinction between the 'thing' and the '*noema*.' However, this distinction and the perplexities generated by it can occur only when Husserl's own distinction between empirical or psychological givenness and determinate meaning relations has been undercut.[24] This reading reveals a failure to understand the point and nature of the project of reduction, whereby both empirical contingency and the opacity and unreachability of the Kantian thing in itself are eliminated in favor of an analysis of the possibility of determinate meaning. The engagement with Husserl culminates toward the end of the second section of Adorno's treatment with the following remark: "It is evident that the opposition between *noema* and *noesis* cannot be made the leading principle for a theory of knowledge; the leading principle is much more the opposition between thingly and phenomenal being."[25] Adorno thus both refuses the shift of domain of inquiry brought about by Husserl's neologisms, *noesis* and *noema*, and refuses the program of reduction that would make him hesitate to invoke as neutral between things and appearing this term 'being.' He continues: "Concerning '*noema*' in the sense in which we are allowed to use the word, as the content of all mediated givenness, we know of it only through intentional lived experience, in which it comes to givenness; *noesis* and *noema* are thus inseparable. We can then for the rest of our investigation do without the term '*noema*.'"[26] It is again, to put it mildly, odd that Adorno should rehearse against Husserl's distinction the very feature that Husserl supposes to be its strength, indeed the very point of inventing it: the inseparability of *noesis*, as act, and *noema*, as determinate content of conscious activity. Furthermore, their identity conditions are not the same, since a number of distinct acts can intend the same meaning content; nor do they display the same temporal properties. It is furthermore the task for a transcendental logic to regulate the relation between intending and intended, at this transcendentally reduced level, and to guarantee that the determinate specifications of contents of *noemata* set a standard for distinguishing between misleading and adequate designations of *noeses*.

In the 1930s, perhaps unsurprisingly, Adorno deploys Hegelian terminology more emphatically against Husserl, identifying a problem with the lack of mediation between an ego pole, and a pole of what is attended to in intentionality. Adorno complains that these two are subordinated arbitrarily to an enforced sameness, in the imposition of the notion of a 'pole.' This however disregards the differences with respect to noeses and noemata pointed out above, and he himself goes on to identify the distinction between these two poles with the subject-object distinction. He then proceeds to prove to his own satisfaction that there can be no direct access between them of the kind that he supposes Husserl labors to demonstrate. The lack of dialectical mediation is, however, an objection to a formulation, in terms of subjects and objects, but not to Husserl's formulation, which is precisely not caught up in an unresolved oscillation between mutually exclusive modes of conceptual idealism and material actuality. It is also remarkable that Adorno has to have been unaware of Husserl's attempts in the papers and lectures written during the 1930s to come to terms with a genesis and historical determination of certain, if not all, ideal essences. Some of this material was published in 1954, as *The Crisis of the European Sciences and Transcendental Philosophy*, following up the 1939 essay on geometry.[27] For Husserl, ideality is not to be opposed to historicality, while Adorno overhastily identifies these Husserlian essences as Platonic and as external to history. Husserl, from beginning to end, is clearly in this respect anti-Platonic and aware of the emergence of ideality in historical time. The publication of the essay "On the Origin of Geometry" by Fink in 1939, in the first volume of the *Revue internationale de philosophie*, does not seem to have informed Adorno's reception here, or rather only seems to have confirmed his mistaken thought that for Husserl all essences exist mathematically in pure space time.[28] For the upshot of Husserl's essay is to show that even for these essences, there are questions of genesis, sedimentation, and erosion of meaning to be explored.

There is undoubtedly an open question about precisely what the connection between philosophy, as rigorous discipline, and history, as the context for actual meaning fulfillments, might have been thought by Husserl to be, but Adorno does not pursue it all that far. Instead, he substitutes the long discussion in part three of *Zur Metakritik der Erkenntnistheorie,* of the lack of dialectics in Husserl's phenomenology; in part four, through a congruence between Husserl and Heidegger on phenomenology, he seems to attribute to Husserl responsibility for Heidegger's affirmations of Hitler. In Husserl's favorite observation concerning the universal plague leading to the extinction of human life, without bringing the slightest danger to that phenomenological remainder, the pure ego, Adorno appears to trace the precursor of that nihilism which he attributes to Heidegger. This nihilism can be understood to develop out of the being toward death of *Being and Time,* into the nihilating nothingness of the inaugural lecture "What Is Metaphysics?" (1929) and the Rectoral Address of 1933, and on into the alarming tone of the analysis of violence in the lectures *Introduction to Metaphysics* from 1935–36.[29] The reference concerning the universal plague is to section 49 of *Ideas I,* where absolute consciousness is adduced as the residuum of the abolition of the world (*Weltvernichtung*). This supposed continuity is, however, entirely spurious, even within Heidegger's texts, which rather form a critique of nihilism, and certainly with respect to any supposed continuity between Husserl and Heidegger. There is, however, at least a consistency in the failure to consider that Husserl may have a notion of history, in parallel with his notions of logic, and of rigorous disciplinarity, separate from and in contestation with those of Hegel. There is throughout a problem with Adorno's presumption that the idealisms of Kant and of Hegel exhaust the possibilities for idealism, and with his refusal to allow for a third idealism that is less irreducibly opposed to an inheritance of empiricism and positivism than his reconstructions of Hegel's and Kant's views.

Excursus on Kant

My view is that Husserl's transcendental philosophy, even when still only implicit in the *Logical Investigations,* provides much more than a theory of cognition; and that it is to be distinguished from Kantian transcendentalism, to the point of promising an alternative account of transcendental aesthetics, not separable from cognition, and not privileging the space-time of theories of knowledge, or indeed of mathematics, above the space-time of making sense of human existence. For specific human existence is predicated of all Husserl's inquiries about thinking, and this is why there must always be a repetition of a reduction to an ideal ego, in the attempt to neutralize the effects of such specificity. The confirmation or refutation of such neutralization lies in the possibility and impossibility of re-enacting reduction. Adorno identifies in Husserl an adoption of a timeless transcendentalism, direct from Kant, and to this he returns in his 1959 lectures on Kant's *Critique of Pure Reason* (1995).[30] In the writings of the 1930s, however, it emerges that Husserl is committed to a drastically revised notion of transcendentalism, for which apriorism is not to be opposed to the thought of ideas developing in time, in specific historical circumstances, and is not separable from an articulation of time. Thought for Husserl is thus subject to the vicissitudes of historical process, and sedimentation. This is re-thematized by Heidegger, as a process of erosion and erasure, which is then subjected to the Heideggerian absolutization as the forgetting of being, *Seinsvergessenheit,* memorably culminating in an oblivion of being. Husserl's own position is rather more nuanced, and deserves to be pursued through the 1920s in the lectures on active and passive synthesis and on transcendental logic.

Adorno declares in his first lecture on Kant: "Thus this interest in synthetic *a priori* judgments is connected with the fact that Kant really does require truth to be timeless."[31] This notion of a 'timelessness' of truth requires careful examination, for Kant hypothesizes several forms of time, even in the first *Critique*. There are the conceptions of time and space set up, in advance of the analytic of concepts, as pure forms of intuition, which provide the backdrop for a determination of time on each occasion of a schematization of concepts, when sensibility and reason are set to work, together to produce knowledge of repeating patterns, as re-identifiable entities. There is then a categorial determination of time, in the analytic of principles, in the discussion of the analogies of experience, with time there determined as permanence, succession, and co-existence. There is then an indication of further dimensions of time, which cannot be determinately thought, in relation to the Ideas of Reason, intimated in the postulates of empirical thought. There is finally the surmised time, in which the task of transcendental critique is to be developed. However, the time of moral judgment is a quite other time, and only the eschatological time of divine judgment provides the horizon of reflection required for secure and incontrovertible moral judgment. Human beings, by contrast, get their moral judgments wrong, and even if right, cannot know that they are right. Famously, the chasm between pure reason and practical reason is to be bridged by the third *Critique*, but even more importantly, the gap between the time of human judgment and the time of divine judgment is intimated as a problem in the third *Critique*, in the analytic of the sublime, and again in the separation of an idea of divine providence from that of a human prognosis. This last is developed in the essay on whether the human race is improving, deteriorating, or remaining on an even keel, in "The Conflict of the Philosophy Faculty with the Faculty of Law."[32]

The relation between the orderly forward directed time of causal sequences, and the interrupted time of judgment is set out in outline in an interruption of the harmonious order of judgments of taste, in a drawing out and slowing down of time, in the formation of judgment, and in a suspension of time, in the experience of magnitude and might introduced in the analytic of the sublime.[33] It is important first to mark a disagreement with Adorno's reading of Kant; and, second, to refuse his elision of the differences between Husserl's transcendental inquiries and Kant's apriorism, which with somewhat more reason, although still not without the possibility for challenge, can be thought to be ahistorical and timeless. As a marker for the manner in which it might be important to attend more carefully than Adorno does to differences between Husserl and Kant, I should in conclusion like to draw attention to an ambiguity in the 'Principle of All Principles', from *Ideas I*, section 24, which is invoked by both Adorno and by Derrida in *La voix et le phénomène*. Neither of them marks a significant shift in Husserl's sentence, in part because each is influenced by Kant's determination of the notion of intuition, thus concealing from them both the change in the scope of intuition resulting from Husserl's innovations. I shall give first the German and then the English:

Doch genug der verkehrten Theorien. Am Prinzip aller Prinzipien: daß jede originär gebende Anschauung eine Rechtsquelle der Erkenntnis sei, *daß* alles, *was sich uns in der* 'Intuition' originär (*sozusagen in seiner leibhaften Wirklichkeit*) darbietet, einfach hinzunehmen sei, als was es sich gibt, *aber auch* nur in der Schranken in denen es sich da gibt, *kann uns keine erdenkliche Theorie irre machen.*[34]

But enough of such misdirected theorizing. As principle of all principles, no such suspect theory can make us go wrong: that every originally given intuition (*An-*

schauung) forms a justified source for knowledge, all of that which offers itself in 'intuition' (*Intuition*), that is in a living reality, is simply to be accepted as what it gives itself out as, however, only within the limits within which it gives itself.

It would of course be worth pursuing the differences between these limits, which are determined on each occasion of givenness, and the limits, set out once and for all by Kant, which sustain and mark out the reliable application of concepts. Neither Adorno nor Derrida however draws attention to the shift from *Anschauung* to *Intuition*, and neither considers its significance. It is the shift from passive synthesis, a habituality in a surrounding world, to active cognizing, in a clarified horizon of lived reality, and from a passive givenness, to a positing of the evidential status of the evidence. This is a shift from the active existentially committed German form to the neutral or suspended Latin form, marking for Husserl a shift from a level of phenomenological psychology to that of a reduced transcendental phenomenology, which speaks Latin. Now it might be possible to challenge this shift, and to argue for the greater philosophical potency of the ordinary language use, uncorrected by any attempt at a pseudo neutrality, but what is revealed is a process of detecting in the ordinary language use the transcendentally given, but perhaps linguistically inarticulable, neutral form. Granted Adorno's attention to and satire with respect to the workings in Husserl's text of notions like "*erledigende Arbeite*" (tasks to be accomplished, rather like a shopping list) and "*Innerlichkeit des Leistens*" (interiority of achievement), it is odd that this more obviously philosophically inflected modulation should pass unnoticed.

Through Heidegger's reading of Husserl, as summarized in the 1925 lectures *History of the Concept of Time*, the themes of transcendental, or categorial, intuition; of apriorism; and the innovation of the concept of intentionality come to the fore.[35] What is repressed is the role of reduction; the insistence on the parallelism between phenomenological psychology and transcendental phenomenology; and the evolution of the analysis of internal time consciousness into a questioning of a connection between thinking time and thinking essential structure. This last might have been developed into an analysis of temporal and historical indices for all ideal essences, not so far from Benjamin's proposed theory of knowledge, which both Benjamin and Adorno conceive as oppositional to that of Husserl. There is then the hidden cargo of Adorno, in writing *Zur Metakritik der*

Erkenntnistheorie, attempting to do justice to Benjamin's critique of phenomenology, although without Benjamin's gift for transforming critique
into affirmation. Through Adorno's readings of Husserl, what emerges is
more negative than Benjamin's passing remarks about Husserl. In their
over-determination these readings reveal the challenge that Husserl's notions of scientificity, of logic, and even of ahistoricality, pose to Adorno's
presumption that Hegel is best on logic and science. My proposal by contrast is to read Husserl as providing an open-ended thinking of time, resistant both to Adorno's critique and to Heidegger's appropriation. It may
be developed into an understanding of a fluctuating role for conceptions
of history in thinkings of time, which, with Heidegger, gets blocked by
the appeal to the opacities of the *Ereignis* and *Enteignis* of being, and, with
Adorno, turns into a petrification of time in a naturalized history, em-
balmed by the movements of commodity fetishism. This intensified notion of commodity fetishism is in my view opposed to a political reading
of Benjamin's notion of natural history, which might rather be aligned
to Husserl's account of historical aprioris. By contrast the petrification of
time, analyzed in critiques of capitalism, seems to have something oddly in
common with Heidegger's notions of an enframing technicity, as a stalling
of the ebb and flow of history.[36]

Polemical Last Paragraph

There is something startlingly irrelevant about the arrival of Hitler's name on the scene in Adorno's discussions of Husserl, a brutality that
Adorno performs, without regard for Husserl's own experiences as a con-
vert Protestant, pursued even in his manuscripts by Hitler's minions. There
is something also rather desperate about Adorno's attempts to prove that
everyone else in the world, except himself, is contaminated by proximity to a black-shirted heritage, when even Heidegger seems to have drawn
the line at brown shirts. As remarked, there is something distasteful about
Adorno's observations on Husserl, drafted in the 1930s in the safety of his
Oxford exile, when Husserl was in there, in Prague, well into his seventies,
trying to contribute as best he could to the formation of a spiritual and intellectual resistance to the coming disaster. It ill behoves the philosopher
to abandon the name 'rigorous science' in favor of cheap polemics, and

it is Husserl, not Adorno, who takes up the task of thinking, not in the name of humanity, or in the name of Auschwitz, or even in the name of truth, but in his own name, painfully signing and owning every twist and turn, every grammatical inflection and hard-won insight. These twists and turns, as is now known, drove Heidegger, with his task of redaction, to the irritated expostulation that Husserl had got lost in his own manuscripts, but it is this care, this detailed work, this personalized craftsmanship, that I seek to draw attention to here, and for which I seek to justify the name 'poietic epistemology.'

CHAPTER FIVE

Adorno and Heidegger on the Question of Art: Countering Hegel?

Nicholas Walker

Much has been written of the famous "failure or refusal of communication" between two controversial thinkers who have proved so variously and unpredictably influential, throughout a fluctuating and remarkable reception history, who have both continued to remain stubbornly and resiliently 'present' with regard to the central concerns and preoccupations of recent and contemporary critical thought. And this despite the frequently proclaimed death or obsolescence of the kind of thinking each thinker in his own way allegedly represents. (Karl-Otto Apel and Jürgen Habermas, for example, have explicitly questioned the continuing relevance of great 'one-man philosophies' in favor of an apparently more fruitful, and certainly more modest, interdisciplinary conception of philosophical thought.) If, as we are commonly assured, communication proper essentially involves *mutual* response and engagement, then the emphatically one-sided literary relationship between these two striking authorships can hardly qualify as a meaningful reciprocal exchange. While there is no doubt of the constant, if polemical, reference to Heidegger in Adorno's work, from the beginning of his career onwards, at the very end of his life Heidegger is recorded as bluntly remarking: "Ich habe nichts von ihm gelesen [I have read nothing by him]."[1] He had of course inevitably read *about* Adorno. Despite this lack of reciprocated engagement, however, both Heidegger and Adorno had certainly read Hegel intensively and had long pondered the significance of the Hegelian legacy, not least in the domain of art and aesthetics. If we wish to open up one possible avenue of approach for a meaningful posthumous comparison between Adorno and Heidegger, and explore why such a comparison appears both tempting and difficult, it may be instructive to take Hegel as a kind of *tertium comparationis* in this regard.[2]

I

Heidegger has claimed that every thinker has only a single thought. If we would seek out the relevant master concept, or family of concepts, or the dominant and recurring set of metaphors that find expression throughout Hegel's work, we could do worse than consider the following. In the *Encyclopaedia Logic,* Hegel describes the subject-matter of the work as that "self-identical thought which sets itself over against itself in order to be itself, and in this other to be at home with itself."[3] And in the first of the concrete philosophical sciences of the *Realphilosophie,* the philosophy of nature, Hegel tells us: "spirit finds the counterpart to its own essence, that is, the concept, in nature. . . . Since the inner essence [*das Innere*] of nature is nothing other than the universal, then in thinking this inner essence we are at home with ourselves."[4] Finally, in the philosophy of spirit that closes the circle of the system, Hegel declares: "The purpose of all philosophical knowledge is simply this: that spirit recognize itself in everything on heaven and earth. For spirit there is nothing whatever that is entirely other."[5] This felicitously captures the Hegelian claim that the ultimate burden of 'speculative' philosophy, as the telling epithet implies, is self-knowledge and self-recognition in otherness, however opaque and recalcitrant such exteriority might at first appear. The most appropriate metaphor of Hegel's thought, at once suggestive and provocative, in some contexts apparently intolerable, is the figure of "being-with-oneself-in-the-other" (*im Anderen bei sich selbst sein*), or, as Hegel phrases it, among other places in the lectures on aesthetics, of being *einheimisch,* of being-at-home-in-the-world (*in der Welt zu Hause sein*). If there is a sense in which all philosophy ultimately concerns the matter of dwelling, the thought of Hegel does so expressly. This figure is the positive formulation of the central and contested speculative concept of 'reconciliation,' the negative counterpart of which is the influential though now seemingly obsolete concept of 'alienation' or 'estrangement' (which should not simply, despite a long and unfortunate tradition of interpretation, be identified with the idea of externalization or objectification in Hegel). All of these interrelated concepts and metaphors play a central role in Hegel's lectures on 'aesthetics.'

Hegel tells us on the first page of the text as we have it that the very title of his lectures is misleading and inappropriate. What he offers here is an emphatic philosophy of art, of *works*, rather than a more traditional inquiry into the range of the aesthetic in general, oriented toward a specific kind of feeling or perception and its corresponding objects, whether humanly fabricated or originally given as 'first nature.' The subject-matter of Hegel's aesthetics concerns the matter of the subject, and thus a certain kind of artifact: 'things' in a broad sense, at once sensuous and made, ranging from the palpable materiality of architecture at one extreme through to the evanescent 'products' of music and literature at the other. Hegel notoriously begins by excluding, or at least severely limiting, the relevance of first nature as the ultimately appropriate object of aesthetic attention, whether directly in its own right as 'natural beauty,' or even indirectly as a principal theme of artistic depiction. This cannot mean that nature is simply secondary or dispensable in Hegel's perspective; it rather presents itself contrastively in a symptomatic manner, as a necessary but not sufficient condition of the aesthetic in the fullest sense. Nature is the 'other' of art, but equally and inevitably the material source of all artistic fashioning, furnishing the ineliminable medium, the body that is to be enlivened and infused with spirit. Hegel's philosophy of art, like his entire philosophy, essentially concerns the matter of incarnation. It thereby paradoxically embodies a theologically inflected 'humanism' of a specifically modern kind. Nature presents itself, offers itself, as the scene and site for the embodied self-manifestation of spirit in and through its own other. Hegel expresses this governing conception in the lapidary formula "Spirit is the truth of nature," or in the claim that "the existence [*Existenz*] of spirit" is "the ultimate end [*Endzweck*] of nature."[6]

A couple of passages in the lectures on aesthetics are particularly instructive in the present context, and systematically illuminating for the interpretation of Hegel's thought as a whole. He attempts to identify the specific "human need" (*Bedürfnis*) to produce, and to encounter, works of art. For it would seem there are better, more obviously realistic, useful, and direct ways, as Hegel says, to accomplish, "*ins Werk zu richten,*" our ends and purposes.[7] What then is the *fons et origo* of art? Hegel tells us:

> The universal and absolute need from which art . . . arises [*quillt*], has its origin [*Ursprung*] in man as a *thinking* conscious being who draws out of himself, and makes explicit for himself [*für sich*], that which he is, and everything that is [*was überhaupt ist*]. The things of nature are simply immediate . . . , but man as spirit doubles himself [*verdoppelt sich*], insofar as he is, like the things of nature, but is at the same time for himself, beholds and represents himself, thinks, and only through this active being-for-self becomes spirit.[8]

He does this "theoretically" by "bringing to conscious awareness everything that stirs, wells, and drives within the human breast, by recognizing nothing but himself in what is called forth from within [*dem aus sich selbst Hervorgerufenen*] and in what is received from without [*dem von außen her Empfangenen*]." He does so "practically" insofar as he is driven

> to produce and to see himself in what is immediately given to him and externally present for him. He accomplishes this by transforming external things, impressing upon them the seal of his own inner being and finding there his own features. Man does this in order, as a free subject, to divest the external world of its alien and unyielding character [*Fremdheit*] and to enjoy in things simply the external reality of himself. The first impulse of the child already harbors within itself this practical transformation of externality; the boy casts a stone into the river and admires the spreading rings that ripple through the water as something in which he can behold his own being and work [*des Seinigen*].[9]

Hegel is articulating a kind of 'anthropological *a priori*' of the art impulse, conceived in a striking, perhaps perilous, proximity to labor, as a specific form of self-expression in exteriority (a thought originally suggested by Schiller and typically elaborated in the Marxian tradition down to the later aesthetics of Lukács). In sum: "The universal need of art is the rational one of having to bring the inner and outer world to spiritual consciousness. . . . It is this freely rational character of human beings in which, like all action and knowledge, art also finds its ground and necessary source."[10]

After providing this general outline of a speculative subject-object, fleshed out here in the medium of art, Hegel turns to the specific historical concretion and development of this structure and attempts to clarify how artistic activity, including both the production and reception of works, relates to other neighboring, or competing, spheres of cultural life and thought from which it can neither abstractly be divorced nor immediately be identified. A central problem of Hegel's thought thus emerges from the apparently necessary but nonetheless subordinate place of art within the overall economy of absolute spirit. Hegel struggles to explain how art, as a specific shape of embodied spirit, can be autonomous, or at least auto-telic, in a kind of sublated Kantian sense, while simultaneously articulating in sensuous form "the highest needs and interests of the human spirit" in its actual historical unfolding. Attempting to justify the truth moment behind the Kantian claim that the work of art, on analogy with the living organism, must somehow harbor its end within itself, as *Selbstzweck,* if it is to present itself as more than an instrument employed essentially for the sake of something else, more than a tool that would, by contrast, be generally inconspicuous in its own right. It must set itself off as an *ergon,* something made but not merely used, that emphatically calls attention to itself. Hegel speaks of the *"Bestimmung der Kunst,"* of its sense and intrinsic purpose, an expression that we might also appropriately render as the vocation or 'calling' of art. If all things are what they are 'in themselves' only 'for another,' and are disclosed as such intrinsically 'for us' as spirit, this is true pre-eminently of the work of art: "it is essentially a question, an address to the echoing heart, a call to the soul and spirit."[11]

But the central difficulty of Hegel's approach only reappears in this wavering and uncertain dialectic of internal and external determination, of intrinsic as opposed to extrinsic features of aesthetic form and content. If art initially seemed to enjoy a privileged, non-instrumental status through belonging to the highest sphere of his philosophy, that of *absolute* spirit (an idea already announced in the *Earliest System Programme* of 1796), it also seems progressively displaced once it is inscribed within an ineluctable teleological dialectic that itself circumscribes and effectively relativizes the concrete identity of form and content that was supposed to be a specific and defining feature of art itself. For it has never satisfactorily been explained how, at least for an authentically dialectical philosophy, the 'same' content *can* be presented under a 'different' form or medium (and for Hegel that content is ultimately nothing less than concrete freedom as reconciled self-possession in externality). Hegel makes this central and problematic claim in relation to both art and religion, something that from the first provoked grave disquiet among the more perceptive of his students and critics. The conservative and 'apologetic' defenders of Hegel are fond of citing his pronouncement that "religion can exist without philosophy, but philosophy cannot exist without religion,"[12] as if this resolved rather than reformulated the difficulty. On this account of "sublation," or *Aufhebung*, the rational hermeneutic of philosophy is merely needed to bring the matter of experience to its own conceptual articulation (*auf den Begriff zu bringen*), is "merely" required to translate (*zu übersetzen*), as Hegel repeatedly says, the authentic content from the given language of intuition and representation (of sensuous and pictorial image, of symbol, allegory, analogy, and metaphor) into the proper form of the concept. But the entire problem lies in this disingenuous 'merely.' A weak interpretation of this translation seems inevitably to reduce the work of philosophy to an otiose 'repetition,' an unnecessary supplement to that which allegedly precedes and conditions it. Some readers eagerly welcomed the radical implications of a strong reading of the labor of the concept, with respect to religion at least, for the implicit 'esoteric' content could now be spelled out explicitly without disguise in the 'exoteric' language of philosophical anthropology—to be 'radical,' as Marx observed, was to go to the root of the matter: to man himself. Others insisted, like Kierkegaard, that the authentic sense of the original could not meaningfully survive the rigors of such speculative translation. Over half a century later, Benedetto Croce, with Italian neo-idealism in general, was more than happy to embrace this conclusion in relation to religion, but was scandalized by the other, intimately related, stone of offense, by the 'immense paradox' of a monumental, indeed memorial, aesthetics that exhibits art as already well and truly dead ("bella e morta"): "Hegel buried art and left philosophy to write its epitaph."[13] It was probably through Croce that the theme of the so-called 'death' of art, and almost certainly this expression, re-emerged as a central philosophical question. We know, of course, that nowhere in the surviving texts does Hegel himself speak of the 'death,' or even unambiguously of the 'end,' of art, although he does refer suggestively to its "dissolution," or *Auflösung*, an idea that plays upon the historically accomplished transcendence of the 'religion of art' and the emergence of a new perspective for 'the modern artist.' With an obscure allusion to an already obscure poem of Goethe's, he writes:

In contrast with the time when the artist, owing to his nationality and his own epoch, stood essentially within a definite view of the world and manner of artistic production, we now find an absolutely opposite standpoint. . . . The artist now stands above determinate and traditional shapes and forms and moves freely within his own spirit . . . and art now takes as its modern saint the human being [*den Humanus*] as such, the depths and heights of human sensibility, the universally human in its joys and griefs, its aspirations, deeds, and destinies. . . . For art now . . . is opened up to all that human beings in general have the capacity to make their own.[14]

However much we may admire, and strive to preserve, the great artistic expressions of religious culture—and specifically of Christian devotional art—Hegel tells us that "we no longer bend the knee."[15]

II

There may be no uncontroversial interpretation of this troubling question concerning the 'fate' of art, its contemporary predicament and future possibility, at the climax, or anti-climax, of Hegel's lectures. But, like the closely related themes of the 'death of God' and the 'end of history,' the issue has continued to provoke reflection, positively and negatively, in a variety of senses and contexts, inevitably caught up as it is in the turbulent wake of Hegel's influence. For Adorno, the apparent supersession of art, and in a highly qualified sense of religion as a discourse of redemption, through the concept cannot simply, should not simply, be undialectically negated or abstractly reversed by decree, by transforming the inherited language of philosophy immediately into the oracular postmetaphysical diction of an entirely 'new thinking,' or by dissolving the distinctions of philosophical discourse, with its sedimented traces of material social and historical truth, into a universalized play of rhetoric. But the work of thoughtful interrogation that remains does involve an 'aesthetic theory,' a theory of art and its possibilities and a theory aesthetic in its own form, responding appropriately to and circling around the 'object' it would know and illuminate. Adorno thus repeats, in a self-consciously critical and transformed key, Hegel's insight that for us, in modernity, reflection has already penetrated the domain of art itself. If philosophy still emphatically requires art as the other it is to comprehend, though not suppress, art in turn requires the practice of interpretation or *Deutung.* Returning here to a fundamental insight of Kant's concerning the fecundity or discursive inexhaustibility of 'aesthetic ideas,' the work of art thus remains something sphinx-like for Adorno, in contrast to Hegel; it represents a kind of persisting "enigma," or *Rätsel,* and calls for critical commentary to let it speak.

Adorno rejects the presumed autarchy of philosophy, and the associated chimerical ideal of a fully transparent or self-grounding 'absolute,' that is, presuppositionless, thinking that circles upon itself, and the concomitant suggestion that the self-recognition furnished by any 'pure' speculative philosophy is either theoretically or practically capable of articulating the reconciled dwelling that it seemed to promise. Here, too, however, there is no undialectical reversal of 'system' when Adorno explicitly eschews any kind of linear methodical march from first principles or absolute beginnings to supposedly inescapable and all-embracing conclusions. His critical mode of exposition produces not a system, nor what Hegel would regard as the opposite of one, namely an indiscriminate congeries of disconnected observations or unrelated *aperçus,* but something more like a web or 'constellation,' to use the term he seems to have adopted from Benjamin. One might describe his approach rather as a liberated contextual holism for which nothing is a brute limit out of bounds for thought, nothing merely 'external' to understanding and interpretation. Though frequently and understandably associated with the Romantic form of the 'fragment'—which also bespeaks a whole that is never fully given or present—the micrological image of the monad perhaps seems more appropriate. And while Adorno suspects the ideologically compromised ideal of 'harmony,' of the concrete universality allegedly embodied in the classical conception of organic system, he does not pursue 'dissonance' for its own sake as the transgressive other of identity or totality. Hegelian reconciliation must rather be denied "for the sake of the reconciliation which absolute idealism betrayed," not exchanged for a generalized, and romanticized, agonistics or for a perpetually re-enacted aporetics always already structurally inscribed in the very movement of thought and language.[16]

Emphasizing the ideological character of the inhospitable 'home' that apologetic philosophy would have us make our own, Adorno turns back to a persisting 'autonomy' that is not celebrated in a formalistic sense as a supposedly intrinsic feature of timelessly aesthetic objects or an invariant form of specifically aesthetic judgment or perception that would always correspond to their relevant objects in advance. There is no question of a nostalgic return to or re-invocation of the kind of communally shared art that Hegel and so many of his contemporaries had identified with the life of the *polis* and that Wagner would initially attempt to rejuvenate under Young-Hegelian influence by appeal to the "all-embracing artwork" or later to the even more dubious "consecrated stage festival drama." The truth-moment of the end of art *qua* religion of art, the undeniable contemporary centrality of the arts of concrete subjectivity and interiority, as Kierkegaard would describe them, of emancipated literature and absolute music, could not be willed away, and disenchanted exteriority cannot be banished at a stroke and its opposite conjured forth by apostrophizing a pre-modern, pre-autonomous, pre-aesthetic concept of art as the epiphany of the rediscovered sacred.

Adorno has been accused of concentrating almost exclusively upon a highly restricted period of art history and the theorizing associated with it, upon the age of autonomy. Hegel and other idealist thinkers of early modernity had found it necessary to disqualify or at least dislodge the traditional primacy of 'imitative' theories of art and representation in order in their different ways to emphasize the specific dignity of art as a unique form of human creativity and experience. This displacement of the concept of *mimesis,* and of the kind of epistemological and ontological 'realism' traditionally associated with it, advanced hand-in-hand with a stronger conception of individual genius and a different emphasis upon the expressive moment involved in both the production and reception of art and upon the distinctively vital and organic character of the work of art itself. This development possesses epochal significance as a symptomatic manifestation of what Charles Taylor has with some justice called the "expressivist paradigm," and it testifies to a simultaneous emancipation from a theological-metaphysical model that privileges 'divine' creation prior to and independent of human existence and contrasts the eminence of the 'works of God' over against the derivative 'works of man,' over against human self-creation in the domain of culture and 'second nature.' The historical supersession of this model is amply recorded in Hegel's explicit attempt to dismantle 'imitation' as the most appropriate concept for articulating the true significance of art, or of our relationship to the world in general.

At first sight, therefore, it appears somewhat provocative for Adorno to rehabilitate an expression that is so strongly associated with an apparently obsolete and pre-modern approach to artistic production. But again, the reintroduction and reformulation of this ancient term represents no abstract negation of a characteristically Hegelian and in some respects typically 'modern' claim. It does, however, reflect an emphatic turn to the 'object,' a reorientation of thinking toward an intellectual, affective, and somatic *responsiveness* to and fully acknowledged *dependency* upon something that is also always already mediated, whether as nature or as art. This ineliminable 'something' is never reducible to the subject's autarchic 'work,' to a pure spirit that would transform what it touches into a transparently reflected image of its own activity and treat the source of all making solely as resource, as the passive material, instrumental stuff, or inert substrate of human appropriation. In this connection, Adorno formulates his critique of idealism and his own differentiated 'realism' in a surprisingly straightforward way: the object that is given to the subject can continue to be on its own account, whereas the subject can never be without the object. But the latter can only show itself, and manifest the wealth of its own untapped possibilities, in cognitive and affective relation to its responsive and dependent other.

Adorno's deployment of 'mimesis,' in an interrelated variety of senses that also embraces anthropological and psychoanalytic elements, must be interpreted as an urgent 'corrective' undertaken in the light of his complex double reading of idealism and its ambiguous legacy. In the late essay "On Subject and Object," Adorno proposes the "priority of the object" as a revision of idealism that does more than invert the primacy of active subjective-spontaneous experience for a more passive and obedient reflection of what lies beyond its own control. (Adorno's polyvalent concept of 'mimesis' can also be read as a critical alternative to the dubiously 'realist' and ideological resuscitation of Hegelian aesthetics in the later Lukács and his attempt to differentiate and reformulate the Marxian *topos* of "*Wiederspiegelung*" by appealing to a historicized concept of 'imitation.'[17]) Since Adorno's complex and ramifying concept of mimesis emerges primarily from his analysis of the *dialectic* of Enlightenment as a progressively self-totalizing process of rationalization, there is no question of reverting to the objectivity of nature as the passive other of active self-determining subjectivity. For the task is to question the seemingly exhaustive duality of spirit and nature in terms of a presupposed, fixed and fixated, opposition between pure autonomy and sheer heteronomy, to reveal the character of this opposition as a 'result' with a reconstructible historical genesis that need not remain legislative for all future experience.

The acknowledgment of a necessary and precarious 'autonomy' in the domain of art neither endorses a narrowly construed aesthetic formalism nor recommends a conception of 'pure' culture indifferent to an inferior realm of concrete and material need; rather, it emphasizes the specifically artistic mediation of relevant content in a specific social and historical context. The 'content' must be sought precisely in and as 'form,' rather than read off from the work of art as independently identifiable or discursively reproducible 'message.' Adorno thus speaks expressly out of his own historical situation and responds directly to the pressing question of art's present or future possibility as a distinctive way of disclosing truth, of art's own continued 'right to existence.' Adorno is not interested in specifying some trans-historical function of art that could be captured in an essential and universal 'definition,' but in addressing the question concerning its changing role and potential, or imminent loss of it, under the specific social, political, and economic conditions of an ineluctably 'advancing' modernity. The fact that he effectively accords to art a single and decisive calling for us today—although it continues to perform, as it has always done, a variety of different functions and purposes of greater or lesser local significance in personal, social, cultural, and political life—arises from his commitment to the 'absolute' dimension of the idealist aesthetic tradition, which had always ascribed to art a unique and irreplaceable task in relation to what Hegel calls the "higher needs and interests of the spirit." Whether in Kant or his immediate successors, the question that we address to art—and art addresses to us—possesses a categorical status insofar as it ultimately concerns the 'interests of reason' and cannot be exhausted by reference to the undeniable contemporary role of art as entertainment, diversion, or optional leisure activity, etc. This is so, whether we speak of the aesthetic as a specific kind of human experience or as responsiveness to objects (where the latter can properly be approached neither in a 'neutral' theoretical nor in an 'interested' technical manner, but must touch and affect the inner-most character of the embodied subject in the free exercise of its sensuous and intellectual powers in response to something that is also 'given' to it) or whether we consciously enrich and expand the relevant concept of the 'cognitive' character of aesthetic experience and defend the disclosive po-tentiality of art as a locus not of informative but of transformative 'truth.' In the broadest sense Adorno's orientation is essentially 'ethical': art mat-ters as an implicit questioning of what it means not merely to live—or to live on—but to live well, to live a properly human life. And it already tells us much if the irreality of art seems to matter little or not at all, or perhaps only as solace, when compared with the self-denying rigors and demands of what is threateningly called 'real life.' If charged with an 'idealist' and anachronistic over-valuation of art and the aesthetic, Adorno might well endorse Hegel's remark that "the enormity of spirit's loss may be measured by the paucity of what satisfies it."[18]

III

Heidegger's critical relationship with Hegel seems, in contrast to Adorno, to be at once more massive and more elusive, with a tortuous and interesting intellectual prehistory in Heidegger's early development as a thinker. Heidegger's attitude to his speculative predecessor moves from one of initially admiring emulation, as documented in the striking enco-mium at the end of his *Habilitationsschrift* of 1916, through an apparent extreme of polemical distance throughout the 1920s, explicit at the end of *Being and Time,* to an arguably more differentiated engagement in his later interpretations of the tradition. It might be claimed that Heidegger, after reacting violently against his own scholastic theological and philosophical background and emphasizing the autonomy and priority of philosophy in a militantly 'atheistic' stance toward the traditional 'system' of Christianity, always tended to interpret Hegel in an overly conservative 'metaphysical' way. Certainly in *Being and Time* Heidegger's hostility to the characteristic language of post-Kantian idealist philosophy, and especially to its concep-tual rapprochement with a semi-secularized humanistic form of modern Christianity, finds exemplary expression in his vigorous attempt to forge a distinctive philosophical vocabulary of his own and to eschew the inherited conceptuality and terminology of 'subject,' 'ego,' 'person,' 'soul,' 'life,' and, perhaps especially, of the theologically saturated language of 'spirit.' Heidegger articulates a radically immanent this-worldly transcendence and simultaneously draws upon a subtly transformed religious rhetoric in explicating the intrinsically disclosive, but inescapably finite and mortal, character of human existence explicitly re-conceptualized as a unified but articulated structure of being-in-the-world. Although he already takes considerable pains to distinguish the project of fundamental ontology from anthropology in its usual naturalistic or cultural sense, renaming and rethinking the 'nature' or 'essence' of the finitely free being that we in each case are as *Dasein,* he can nonetheless appropriately describe his own kind of hermeneutic phenomenology as related to a sort of "*a priori* anthropology"[19] (analogously to the sense in which Kant's critical philosophy has been described as a "transcendental humanism"). Heidegger reworks the Copernican Turn in his own way, rejecting the naturalistic understanding of human existence and the way we allegedly 'know' the world and relinquishing the God's-eye view and the contemplative bias he associates with the metaphysical tradition.

It is not entirely surprising, therefore, that *Being and Time* would often initially be read in subjectivist and existentialist terms or, subsequently, in a reductively pragmatic or functionalist manner that privileges the human being, oriented by its particular interests and purposes, at the center of the world in place of God as highest being and maker. Emphatically repudiating the vaunted primacy of 'theory,' of a purely spectatorial cognitive stance, Heidegger's analysis could easily be construed as predominantly instrumental in character. In this context two striking, and arguably related, omissions, or at least instances of relative neglect, seemed to appear at the heart of the fragmentary *Being and Time*: the realm of 'nature,' as anything significantly other than the objectified correlate of scientific-theoretical projection (along with the specific mode of being peculiar to non-human 'life'), and the realm of art and the problem of the 'aesthetic' dimension in the modern sense of the term.

It has often been remarked that the earlier Heidegger showed surprisingly little real interest in themes that emerged into such prominence later: the question of poetry, language, and art in the 1930s, and that of 'nature' conceived in terms of *phusis* later still. This is seriously misleading inasmuch as Heidegger's first encounter with Hölderlin, and with the works and writings of van Gogh, for example, actually predated the Great War. In lectures delivered shortly after the end of the war, Heidegger is already quoting Sophocles, in Hölderlin's translation, to illustrate the striking difference between the objectivistic conception of nature (and specifically the earth, as motion, extension, and matter) and the way in which the world is primarily disclosed to the concernful dwelling that always already characterizes human existence and permits things of different kinds to show themselves, in a potentially complex variety of ways, as mattering to and for us.

Nonetheless, the analysis of so-called 'gear' or 'equipment' (*Zeug*) and the priority of the ready-to-hand in Heidegger's discussion of world, together with the relatively undeveloped account of language in the full range of its possibilities, have also served to conceal some of the implications of the work (both with regard to a non-, or less than, objectivistic perspective upon 'nature' and a non-, or more than, subjectivistic perspective upon the affective human dimension of attunement and the phenomena traditionally described in terms of 'expression'). If readers had accorded as much attention to Heidegger's discussion of existential spatiality, the place of dwelling, the house and church to which *Being and Time* also alludes, as they had to the tools that furnish one case of the ready-to-hand, if they had pondered the further implications of the "wherefrom" as well as the "wherefore" of such artifacts—of the material cause as well as the final cause that resides 'in another'—they would not perhaps have been quite so surprised by the apparently novel turn of Heidegger's thinking in the writings of the succeeding years. But it remains true that the aforementioned absence of any explicit discussion of works of art, or of living beings, neither of which can appropriately be understood solely through the two categories of the ready-to-hand and the present-at-hand, has strongly contributed to a foreshortened interpretation of *Being and Time*.

The essay "The Origin of the Work of Art" does of course extend and deepen some of the relevant themes intermittently suggested if not always explicitly broached in the earlier work. A painting *of* equipment, though fabricated, is not *like* equipment: it resembles an end in itself or an ultimate "for the sake of which" like that which characterizes *Dasein* itself. It is not destined to any particular use or purpose, but shows up in its own right and shows forth the true character of what it presents in the context of world and earth. The work 'works' by bringing out, or de-familiarizing, what is otherwise overlooked, or taken for granted, in our immediate use of and absorption in things and is marked by an indissoluble identity of medium and content that cannot be divorced into anything like material base and signifying superstructure. The work can be 'understood' neither through detached inspection as an object nor through pre-reflective utilization as an implement. Nonetheless Heidegger is reluctant to repeat the traditional modern appeal to a certain kind of subjective experience and a supposedly 'disinterested' standpoint that might itself appear all too contemplative. He is equally unwilling, in a way that acknowledges the autonomous or self-standing character of art, to re-invoke the language of 'imitation' or 'depiction' or to separate out the 'thingly' givenness of the work from the 'meaning' it is supposed to bear (lest it become a merely provisional symbol or propaedeutic allegory that points away from its emphatic presencing in the direction of an ideal sense independently reproducible by the 'mind'). Even more clearly, the ineliminable 'earthy' character of the work, in its very constitution and through the play of concealment and unconcealment it enacts, excludes its interpretation in terms of a mere vehicle and prevents its subordination to an allegedly superior or more transparent conceptual truth. The account implicitly presents itself as a foil and contrast to any idealist approach that would 'demote' (*herabsetzen*, as Hegel often puts it) the sensible material of art as a 'means' of expressing a higher content.

The work opens up and unveils the being of beings. In the lyrical description of van Gogh's painting, which allegedly discloses a world, Heidegger makes his first reference to 'earth.' But this discussion appears simply preliminary to the fuller and memorable evocation, we might say celebration, of the only other concrete 'example' of a work of art (or work of 'art-religion' as Hegel or Schleiermacher would say): the generically identified but eloquently invoked temple. Neither the painting nor the temple, in this account, could properly be described as 'aesthetic objects.' Hegel expressly alludes to a Greek temple when he introduces his discussion of the 'system of the arts,' and this is not described as a 'purely' aesthetic object in a remotely formalist sense either. In Kantian terms we should have to speak here of 'dependent beauty' and refer the thing to the purpose it subserves; Hegel also invokes this 'purpose' as the appropriate housing of the god where the people gather in commemoration of their own essential historical world in a particular and special place shielded from the raging elements, etc. Heidegger seems deliberately to echo, and profoundly transform and intensify, Hegel's account. For the latter, the temple represents the first, though ultimately rudimentary, form of art-religion in which man makes himself at home in a meaningful world embracing the communal life of a culture as it defines and understands itself through its gods.

What Heidegger calls 'great art,' in this essay at least, seems limited to the kind of work—at the level of creation, address, and preservation—that first founds and reveals the tasks and standards of the collective historical existence of a people in its distinctive place (and it is far from clear what the role and status of Heidegger's first example of the painting occupies in this respect). Heidegger's recurrence to the supposed thesis of the end of art, at least with respect to its highest vocation, both at the close of his essay and on subsequent occasions, indicates the paradigmatic role of Hegel as a foil to his own investigation. It has been claimed that the essay represents a simultaneous retrieval and 'destruction' of Hegel as the exemplary culmination of a metaphysical understanding of art: the 'great' art whose death Hegel allegedly analyzes, confirms, and accepts is reclaimed here at least as an imminent possibility of the present beyond the distorting and reductive confines of a merely individualistic and subjective 'aesthetic consciousness.' Hegel, however, certainly did not regard 'great art' as essentially coterminous with the (vanished) truth of art-religion, or art in its capacity to shape and present an entire world in exemplary and privileged form. He acknowledged the fundamentally transformed character of its role in modernity—its loss of immediate solidarity with an inherited religious or metaphysical substance—without wishing to understand art in purely aesthetic terms of subjective experience or individual taste. But the thematic of the aporetic 'autonomy' of art remains after the collapse of speculative idealism and its failure to sublate without remainder the more than aesthetic question that art persists in posing. We might then interrogate the acknowledged autonomy of 'modern' art less as the expression of an inadequate conception of art itself than as the appropriate self-reflection of its own critical character as the internal antithesis of society. We might with Adorno undertake a critique of the conceptuality of German idealism from within the tradition itself, not so much eschewing or immediately replacing its vocabulary as exploring its limits and hitherto untapped potential with regard to the experience from which it lives, which it both reveals and conceals, but has failed, for more than philosophical reasons, to redeem. And here an intriguing possibility for posthumously encouraging the difficult 'dialogue' of which we spoke at the beginning would be to address a poetic thinking that arose within the context of the post-Kantian idealism, which it partly furthered and certainly questioned. For the 'spirit' of Hölderlin could equally be said to hover over some of the densest and most characteristic reflections of Heidegger and the later Adorno, although little more than a hint in this regard can be suggested here.

Hölderlin's work was initially governed by the thought of a comprehensive, non-coercive reconciliation of the harsh polarities and disabling dualisms apparently bequeathed by Kantian thought, and principally the bifurcation of subject and object articulated as a fixated opposition between spirit and nature. Yet he equally insisted upon an anti-identitarian, literally 'anti-monarchical,' perspective that resists the institution of a single controlling principle—as in a metaphysical first philosophy—that threatens to suppress diversity and differentiation. He draws attention to the fundamentally enabling character of reciprocal interaction, on the intellectual, affective, and somatic level: "It is to the good that . . . no one power alone rules in heaven or earth. Absolute monarchy everywhere cancels itself since it has no objects. . . . Everything touches every other thing, is touched even as it acts on others."[20] The affirmative conception of finitude and fragility, within and beyond the exclusively human domain, the expressly acknowledged interdependence of subject and object, art and nature, each calling forth and revealing the significance of the other, evokes an ethics of gratitude that transcends a traditionalist ideology of subservience or deferential passivity. For Hölderlin also accepts the intrinsic dependency of the 'divine' dimension, which is no transcendent causal agency, upon the sphere of mortal human experience. While repudiating the metaphysical conception of an infinite creator God external to and independent of the created world, there is a sublimated theological residue in this emphasis upon human 'creatureliness' within the economy of nature, upon the privileged vocation of man as the finite site of the self-manifestation and self-enjoyment of life through the indispensable cultivating—

the fostering, tending, and protecting—addition of human 'art.' This projected vision of reconciled dwelling invokes a transformed relationship to inner and outer nature. Hence Hölderlin can describe art and the philosophy that attempts to illuminate it, in a very Adornian spirit, as a *paradoxon,* a kind of active service, or *Dienst,* that responds to something we have not created ourselves—something that is not simply "the work of human hands," but nonetheless needs such a response to be fully itself.[21]

By contrast, we might do well to consider a famous passage from the *Philosophy of Spirit,* where Hegel speaks of the "sovereign ingratitude of spirit."[22] Spirit, as it were, lives off nature and comes to be in dependency upon nature, which it simultaneously sublates and turns into a means of its own realization, thereby giving rise to an "ingratitude" (*Undankbarkeit*). The contrast between Hegel's ingratitude of spirit and Hölderlin's notion of active service, which emerges from an internal critique of idealist thinking in reflecting on art and nature, perhaps provides us with the means to articulate a certain proximity to Adorno and Heidegger, even though Hölderlin has nearly always been claimed pre-eminently by Heidegger and as Heidegger's own poet of poets.

CHAPTER SIX

Beyond Critique? Art and Power

Krzysztof Ziarek

When it comes to the notion of critique, art raises quite particular problems, in part at least because artworks refuse to submit themselves to the parameters of critical inquiry and, on occasion, appear to undo the very framework that makes critique possible and valid. The problem inherent in critiquing art is a specific one, as it concerns the difficulty involved in understanding how or in what manner art itself can be envisioned as critical: both as a source and as a work of critique. In short, the difficulty with furnishing a critique of art lies in artworks' particular resistance vis-à-vis the very idea of critique, that is, in a real conceptual quandary that interpreting art as a form of critique entails. The way in which an artwork "works," that is, its specific artistic "language," as both Adorno and Heidegger like to refer to it, is not a language of critique. On the contrary, it is a language that needs to be translated into a more familiar discursive practice or optics, which would make interpretation, critical engagement, or assessment possible. As Heidegger might put it, what an artwork "says" takes place as if through words and yet is not equivalent to them, and this is the case even, or perhaps especially, in poetry, which Heidegger sees, already in "The Origin of the Work of Art," as paradigmatic of this idiomatic language of arts. There is thus both a need to render art's 'language' into words and to recognize that this operation involves an inevitable mis-saying or mistranslation, even when we deal with language arts, such as poetry or prose, or more broadly literature. Yet the problem here lies not just in the inadequacy of translation, or in the eventual inability to render fully the idiomatic languages of various arts into a critical discourse. Rather, at issue is art's distinctive capacity to outstrip and undermine critique, that is, to void, or perhaps even to transform, the very parameters within which critique operates and becomes recognizable as critique, and which critique also, by default, reconfirms and petrifies. What I am going to suggest here is that this idiomatic force of art, by calling into question the operations and powers of critique, becomes, in a very specific sense, more radical than critique. Ultimately, this distinct 'radicalism' of art consists in its capacity to bring into question the very notion of power by means of which critique invests its own procedures with the ability to critique and the authority to judge. The purpose here is not to diminish or disable critical thinking but to indicate instead that art's 'language,' though it always calls for critique and interpretation, remains of a different order and force than critique itself. What this also implies is that the idea of critique cannot do justice to how art works, to how its idiomatic language operates. To put it briefly, the force of art works otherwise than critique.

What underlies this 'critical' predicament is the broader issue of art's relationship to empirical reality and social practice. The manner in which art can be thought of as critique is linked to, even coded into, the very form that the relation of artworks to society takes. The issues of critique and praxis are folded into each other and constitute the parameters of the modern discussion of art vis-à-vis the social sphere. This double issue of art's critical force and its connection to society emerges with particular poignancy in modernism, especially in the artistic and social radicalism of the avant-garde. The accent that the avant-garde places on the critical force of art has to do with the phenomenon of the 'death' of aesthetics and the consequent change in art's function announced in the radical works of the avant-garde. Responding at least in part to the intensifying aestheticization of experience, the avant-garde undertakes a radical de-aestheticization of art. Such de-aestheticization does not simply mean divesting art of beauty and aesthetic pleasure but entails also a more 'revolutionary' disinvestment of art from aesthetics, that is, from the conception of art as essentially an aesthetic phenomenon. What emerges instead, especially in Futurism and Dadaism, is the practice of art as an event, which attempts not only to undo the aestheticization of experience but also to undermine the traditional aesthetic idea of art. Futurism, Dada, Surrealism, and their aftermath recast Hegel's notion of the end of art: what comes to an end for them is not art but, instead, aesthetics, or the aesthetic concept of art, which construes the artwork in terms of aesthetic experience, pleasure, judgment, and their correlative, commodification.

In the aftermath of this displacement of aesthetics, it is precisely the question of the critical force of art that comes to define some of the most trenchant artistic practices and theoretical reflections characteristic of the twentieth century artistic and literary scene. When art is stripped of its aesthetic functions, the problem of redefining its social role becomes of particular importance, even of historical urgency. Either art progressively merges with the culture and entertainment industry, or it inaugurates a new modality of the critical relation to the social sphere. The avant-garde's disavowal of aesthetics as the horizon of art's existence does not mean that art becomes immediately political, or that its critical function becomes transparent, easy to grasp and evaluate. Rather, what the avant-garde makes apparent is the need for a rethinking of the way in which art can be considered critical. As I have already suggested, such a reconceptualization of art's relation to the social brings into question the very notion of critique.

I

The strained relation between art and critique is perhaps the most interesting and, at the same time, the most difficult among the tensions running through Adorno's *Aesthetic Theory,* because this particular tension redefines the horizon within which contemporary art can be thought of *as* critical. Throughout *Aesthetic Theory* Adorno insists on the importance of interpreting art, even of producing a philosophical critique of art, which he himself is in the process of constructing in his book. Yet, even more insistently, he keeps claiming that art undermines all such attempts, calling into question the very discourses—social, philosophical, aesthetic—that attempt to define art and distill its critical functions. This difficulty is literally composed into the form of Adorno's text, which, as soon as it appears to succeed in defining art's role in a historical and semi-systematic manner, restores the paradoxical status of art, as if trying to continuously undermine the theoretical pretensions of its own argument. This is why the somewhat recondite character of Adorno's formulations in *Aesthetic Theory* may be due as much to its 'programmatic' understanding of art's paradoxical relation to society and its forms of critique, as to the fact that the text remains unfinished. This difficulty comes to a head when Adorno announces that "real denunciation is probably only a capacity of form, which is overlooked by a social aesthetic that believes in themes."[1] This remark makes clear that the social and political criticism evident in art is not sufficiently critical for Adorno, because it remains caught in the very discourse that, even if used to criticize society and to try to open a path to transformation, implicitly legitimates the status quo it tries to call into question. As it buys into the critical claims and adopts the discursive strategies that modern society makes available to it, such art—for instance, Brecht's work—finds itself, against its explicit aspirations, in complicity with what it intends to criticize. In spite of its polemical and 'negative' surface, art that employs accepted discursive and representational practices to advance its claims fails to critique and transform the parameters structuring social praxis and thus, contrary to its objective, legitimates the status quo. Because politically engaged art operates in socially recognized idioms, the 'critique' at work in such art remains fundamentally positive, and thus false, incapable of the requisite labor of negativity. By contrast, progressive aesthetics for Adorno is a constant labor of the negative on the level of form, irreducible to social criticism and untranslatable into critical pronouncements.

The fact that form for Adorno is probably the only truly critical capacity brings the problem of the relation of art and critique into focus. On the one hand, what needs to be understood is how form works as critique, that is, how it "negates the categorial determinations stamped on the empirical world"[2] and possibly revises the parameters of social practice. On the other, it should be remembered that this critical force specific to art gains its strength at the expense of other forms of critique. The critical capacity invested in art's form calls into question, perhaps even disqualifies, critique as such, disclaiming critique's apparently revolutionary force. Seen in this way, art in modernity acquires a double task, a task that defines artworks as a peculiar paradox: art is to be a critique, and, at the same time, in order to function as such, it needs to undermine the very parameters that make critique possible. Thus art is the paradox of the necessity and the impossibility of critique. In the context of Adorno's *Aesthetic Theory*, it is possible to say that, in a sense, what we encounter in modernist art is a critique in the negative, by which I mean not only that art performs the negation of social practice but that it also undermines its corollary forms of critique. This is to say that art is critical by way of negating even the absolutely requisite critique of domination and the absence of freedom pervasive in modern societies. Nowhere would Adorno suggest that the forms of social, political, or philosophical critique that issue from modern social praxis are not important; in fact, he would insist that they remain indispensable. However, the paradoxical autonomy that art achieves in modern society gives it the opportunity, and the task, to call into question, and thus in a way to radicalize, the patterns of critique that are possible within the social sphere. For Adorno, critiques, no matter how negative or revolutionary, are necessarily fashioned within the categorial determinations available within the social world, and as such they cannot, despite their critical force, undermine the very praxis from which they issue and within which they operate. Art, on the other hand, by virtue of its autonomy, can negate society in a more radical manner. What this capacity to negate or denounce figured as art's form implies is that art has the specific force to call into question the forms of critique available in the social sphere.

This paradoxical situation describes the enigma of art, which Adorno signals in various contexts throughout *Aesthetic Theory*. Let me mention the most important one here. Claiming that art has "the immanent character of being an act,"[3] Adorno underscores the paradoxical capacity of art to be both less and more than praxis. Less because art's act seems ineffectual from the point of view of pragmatic action: art does not do anything. Yet art is at the same time more than praxis because it undermines the very parameters on which the conception and the actualizations of practice depend: "Art, however, is more than praxis because by its aversion to praxis it simultaneously denounces the narrow untruth of the practical world."[4] Art becomes of social importance precisely by virtue of calling into question, as Adorno would say, the very terms on which social praxis operates.[5] Being both more and less than praxis, art calls into question the narrow sense of praxis, and thus of any form of politics that stems from this practice.

As Adorno puts it, for art, action understood within the parameters of social praxis is "a cryptogram of domination."[6] Therefore, the primary question emerging from modern(ist) art is the critique of domination, or, to
evoke Heidegger, of machination and manipulative power, which serve as
the template for action and praxis. For Adorno, art is emphatically not an
alternative site for political critique, for a kind of politics by other means,
or merely an extension (either a representation or an amplification) of social antagonisms or cultural ideologies coursing through the social fabric.
Art is 'political' to the extent that, as an event, it undermines the practices
of power and domination, which serve as the blueprint for politics and action.

One way of looking at this paradox of art and critique would be to
say that art is a more radical critique than other forms of critique—for instance, philosophical, ideological, or aesthetic critiques. The difference between art and other forms of critique would then be a matter of degree, of
the intensity or radicality of critique instantiated in art. Yet the difference
inscribed in art is more 'radical' than that, since artworks call into question and exceed the very idea of critique. Critique—and Adorno's *Aesthetic
Theory* is aware of this problem—is a form of power discourse, and as such
participates in practices of domination in spite of its subversive intentions.
Even though critique is a negative idiom, a counter-discourse to power, it
nonetheless inscribes itself within the operations of power and its discursive articulations. In short, critique needs the power of negation to achieve
its goal, and it is this necessity that always already 'compromises' critique
in the specific sense in which it renders critical discourse part of the operations of power, making it, often against its wishes, into "a cryptogram of
domination," as Adorno puts it. By contrast, artworks, I would argue, can
undo and desist from power, which means that art is a form of 'discourse'
whose radicality consists in undermining power's pervasive hold on contemporary reality.

II

To clarify how art may be seen as more 'radical' than critique, and
as calling critique into question, I propose to rethink what Adorno regards as a critical lacuna in Heidegger's work, namely, the absence in it of

critique and of the force of negativity. In the 1960–61 lecture course *Ontologie und Dialektik*,[7] largely devoted to an implicit polemic with Heidegger's thought, Adorno defines critique as a decision, a confrontation between two different moments: the concept and the object, an opposition in which the conceptual moment becomes fulfilled in the object while, in the same gesture, the object is shown to correspond to the concept.[8] In short, at stake in the critique is the requisite mediation between the concept and the object, between the subjective and the objective moments. A page later Adorno declares that "the concept of critique, as far as I can see, has no place in Heidegger's philosophy."[9] One could say, adapting here a distinction Heidegger often makes in his work with regard to science, that this statement by Adorno is quite correct and yet remains untrue. Adorno is correct in suggesting that the idea of critique as requisite mediation does not play much of an explicit role in Heidegger. However, the conclusion Adorno draws from his own assertion, namely that Heidegger's thought is therefore not critical at all, is obviously untrue. For, rather than focusing on the conceptual and the objective and their consequent mediation, Heidegger is interested in the notion of the event (*Ereignis*) as the unfolding of the space-time in which dialectics and mediation become possible in the first place. Critique in Adorno is based on the notions of negation and mediation, while for Heidegger, the event, which inaugurates the very space for mediation, has a nihilating force that is more radical than negation. This is the case because it is nihilation that makes differentiation, and with it also negation, possible. As the refusal of grounding, nihilation is, in Heidegger's words from his lectures on Hegel, the "highest guarantee" of differentiation and decision.[10] It is thus the temporal, nihilating force of the event that ensures the possibility of critique and transformation. Neither immediate nor indeterminate, this nihilating force of the event allows for difference, determination, and mediation to be put into, and maintained in, play.

These remarks make it possible to see Heidegger's thought as a deliberate attempt to radicalize, as he explicitly states in *Hegel* and in *Besinnung*,[11] the notion of negativity, and with it also the idea of critique, beyond the dialectical schema. Unfortunately, Adorno misses this point when he claims that Heidegger's thought of being evacuates the force of negation and critique. What interests Heidegger are not the metaphysical mechanics or the dialectical forms of critique but the ensuring of a continuous opening up of the space in which radical critique would still be possible. In other words, what is radically critical for Heidegger, radical in the sense of keeping the origin in play, as he puts it in *Besinnung*,[12] is the event understood as the unfolding middle of differentiation, the middle that opens, as it were, prior to difference and negation. Without being reducible to affirmation or complicity, what the event in the Heideggerian sense, but also in the shape that it takes in avant-garde art, instantiates is an otherwise to critique. It would be a mistake to see this otherwise as uncritical, or as the absence of critique, for it is, in fact, critical *otherwise*. To put it differently, its force, operating beyond a yes and a no, and thus beyond mediation, is more radical than any form of critique. And this critical radicalism of the event is such that it calls into question even critique itself.

This is not the place to show how this critical radicalism of the event is tied in Heidegger's thought to art, poetry, and language. Suffice it to say that it is art, and specifically its force of *poiesis,* that for Heidegger constitutes a particularly important modern mark of the event's futural, radically critical, potential. This force of *poiesis* works in an enigmatic way, and what is specific to this enigma is how art manages to refuse the terms of power, desisting from power and dissipating it. In the late 1930s and 1940s, Heidegger explains power as *Machenschaft,* as machination and manipulative power, which organize reality into a state of what he calls a "total war."[13] Armed conflict issues from this total mobilization of modern being into the terms of power, where power comes to be understood as practices of *machen*: that is, practices of making, production, or manipulation. In a later essay, "The Question Concerning Technology," Heidegger defines power as technicity, that is, as a modern way of disposing relations into the *Gestell,* or the enframing,[14] which can be understood as a set of practices through which what is becomes constituted essentially in terms of how it is posited, produced, regulated, and ordered into a standing reserve (of resources). Those practices become operative within the overall frame that shapes being into multiple terms of availability: as resources, whose existence is defined through use, manipulation, and production, or more recently as information, which is intrinsically determined as available for exploitation, storage, and reprogramming. If power operates in ways that render the actual as available, such power is intrinsically technical. By contrast, the artistic force of *poiesis* eschews and empties power: instead of rendering available, it 'lets be,' as Heidegger puts it. It lets be in the specific sense in which it releases what is from the technicity characteristic of modern power, which produces and creates by putting in place and enforcing availability and machination.

III

This difference between rendering available and letting be, though only later fleshed out in these terms, is already suggested in "The Origin of the Work of Art," through the distinction Heidegger draws between what happens with material in equipment and in the work of art.[15] In art's characteristic revealing of its material, what is put into question is the status of the artwork as a produced/created entity, in which the material, through the process of creation—a sub-genre of production—receives an artistic form. In this way, the materiality of the work of art calls into question the primacy of production, that is, of making, designing, and creating, which involve the fashioning of the material toward an end, an aesthetic end in the case of art. Thus, it is not only the *Gestalt,* the figure inscribed in art's material, but also the very materiality of the artwork, that marks the tension and the possible reversals between *techne* and *poiesis.* We could say, therefore, that the matter of art, which for Heidegger spells the end of the metaphysical idea of art and its various aesthetic incarnations, is intrinsically connected with the artwork's materiality, materiality that is never simply fashioned by the artist, but is also let be, and thus becomes revealed as what it is. Letting the material be, the work of art releases the material from its inscription into the operations of power, namely, from the material's subordination to the processes of production and creation. The event figured in the artwork's figure is a play of concealment and unconcealment, of making and letting be, and in order to be figured as such a play, it requires a different relation to the material: not simply one of production, manipulation, or creation, but, instead, one of letting be and release from power. No doubt the material in art is fashioned and formed, but in being formed it is also released into the very properness of its materiality. As Adorno puts it, in art, the material is dominated in a specific way, which, paradoxically, undoes domination. What I am suggesting here, is that in the artwork, the material is shaped in a way that undoes the very parameters of production and of the creative power to which the material is submitted in the artistic process. In short, in being produced, the work of art undoes production and its intimate correlation with the operations of power. Releasing the material from the operations of power, the work of art calls the techno-metaphysics of power and of production into question not only through its *Gestalt* but also through the characteristic fore-grounding of materiality. The end of art can be seen, therefore, as a release of the material into its materiality, as the instantiation of a different, non-metaphysical relation to the material, a relation which is power-free, *macht-los*—that is, released from power and production. The work of art becomes thus a complex play of power and the power-free, of making and letting be, of creation and the undoing of the very paradigm of creation and production. That is why the artwork continuously figures its own end as art: it produces itself in order to call its own production into question and to release its figure and its material from power. Both in its figure and through its materiality, the artwork thus instantiates an inflection of pow-er into the power-free. It marks in this way the end of metaphysics: not as a specific moment in history, but instead as a repeated release of relations, and with them, of being, from power.

The solidity of the material, its certain impenetrability, which Hei-degger underscores throughout "The Origin of the Work of Art," shelters the figure. But this sheltering is at the same time a paradoxical exposition of any notion of solidity or substantiality to the nihilation, to the noth-ing, intrinsic to the happening of being. What the material in the art-work shelters and maintains in play is the nihilating force of temporality, the futural ungrounding opened by and as the event. The end of art does not mean the end of the artwork but instead indicates the appearance of the artwork's materiality as sheltering the nihilating force of the event. Though, of course, not limited to art, this force is brought to the fore with a particular poignancy in artworks. But why would it be the case that this force would nihilate power and release relations into the power-free espe-cially in artworks? The answer may lie indeed in the artwork's materiality. Since the material in the artwork is produced in a way that, foregrounding it as material, undoes the dominant paradigm of production and the op-erations of power implied in it, the artwork's material comes to inscribe in its very materiality the difference between *techne* and *poiesis,* as well as the inflection of the operations of power into the power-free. The fact that in the artwork the material not only does not disappear into usefulness but, conversely, becomes disclosed and let be as material over and against the power to fashion and to produce marks the force of the power-free. By letting the material be, the artwork performs the difference of letting be from production. In this specific sense, the artwork's material materializes, quite literally, the matter of art: freedom from power (*Machtlosigkeit*).

The force of art lies therefore in its ability to call into question and rework the very paradigm of making and producing (*machen*), disclosing its inscription in the operations of power (*Macht*) and their ways of manipulating (*Machenschaft*) and foreclosing the event of being into resources and products, in which beings and their relations become conduits of intensifying power. Heidegger's rethinking of the work of art indicates how the very idea of production is predicated on the 'disappearance' of materiality, effected by the operations of forming and remaking, intrinsic to the activity of making. What the work of art brings into the open about equipment—tools and instruments, but perhaps also more broadly, products and commodities—is the manner in which materiality becomes inducted and disappeared into power: its being a material is subsumed into power that flows through the relations that make matter into a product (a commodity) and allow it to function as such without regard to its materiality. Rather than foregrounding and letting the material be the material, production accentuates the operations of power that not only make production possible but become 'effective' and intensified through this process. In short, what production brings about is the intensification of being *qua* power, often a literal production of being into and as power relations. By contrast, the work of art transforms the operations of power into an event that is power-free, *machtfrei,* as Heidegger puts it, in just this sense that it releases forces and relations from power: in this event, being happens as *das Machtlose.* "In its essential ground, being is never power and, therefore, also never powerlessness. If we call it the power-free (*das Macht-lose*), this does not mean that being lacks power; rather, the name indicates that being, given the way it unfolds, remains disengaged [*losgelöst*: detached, freed, loosened], from power."[16] Since the happening of being is *macht-los* or *macht-frei*—and Heidegger uses both terms as equivalent to indicate a power-free happening—being can never be made powerless (*entmachtet*). This is the case because rendering something powerless presupposes the binary of power and powerlessness. To be rendered powerless, something has to be already 'power-ful,' that is, it has to exist within the domain of power and be implicated in its forms and operations. Since being happens as free or released from power—this disengagement is marked by the suffix -*los*—it can be neither empowered nor made powerless; in fact, these very terms entail a decisive misrepresentation of being.

In order to distinguish, as Heidegger repeatedly does, this difficult, non-dialectical notion of the powerfree from powerlessness, one can draw upon another key term in Heidegger's work in the late 1930s: *Nichtung*, or nihilation. To begin, the disengagement or freedom from power signified by *das Machtlose* has to be thought as a spatio-temporal nihilation, that is, as the nihilating force of futurity, which always already opens up and 'empties' what is into the arriving future. Heidegger makes a critical distinction between the metaphysical concept of nothingness (as the indeterminate immediacy) and nothingness as nihilation at work in being, when it is seen non-metaphysically as the abyss (*Abgrund*).[17] While within metaphysics nihilation appears primarily as negation or as indeterminate immediacy, Heidegger thinks its force as a release or a freeing, which enables opening onto the future and transformation: "The nothing is neither negation of beings nor that of beingness [*Seiendheit*], nor is it the 'privation' of being, its deprivation, which would also be annihilation, but *the nothing is the first and the highest gift* [*Geschenk*] *of being. . . .* "[18] What Heidegger calls the highest gift or dispensation of being indicates the futural and transformative opening of the event: namely, a freeing and a detachment from, a letting go or a nihilation of, the past's hold on the present, which enables change as intrinsic to being's occurrence. As a release that 'nihilates' all forms of grounds, foundations, identities, or essences, nihilation literally enables the future, bringing about openness to and the capacity for the new, thus ceaselessly putting difference and transformation into play.

Heidegger calls nihilation the "gift of being" to draw attention to the fact that nihilation is characterized primarily by its force of enabling, a force that needs to be thought beyond the notions of positing and negation, because nihilation constitutes the element in which both positivity and negativity become possible to begin with. In "Letter on Humanism," Heidegger remarks that enabling not only can achieve this or that but also can let something essentially unfold in its provenance, that is, let it be. It is on the 'strength' [*Kraft*] of such enabling [*Vermögen*] by favoring [*Mögen*] that something is properly able to be. . . Being is the enabling-favoring, the 'may-be.' [*Das Sein als das Vermögend-Mögende ist das "Mög-liche."*] As the element, being is the 'quiet power' [*stille Kraft*] of the favoring-enabling, that is, of the possible [*des Möglichen*].[19]

The play on and the intrinsic proximity of *Vermögen* (enabling), *Mögen* (favoring), and *das Mögliche* (the possible) illustrate the way in which enabling is to be seen as the opening up of the possibility for something to be, and thus to be what it is. Nihilation, as the futural vector of the time-space opening up out of the event, empties, that is, clears and illuminates (in the sense of *Lichtung*), the space of and for the possible. Nihilation thus enables, makes possible, what exists to be precisely what it is, that is, to be in its possibilities for being. Such 'possibilization' of being keeps opening up and holding open the futurity of transformations, including the eventual non-being. As such a 'possibilization' of being, nihilation for Heidegger indicates an enabling emptiness always already opening onto possibilities for being. Such nihilation occurs, therefore, 'before' and 'beyond' positivity and negativity, and needs to be freed from the 'negative' connotations of negation and nihilism. In its specific sense of the futural possibilization of being, nihilation is more 'negative' than any negation, and yet, precisely by virtue of the radicalism of its nihilating force beyond both a yes and a no, its vector is that of enabling and opening onto the possible.

What is critical to understanding this 'radicalism' beyond negation and affirmation with which Heidegger invests the enabling force of nihilation is its capacity to refuse power, making, and machination. As he puts it in *Die Geschichte des Seyns*: "Being is nothing/Nothing nihilates/Nihilation refuses/The refusal guards."[20] Nihilation forgoes and empties power, and in this specific sense, nihilation can be understood as desisting from making, effectuation, or production. As an enabling, nihilation lets something be in all its futurally opening possibilities for being, which include, among others, being made, manipulated, empowered, rendered powerless, et cetera. In short, the operations of power, with their intrinsic dialectic of power and powerlessness, are rendered possible within, or out of, the 'element' of nihilation, that is, within the time-space opening up, or 'nihilating,' out of the event. Yet as such, nihilation, though always already (mis)translated into the operations of power and making, refuses power. It does not contest, resist, or negate power, nor does it posit a counter-power. Rather, more radically than these operations of power and counter-power, nihilation enables being otherwise than power, making possible an otherwise *to* power. As the element, the 'emptiness,' wherein power comes into being, that is, becomes enabled as a possibility, nihilation remains both 'prior to' and 'beyond' the perimeter and the parameters of power. And it does so by virtue of its more radical 'possibilization' of being than the possibilities created and made by and within the operations of power. Enabling power, nihilation also enables an otherwise to power. In this way, however, nihilation refuses itself to the operations of power it enables and, in this same gesture, makes it possible to be otherwise than power, namely, apart from power and its twin, powerlessness.

This refusal and slipping away from power not only keeps freeing the space-time of history futurally, or into the future, but also guards it as an event. It does so by nihilating beings and the power relations among them, and this nihilation needs to be thought here carefully not in terms of absence or lack but as the event through which and as which history is given. Obviously, in the event, the space is made open for power relations. Yet in the same gesture in which power is made possible, it is also 'nihilated' in the sense that it is held open, by the futural/enabling force of nihilation, to its otherwise, that is, to freedom from power. Making power possible, nihilation also empties power, not into powerlessness, but into a power-free enabling. Seen in the context of historicity and finitude, nihilation enables beings to be more in being (*seiender*), that is, more in terms of historico-temporal happening than of enduring or constancy. As such an enabling, nihilation constitutes the 'gift' of being, in the sense that it releases beings into their event-like occurrence, thus allowing them back into their proper temporality and ground-free existence. Through this distinctive enabling, nihilation 'guards' the historicity of being from disappearance into seemingly solid, posited beings or objects. In a way, nihilation ensures that beings remain open and transformable by keeping in play their historical happening, which 'grounds' by detaching or freeing, as the *Ab-grund*, from grounds, essences, or objectifications. Rethought by Heidegger in this specific way, nihilation cannot be mistaken for either negation or bad infinity. Neither empty nor indeterminate but instead emptying and enabling, nihilation indicates the futural and transformative unfolding of being as event.

By completely transforming the notion of grounding from foundationalism to "grounding" as *Ab-grund*, nihilation enables an opening toward otherness, an openness that is ceaselessly reopened by the very happening of the event. As Heidegger writes in the *Contributions to Philosophy*, happening as nihilation, being enables and enforces otherness.[21] Nihilation gives otherness the force to keep power open to an other mode of relating: a power-free relating. This otherness enabled by nihilation cannot be subsumed into negation or opposition but marks instead the differentiation intrinsic to the event. This differentiation is 'grounded' not simply in difference but in the futurity kept open by nihilation. Furthermore, otherness here is not a matter of identity and difference, since it is inscribed not just on the ontic level of beings and entities, but on the level of the ontological. In short, otherness is there not because there are differences; rather, there are differences because otherness is enabled and 'enforced' by the very mode in which being happens, that is, by its event. To put it briefly, such otherness is 'in force' not by virtue of its power, that is, as a resisting counter-power or a subversive power, or, conversely, as a mark of its powerlessness, that is, as subject to and incapable of resisting power. Rather, such otherness rests on the strength of nihilation, which enables this otherness and lets it be power-free (*macht-los*). Since this otherness is held in play by the 'nihilating' happening of being, it happens beyond both negation and positing, beyond representation, sublation, erasure, or exclusion. What makes this otherness so resistant, so 'other,' to closure is the fact that it is enabled by the nihilation and its power-free sway.

Seen through the prism of nihilation, art's force is, therefore, the force of freedom from power, but a freedom that can no longer be conceived metaphysically. Within metaphysics, freedom pertains to the domain of the subject, and is consequently determined and shaped within the metaphysics of subjectivity. In the non-metaphysical perspective of being as the event, freedom becomes the 'matter' and the 'gift' of being, that is, the matter of whether the very spacing and temporalizing of history can remain disengaged from power. Freedom here entails letting being remain free from power, allowing it to unfold the way that, as Heidegger suggests, it occurs in accordance with its character as the event. This letting be is not passive, because it requires that *Dasein* allow nihilation to have an enabling force. Freedom thus becomes the question of whether and how *Dasein* occurs, of how being-there takes place in relation to the nihilation intrinsic to being. *Dasein* marks the site, the 'there,' where, thanks to its 'gift' of nihilation, being sheds the vestiges of anthropism and holds sway as a power-free event.[22]

IV

Yet this freedom, that is, the power-free happening of the event, keeps being misrecognized by metaphysics as powerlessness. This misrecognition follows from the fact that metaphysics operates in terms of power and the various patterns through which power puts in place, posits, and forms beings and relations in terms of making, representation, and machination. For Heidegger, power cannot fail to misrepresent the power-less as the powerless,[23] and the power-free as a lack or negation of power, because its own perspective does not admit of anything that does not transpire or explain itself in terms of power. In short, power narrows down the 'possibilization' enabled by nihilation exclusively to the terms of power, forecloses power's otherwise, and thus ends up marking all relations with a plus or a minus in regard to power. Consequently, within the power-bound parameters of metaphysics, if something does not present itself as powerful, it automatically becomes powerless and ineffective, deprived of any strength or ability of doing. Since within modern techno-metaphysics, power never operates as simply dominating or constraining but often, even primarily, as productive and creative, what is withdrawn from such essentially productive deployments of power, namely, *das Macht-lose*, or the power-free, is 'sensed' only as lack, that is, as absence of power, as the inability to act or to do anything.[24] In this way, the power-free, the very movement of enabling and 'possibilizing,' which for Heidegger is the "highest deed" because it makes possible and 'enforces' otherness, and thus holds open the possibility of transformation, becomes totally mischaracterized as the inability to do anything and the powerlessness to effect any change or transformation. While it is important to keep a critical distinction between productive manifestations of power, on the one hand, and domination or manipulation, on the other, these different operations nonetheless all 'effect' power, allowing it to circulate and intensify. What needs to be both delimited and transformed, as Heidegger suggests, is precisely this 'effecting' or 'effectuating' character of power, its operation as *Wirkung*: demarcated with regard to the force of nihilation and transformed by being opened up to the alternative of a power-free enabling, which overflows and refuses the effecting potency of power, both its 'productive' and its manipulative efficacy.

To propose a critique of manipulation or oppression, on the one hand, and to extol empowerment and the efficacity of action, on the other, without rethinking and transforming their common nature of 'effecting' things and 'making' them happen, will not critique power as such but rather its oppressive and constraining manifestations, the ones that, in the still-metaphysical terms of good and evil, appear as patterns of 'bad' power, that is, of domination or manipulation. That is why it is not enough, even though it remains extremely important in the current, metaphysical 'state' of technological society, to counter and resist dominating or manipulative power, and why it becomes necessary, instead, to inflect the effecting/effectuating character of power. This would entail a critical transformation of the essence, that is, the *Wesen* or the happening, of power: from production and effectuation to the middle voice of enabling. This enabling is emblematic of the *poiesis* at work in art, *poiesis* which is a doing without making or effecting. This 'poietic doing' consists in a radical opening up of being, and in holding it open, to the possibilities beyond power. *Poiesis* is not only not an inability to act, a powerlessness with regard to the operations of power; instead, it is an enabling to be, and thus to do, in ways free of power. It is a letting that enables something to be as what it is, without effecting, producing, or empowering it: instead, it is a radical 'making possible,' whose 'otherness' and the futurally nihilating force breaks and 'empties' even the subtle, creative inscriptions of power, inaugurating the possibility of a power-free letting-be of forces and relations.

On that point, Adorno comes quite close to Heidegger, at least in *Aesthetic Theory*. The tension between art and critique, which subtends much of the argument in *Aesthetic Theory*, bespeaks art's capacity to dominate its material and the social antagonisms it inscribes, and to do so in a paradoxical manner that undoes domination. To get a clearer sense of how such an undoing of domination, and, in fact, of all effectuation, actually works in art, we have to see art not just as a form of the negative imprint of the social but also as a transformative event that changes the very make-up of action and the 'force' of doing from making and production to *poi-esis*. If critique is still a form of negativity and domination, and thus part of the operations of power, the event at work in art can, by contrast, un-fold prior to the instantiation of power, that is, in a rupture, whose criti-cal force is, paradoxically, emptied and freed of power. I would put it even more strongly: what gives art a critical force of its own is that it can be power-free.

The power-free associated here with art indicates an alternative econ-omy of forces, in which the very makeup of power gets changed because an enabling of a different, poietic doing opens up the scope of possibility beyond power and powerlessness. What needs to be remembered here is that the transformative event at play in art in no way entails indifference to things or leaving them unaffected, since, left as they are, things would re-main always already inscribed into the operations of power. As Heidegger indicates in *Besinnung*, such an event implies neither indifference nor not doing anything but, on the contrary, involves transformation. At the same time, letting be should not be misconstrued as effectuation or manipula-tion, but seen, instead, as working in the middle voice, between activity and passivity, power and powerlessness, without being reducible to or ex-plainable as either one. Far from being some illusory beyond to power, this alternative relationality marks a critical inflection in the very tonality of power, a change of momentum from making to enabling and letting be. In this context, the force of art can be thought of in terms of such an en-abling, that is, as a transformative work and a poietic doing, that shifts the very momentum of relations radically, beyond a yes or a no. This ability to let go of power, to transform relations and to enable their alternative con-figurations, constitutes the power-free force of art. In order to discern the release from power inscribed in this force, art needs to be thought, howev-er, beyond the paradigm of critique, that is, as more radical than critique, for critique remains inscribed, albeit negatively, that is, as a critical nega-tivity and a no, into the capacities and flows of power.

To return to my initial discussion of art's language, what is at stake here is not the translatability (or its impossibility or lack) of art's workings into critical discourse, that is, the interpretation or theorization of art's critical force, but, instead, the transformation of the very grammar of critique by art's idiomatic, power-free language. The radicalism of this idiomatic language of artworks is beyond a yes and a no, just as it is beyond anthropism and its ruling paradigms of making and effectuation. It needs to be seen instead as a non-anthropic (*entmenscht*) event, whose distinctive, power-free futurity keeps nihilating power.

CHAPTER SEVEN

"Were speculation about the state of
reconciliation permissible . . . ":
Reflections on the Relation Between
Human Beings and Things
in Adorno and Heidegger

Ute Guzzoni

It has been accepted for a while now that Heidegger's and Adorno's fundamental thoughts, despite their considerable distance, are indeed
marked by certain similarities, such that it seems worthwhile to bring them
into a productive discussion with each other. The differences that exist between them, perhaps more severe than their correspondences, might be
summed up in the fact that the former thinks *ontologically,* the latter *onti-
cally.* Heidegger's thinking about the history of Being and Adorno's critical
analysis of reality and society operate on different philosophical terrains.
As soon as we look beyond superficial comparisons and differences and
attempt to approach their subject matters and intentions a bit closer, we
will see that it is rather difficult to find a common language and common
ground to express their respective modes of thinking.

Nevertheless, in what follows I will turn to a specific field of consideration that is of importance to both. More precisely, I will search, in
Adorno's and Heidegger's works, for *a specific relation to things,* a relation

that is no longer corrupted by the spell of identity on the one hand and by the oblivion of Being on the other.

I will begin by following the traces of that relation in Adorno, and, on this basis, I will go on to discuss what we can discover in Heidegger.

I

In the second section of "On Subject and Object," Adorno speaks of the "separation of subject and object." The opposite of this separation is considered in two ways: on the one hand, as that which precedes separation—"before the subject formed"—and on the other hand, as the state of reconciliation, within which the "relation of subject and object" would be "put right." Let us look here at the latter.

"Were speculation about the state of reconciliation permissible . . . "— Adorno speaks in a very cautious way. He is convinced that, strictly speaking, such speculation is not permissible. For him the spell of identity *is* absolute, today's life *is* false, the direct gaze upon the object *is* obstructed. There are many statements confirming his conviction that speaking about a non-alienated nature beyond the context of the blindness in which we are caught today must remain a sign of social mutilation and a lie. Adorno says: "He who paints himself a right state" cannot ignore the predominance of the current objectivity: otherwise "all would become distorted."[1]

"Were speculation about the state of reconciliation permissible . . . "— Very rarely does Adorno allow himself to engage in such speculation. When he does so, it is as if he furtively kicks open a forbidden door, or steals a glance through a crack in objectivity at what waits behind it—what waits for a time when an "alteration of the world" will no longer fail.[2] In what follows, I allow myself to participate in his furtive glance and look at what would belong to a 'right' and 'true' life.

Our passage in "On Subject and Object" contains four formulations that describe the "state of reconciliation." Adorno speaks of (1) the communication of the differentiated, (2) the potential of a consensus between humans and things, (3) a realized peace between humans as well as between them and their Other, and (4) peace as the state of differentiation without domination, in which the differentiated elements participate in one another.[3]

Let us reflect more carefully upon these moments, which revolve on the one hand around things differentiated from each other, and on the other around consensus, communication, peace. We will confine ourselves to discussing the relation between human beings and *things*.

The *differentiated* elements that are at stake here are not *separated*. The *separation of subject and object* is indebted—although not exclusively—to the subject's becoming independent with regard to the object. The "mind takes over the place of the absolutely independent, which it itself is not."[4] The subject believes itself to be sublime with regard to nature; it claims primacy in relation to the object.[5] Thus it not only separates itself from the object, but, moreover, it tries to reduce the latter to itself: "Subject devours object, forgetting how much it itself is object."[6] Separation and identification go hand in hand.

However, if the predominance of the subject has become questionable, if instead "the predominance of the object" has asserted itself, then both, humans and nature, enter into a new relation with each other. On the one hand, it is only then that they would become truly themselves, that each *is* in its own way, that is, differentiated; on the other hand, it is only then that they could, in their particularity, realize their differing relations to each other. While identification leaves no room for those who are forced by it *to be* (they lose their own way, and thereby the possibility of approaching each other), the overcoming of separation signifies the recognition of the non-identity and otherness of the particular in its particularity. The non-identical is that which bars itself from the concept and which is always already more than what is grasped by the concept. In Adorno's words: "the other, the alien, whose name not coincidentally resounds in alienation."[7]

By emphasizing the non-identical, Adorno believes he is following Hegel insofar as Hegel attempts, as Adorno says in *Negative Dialectics,* "to meet with philosophical concepts the challenge of what is heterogeneous to them."[8] Even if Hegel insists: "Every existent . . . has truth only insofar as it is an existence of the idea," Adorno nevertheless sees in Hegel a certain trace of something contradictory in itself and of something different, that is, of the non-identical. However, Hegel's idealistic dialectic and Adorno's negative dialectic consider identity and non-identity from contrary points of view. In Hegel, the different or otherness is lifted into the absolute unity that is its truth. Adorno, however, decisively sides with the non-identical. For him dialectic means "that objects are not equaled by their concepts."[9]

"The reconciled state would not, through philosophical imperialism, annex the foreign, but would have its happiness in the persistence of the foreign and the different within the granted nearness."[10] This is decisive for Adorno: the differentiated persists as the foreign, the distant, and the different—even in communication and consensus. Things are something other, differentiated from humans; they must stay preserved in their difference, since by contrast with humans they are natural, material, and resistant—even if they are manufactured—since they are *something*. The otherness of things also signifies that their concepts do not equal them, that they *are more* than they are. This immanent otherness distinguishes them from what surrounds them and at the same time *relates them* to it: their relation to what they are not is essential to them.[11] Furthermore, in their otherness there also lies a relation to what they are no longer, to what has become a sedimented past.

Humans and things communicate with each other only insofar as they are differentiated. "Communication with the other crystallizes within the singular individual, whose existence is mediated through communication."[12] The reciprocal relation between humans and things finds expression in what both of them are; only within that relation are they allowed to be themselves. Communication needs those who relate actively and passively to each other, so that something may occur between them. But in order to succeed, communication, in a particular way, needs *one* of them, namely, the human being who speaks and thinks. Truly, "the cult of mind is put out of commission by the dominance of the object,"[13] yet the real difference between humans and things cannot be denied. It consists in the fact that it is humans who make things speak.

Communication particularly needs the human assistance that occurs when humans experience what is other to them, when they observe it and talk to it and about it. In particular, Adorno speaks of "the long and nonviolent look upon the object,"[14] and of the "lingering look."[15] This look has need of "patience with regard to the matter at hand [*Sache*]"[16] and of a willingness "not to swim with one's own current,"[17] that is, not to rely on what one already knows and is acquainted with. Thoughts must incessantly renew themselves through experience, they must listen to the matter at hand. It is only in communication that the matter at hand determines itself and shows itself as something qualitative; and it is only in communication that thinking and experience reach this matter at hand and so exceed the concept in order to immerse themselves in things as being foreign and different.

Although Adorno often speaks against irrationality and the reception of emotional immediacy, in reference to the reconciled state he speaks of the "love for things,"[18] of the "nestling near to things," and he asserts, that one should remain "in touch with the warmth of things."[19] Love, nearness, warmth—these are words or qualities that we usually know from relations between humans: but they also signify the relation to unobstructed things, which relies upon a consensus with them.

Love, nearness, warmth signify the atmosphere and the common space, in which humans can relate to things. I would like to cite two remarks on Alban Berg, because Adorno seems to have sensed in Berg the issues I am speaking about. "Berg had an exceptional sparing love [preserving and caring, *eine schonende Liebe*] of things and every violence as even every clumsiness in treating them hurt him."[20] And: "The sensibility of the person Berg was long since attuned to the treatment of things. The sparing love and thoroughness he bestowed upon them originated from a feeling of sparing [one could also say: of gentle protection] for what is made; as if he wanted to repair in *things* something of what happens to matter that humans fashion for their own ends."[21]

Both citations speak of sparing love, and we already can remark that this 'sparing' (*Schonen*) in Heidegger is an essential character of dwelling as the human relation to things. I wish to stress the moment of *reparation* involved here. It corresponds to what Adorno means in the *Negative Dialectics* when he says that the love for things signifies rescuing what has been oppressed by the dominating subject. This love for things, which—as opposed to the unreconciled state—is a healing, repairing, and saving attitude, may well be the source of what are among the most beautiful sentences that Adorno ever wrote (even if we might disagree about his view of American landscapes). We find them in *Minima Moralia*. I will quote almost the entire reflection:

Paysage. The defect of the American landscape is . . . that no hand has left a trace upon it. This refers not only to the lack of fields, the uncleared and often bushlike low forests, but most of all to the streets. These are always blasted without mediation into the landscape, and the smoother and wider they are, the more relationless and violent their shimmering course stands out against the all too wild and overgrown surroundings. They have no expression. Just as they know no footprints and wheel prints, no soft walkways along the edges as transition to vegetation, no side paths down into the valley, likewise they miss the mild, soothing, and non-angular character of things, upon which hands or their immediate tools have done their job. It is as if nobody has ever run his fingers through the hair of the landscape. It is uncomforted and without comfort. The way it is perceived corresponds to it. For the hurrying eye cannot retain what it has merely seen in the car, and so fades without a trace just as it itself remains without traces.[22]

The hurried eye cannot cast a long and non-violent look. Only this long and lingering look is capable of getting involved in what surrounds it. The astonishing care—almost awe—that is expressed here is even more remarkable as we know Adorno as a rather sober, 'rational' thinker. However, we often find in him this flash of a different way of treating things, of an attitude that lovingly tends to them, especially where he tries to make the alienated, obstructed, oppressing, and oppressed comportment to the world apparent by contrast.

This becomes evident too in his reflections on giving gifts or on forgetting how to give gifts in *Minima Moralia*.[23] The giving of gifts, which "finds happiness in imagining the happiness of the receiver," belongs to human capacities that "can prosper only when in touch with the warmth of things." This being in touch with the *warmth of things* becomes important to Adorno in the face of the coldness that nowadays characterizes the reciprocal relation of humans. "Such coldness finally strikes back at those who initiate it. Every non-obstructed relation, maybe even reconciliation in organic life itself, is a giving of gifts. He who becomes incapable of this through the logic of consequence makes himself a thing and freezes."

The logic of consequence rigidifies and freezes. It does not allow one to involve oneself with the other as other. Into a true encounter we should bring our own attunement and feeling and our own experience. To be in touch with the warmth of things means to feel them; but to feeling belongs the taking in of the thing just as it does the giving oneself to it, "in order, ideally, to disappear in it."[24] The few places where Adorno allows himself to use the word "happiness" in a positive way usually refer to such encounters, such experiences of otherness without separation or break.

Love, warmth, and nearness. They are not without farness. Nearness as such for Adorno is always in danger of being what he calls "nearest nearness," "immediate nearness," practically undifferentiated fusion. That is also why the word "consensus" usually bears negative connotations for Adorno; it means a consensus that satisfies itself all too quickly with what is and persists. Therefore differentiation and distance, or farness, must come into play. The nearness to humans and to things is the nearness through farness, or farness itself in nearness. "The non-violent observation that generates all happiness of truth is bound to the fact that the observer does not assimilate the object: nearness bound to farness."[25]

Pressure on an object is initially the pressure to assimilate it in an identifying appropriation; it means, as Adorno puts it in *Negative Dialectics,* once again to "make equal to the subject what is not its equal."[26] This assimilation *seems* to lead immediately to nearness, but in fact, it makes it impossible. What is needed instead is the breaking of the one-dimensional relation, the tense togetherness of unifying and dividing. The happiness of truth as the self-developing constellation of humans and things originates precisely from persisting tensions, from farness.

And vice versa. Farness itself needs nearness, if it is not to remain *mere distance.* Absolute otherness, without any relation, isolates individuals and makes them lie coldly beside each other. They have nothing to say to each other, or they must oppress or even destroy each other, since the other appears threatening because of its foreignness. Adorno counters: "Only through the recognition of farness in the nearest is foreignness eased, taken into consciousness." This taking into consciousness is to be understood as the recognition of the other, as admission of its otherness within a relation that creates nearness; it is not to be understood as an assimilation, which could only lead to a false consensus. "The demand of an undiminished, already attained nearness, however, the denial of foreignness inflicts extreme injustice upon the other . . . , 'sums it up,' assimilates it to the inventory of possession."[27]

"*Were speculation about the state of reconciliation permissible . . .* "— "The reconciled state would not, through philosophical imperialism, annex the foreign, but would have its happiness in the persistence of the foreign and different within the granted nearness, beyond what is heterogeneous and what is one's own."[28] The formulations that express the relation of nearness and farness or foreignness and mention love and happiness are signposts, which questioning about undistorted relations can follow. We could add to this the sentences in which Adorno points out how strongly the need for nearness is connected to "archaic barbarism, which consists in the fact that the longing subject is unable to love what is foreign, what is other, is connected to the greed for assimilation and persecution." Again, together with the denunciation of the false state, the possibility of another, of a state of reconciliation, flashes into view: "Were the foreign and alien no longer banned, alienation would scarcely persist."[29] We can also turn it around: were there no longer alienation, the foreign would no longer be banned, it could be loved, and that means it could come into a nearness within which its warmth could be felt and yet its being other and foreign could be preserved.

To conclude what I hope is a nonviolent look at Adorno, I will quote in its context the passage from "On Subject and Object" that underpins my interpretation:

> Were speculation about the state of reconciliation permissible, then neither the undifferentiated unity of subject and object nor its hostile antithesis could be conceived in it; rather, it would be the communication of the differentiated. Only then would the concept of communication—as an objective concept—come into its own. Its present concept is so ignominious because it betrays what is best, the potential for a consensus between humans and things, to information between subjects according to the requirements of subjective reason. The relation between subject and object would be put right, even in epistemology, in the realized peace between humans as well as between them and their other. Peace is the state of differentiation without domination in which the differentiated elements participate in one another.

II

The question of the relation of humans to things in (the later) Heidegger meets with difficulties quite different from those we met in Adorno, though the topic is common to both. While the problem in Adorno consists in the fact that there are only a few occasions where he looks beyond the spell of identity and alienated existence, the difficulty in Heidegger originates from the fact that the question of thing and world—that is, of a non-objectifying thinking—becomes more and more central in his later works, while *humans themselves* and their actual relation to things increasingly fade into the background.

Just as Adorno diagnoses for our times the primacy of the subject of "false objectivity," of reification, and the loss of all qualities as such, Heidegger points out that we live in a time in which comprehensive machinations, objectification, and general calculability are dominant because "'world' has become unworld."[30] It is implied in this unworld that humans stand in the middle of the consideration as the subjects of that calculability. While in Adorno the totality of the social and real force of identity nearly always *forbids* the question of the other as such, the abandonment of being in Heidegger inversely *demands* sensitive reflection, *Besinnung*; it asks for a thinking that prepares for a change and is no longer calculating but reflects in a sensitive way.

By questioning thing, world, and language Heidegger wants to prepare a path on which, in the future, an other might turn to us. What is decisive is that thing, world, language, and, not least of all, thinking itself are to be thought in another way, and that means also and above all, that they are no longer to be primarily related to *humans*. Thus, if we ask whether we can find in Heidegger, too, something like "love for things," like "nestling close to the object" or the "non-violent look," a reflection on differentiation and communication, on nearness and farness, then we meet with the difficulty that he nearly never treats the relation of humans and things explicitly. Where he does address the topic he is less interested in those who are in the relation than in finding out something about the way their relation is *thought* or about *relatedness* as such. Nevertheless, with Adorno's thought in the background, I will try to show how in Heidegger humans and things relate to each other—or at least *could* relate to each other—if this relation could be "essentially performed, satisfactorily thought, and genuinely spoken."[31]

We meet remarkably often with nearness and farness in Heidegger's later thinking. The lecture titled "The Thing" in particular deals with this issue, the thing, in relation to nearness. In order to discuss nearness Heidegger here looks at *what is near* and accordingly questions a *thing*, "the jar that is near."[32] As Adorno speaks of the "granted nearness" in the face of the pure distance and isolation of alienated singularities, Heidegger turns to the thing that is near in the face of the abolition of "every possibility of farness" as well as nearness.[33]

In a seemingly traditional way he begins by asking "what is a thing?" and then: "what is the jar?" Already the transition from the first to the second question makes it evident that this is not the traditional question "what is?" or the question of essence. More precisely, this change expresses itself already in the formulation of the first question. For it does not say: what is *the* thing?, but: what is *a* thing? The sentence "the jar is a thing" is then already the answer to this question, not only its exemplification. The question of what a thing is shall no longer, as in the tradition, be answered with reference to its objectivity or its substantiality, to its being produced or its reality, but only with reference to looking at a *particular thing*, in this case the jar. A 'substance' and 'something real' are not truly near, because one cannot really have dealings with them.

The thing is a near thing by being a jar. And it is a jar by the jar's behaving like a jar, that is, by containing and pouring liquid. In its containing and pouring the jar exceeds itself or, better, it brings itself into a wider realm of happenings. Things are *related* things. In Adorno's terms we could say that they are in communication with each other, as they themselves, as particulars, in the specific, always *different* way of *their* thingness. The jar does not contain or pour liquid in general, but rather milk or water or wine. Thus it already relates in its own way to *earth* and *heaven*, to humans, whom Heidegger calls the *mortals*, and to something immaterial, which he calls the *divine*. The jar, a thing, gathers those four dimensions of the world, the fourfold, and lets them, so gathered, occur. So it is said of the bridge: "The bridge is a thing and only this. Only? Being this thing it gathers the fourfold."[34]

This gathering is thought by Heidegger as the bringing near of the far. "Nearness brings farness near as the far."[35] By bringing the world-dimensions into play with each other, the things hold them apart as well as together. An important and remarkable difference to Adorno's concept of nearness and farness lies in the fact that for Heidegger nearness and farness are not characteristics of the relation of humans to things, but rather, on the one hand, they themselves determine thingness and, on the other hand, they are something like the space within which the thingness of things and human involvement with them can begin to take place.

In these reflections on nearness, on world and thing, and on the repulsive loss of farness, humans play a nearly secondary role, or at least the second role. In the fact that nearness remains absent, the repelling shows itself, the "repelling that repels all that is out of its former essence."[36] What repels is nothing human. For Adorno, nearness is a nearness granted by humans—for example, the nearness of nonviolent observation, which originates from humans and remains related to humans. In Heidegger it belongs to openness itself, to the relatedness that swings in the twofold of farness and nearness, of range and while, of unconcealedness and concealedness. It is only within the space of this openness, which is the "nearness of farness,"[37] that a relation between humans and things can arise.

For Heidegger there are first of all two features that characterize this relation: the *sparing* (*Schonen*), which I mentioned already in relation to Adorno's "sparing love," and "releasement toward things" (*Gelassenheit*). "By sparing the thing as thing we inhabit nearness," says Heidegger in "The Thing."[38] Nearness is the space in which humans dwell, that is, live when they truly are able to be human. Dwelling and sparing are fundamental features of the human being's being-in-the-world. Just like things, humans in their own being are related to the fourfold of the world and are determined by it. Their specific relation to the world is called dwelling. They not only *are* in the world, but they inhabit it, are at home in it, belong to it as to the space that shelters them. They actualize this belonging when they let that which surrounds them remain in its essence, in itself, when they give it its own space, when they spare and gently protect it. "The fundamental trait of dwelling is this sparing. It pervades dwelling throughout its entire range. We see the range when we consider that humanness lies in the dwelling and namely in the sense of mortal's stay on earth."[39]

This stay on earth is "always already a stay with things."[40] The fourfold relation of dwelling to world gathers around *things*, concentrates dwelling in things. This is a sparing. "Dwelling spares the fourfold by bringing its essence into things."[41] Two years earlier, in 1949, Heidegger had said in "The Thing": "Insofar as we spare the thing as the thing, we inhabit the nearness."[42] What is spared at first is the fourfold, the *world*, and then later it is *things*. Yet the difference between the two statements is not great. In both cases humans let their relation to thing and world be as a reciprocal gathering in an active sense. Thus, sparing gathers things into the world as well as world into the things.

This double use of 'sparing' clearly shows that sparing for Heidegger is not the loving relation to particular things as such, as Adorno remarked in reference to Alban Berg, but rather the relation between world and thing; it names the ontological task that within the game of the world is assigned to humans. This has little to do with love, warmth, and nearness in Adorno's sense.

The comparison between Adorno's and Heidegger's views of an undistorted relation of humans to things leads to an insight that is unexpected at first glance. Considering their respective styles of thinking and writing and their different intentions as well as what we know about them, we could have suspected to find rather in Heidegger than in Adorno traces of an 'affective' inclination toward things. Characterizing them in a rather superficial way we could say that Adorno is a city person, while for Heidegger his rural origins were significant throughout his whole life. One might then assume that Adorno is the cooler, more intellectual thinker.

And so it is quite astonishing that Adorno can speak of "being in touch with the warmth of things," while in Heidegger—even where he speaks of jars, bridges, and houses—we meet with a rather sober, and not particularly concrete, analysis. For him, only this kind of analysis is capable of showing something about the fundamental traits and features of the world-play and about the way things and humans are woven into it. In the passages I quoted, Adorno evokes images of a non-alienated being with things; even so, he does not discuss the implied play of nearness and farness in its fundamental ontological relevance.

Heidegger, however, speaks from the opposite point of view. For him, to philosophize about empirical human behavior belongs to an inadequate anthropology. He wants to question and learn something about the mortal stay on earth, about the fourfold of the world, and about things. His intention understands itself as belonging to the history of being; that means that it brings its thinking as a careful participant into the occurrence of being and world. Thus he wants to help make possible that "mortals . . . attempt in their way to bring—out of themselves—dwelling into the fullness of its essence."[43] In these mortal humans there is no subjective will at work, yet they bring themselves into the occurrence of being; it is being itself that demands and claims the dwelling and thinking humans, announces itself to them, and approaches them. In this sense Heidegger can speak of "the solid relation of things to us,"[44] and especially of the "relation of being to humans."[45]

The ontological demand also determines the discussions of what Heidegger names "releasement," *Gelassenheit*. Releasement characterizes a thinking that involves itself with what it has to think and does so by letting itself be determined by it. It waits for it, brings itself into the nearness of its farness. This releasement stands in radical opposition to the calculating relation of humans to the whole of the world and to the objects that humans attempt to violently seize in a technical and scientific manner. Released thinking is neither active nor passive; it is neither the grasping of the modern subject, which attempts to get things into its grip; nor does it exercise a mere disinterested spectatorship. Instead, it originates out of an attentive questioning and listening and a sensitive reflection. These characteristics indeed immediately remind us of Adorno's patient attentiveness and of the long, nonviolent look.

Releasement turns not only to the jar and the bridge, that is, to things of a sparing and dwelling use. But it also refers to "technical objects," when we succeed in letting them be in and as themselves. Heidegger says with respect to this released attitude toward technical objects: "Our relation to the technical world becomes in a strange way simple and calm"; and he calls this the releasement toward things,[46] in which we can also hear a resonance of Adorno's "love for things."

Sensitive reflection is affiliated with the "openness for the mystery"; we can understand this openness as the ontological dimension of the concealed and concealing origin of things, as the dimension of the occurrence of being itself. The openness for the mystery is akin to the reserve that Heidegger elsewhere calls the "fundamental attunement of the relation to Being" and to which belongs the "awe before the most far."[47] Perhaps this reserve and this awe before the mystery prevent us from retaining the genuine warmth of being in touch with things. The "coming near to the far," of which Heidegger speaks, traverses an openness that is perhaps less familiar to us than Adorno's space of happiness and no-longer-alienated foreignness. But it is Heidegger's space of farness and foreignness that makes a relation of nearness, of love, of sparing, and of released comportment toward things ontologically possible.

To conclude I will take a comprehensive, comparative look at the meaning of the differentiated and the communication of the differentiated, as well as at foreignness and nearness in Adorno and Heidegger. Both speak of the constellation of thinking and being—we could also say, of humans and things. In Heidegger, this constellation is the belonging together of being and humans that is determined by the history of being. Adorno conversely refuses to see it as prior to those who are in constellation with each other. It is their communication that creates itself out of the "inadequacy of thought and matter," and its truth lies in "becoming constellation,"[48] that is, "the constellation of subject and object within which both fuse with each other."[49]

Adorno primarily intends to teach us to experience the differentiated and foreign. This is the particular, the non-identical, that which is and remains other to the other and to itself, when it is nonviolently and patiently taken in. Only then may it be differentiated in such a way, when the loving inclination of human handling and observing gives it a space of granted nearness. The "potential of a consensus between humans and things" would be realized if there were such a space of openness and of "realized peace." "The reconciled state . . . would have its happiness in the persistence of the foreign and different within the granted nearness."[50]

Of first importance for Heidegger is the relation—or better, relatedness—and with it the realm or space that is opened by it. He calls the modern subject-object relation into question by understanding humans and things in the space of the world, which he understands as an occurrence of unconcealing and concealing, as a moving *to* each other, *with* each other, *confronting* each other. He attempts to think an occurring relatedness that is at once nearness and farness. This "play of the world" occurs *before* those who relate to each other in the world and as the world, even if the world is opened and preserved by those who relate to each other within it. Humans and things are particulars and others, because and as long as they join the language of the world and remain within it.

CHAPTER EIGHT

The Struggle of the Self Against Itself: Adorno and Heidegger on Modernity

Josef Früchtl

The General Thesis

To reflect upon modernity is inevitably to reflect upon the self.[1] This is the general thesis that forms the basis of the following discussion. Hegel was the first to formulate this as the basic question and problem of modern philosophy, and in recent times it has been taken up once again by thinkers who otherwise represent the most varied theoretical perspectives on the present. Thus Habermas, provoked and challenged by the protagonists of so-called post-modernity, has felt called upon to defend the cause of modernity and those *maître-penseurs* (to use André Glucksmann's expression) who have been criticized so vehemently in this connection, namely the heritage of Kant, Hegel, and Marx (though not Nietzsche). Richard Rorty, the principal American representative of the post-modernist challenge, has expressly taken up the alternative and competing cause through a vigorous defense and rehabilitation of the Romantic tradition and its ideal of human self-creation through art and artistic sensibility (a strategy that will hardly come as a surprise, at least to German readers). There are also of course numerous French representatives of this challenging current of thought. Thus Michel Foucault, in *Les mots et les choses* (in English translation, *The Order of Things*), attempted to describe modernity from a theoretical-historical perspective in terms of the 'episteme' of 'Man,' understood as subjectivity; in *Surveiller et punir* (*Discipline and Punish*), he appealed to a genealogical theory of power to reinterpret modernity in terms of a fundamentally 'disciplinary society': the development of subjectivity here represents a process of discipline and regulation, and vice versa. The specifically modern form of rule and regulation transforms those who are ruled and regulated into 'subjects' insofar as they learn inwardly to rule and regulate themselves. Jean-François Lyotard, in *La condition postmoderne* (*The Postmodern Condition*), attempted to identify modernity as an epoch grounded in a self-legitimating discourse that is articulated through various 'grand' or 'meta-' narratives. Unlike the post-modernity invoked by Lyotard himself, modernity requires a specific grounding or foundation, derived from within itself, and the appropriate model here, as originally suggested by Descartes, can be provided only by the ego or subject. Again, like Rorty, Charles Taylor has emphasized the romantically accentuated expressive dimension of subjectivity for a proper understanding of modernity (this was already a major theme of Taylor's large book on Hegel, which he has further systematically developed in *Sources of the Self*). But the identity of the modern age is also nourished by other important sources, religious and rationalist ones, and Taylor himself wavers between a post-modern emphasis upon the inevitable internal conflict of these different sources and a kind of classically modern overall synthesis that is reminiscent of Hegel.

To reflect upon modernity is thus, indeed, to reflect upon the self. But to reflect upon the self is therefore to thematize its different dimensions and their internal relationship to one another, for the self or the I, as Hegel above all had already shown, cannot be grasped as a simple unity. The I that knows itself as I thereby negates its apparent identity and sustains itself (both preserves and acquires itself) as a duality, as an I that equals I. Whoever says 'I' has always already doubled himself and implicitly said 'I' twice. This is why 'diremption' and 'self-othering,' or 'externalization' (*Entäusserung*), are basic concepts in Hegel's philosophy, even if the fundamental underlying motif here (that something is itself and its own opposite) has a theological origin and is essentially a secularized form of the Christian doctrine of *kenosis* as the self-othering of God in the incarnation.[2]

The German Romantics, philosophers and writers like Schelling, F. Schlegel, and Novalis, also dramatized this inner contradiction within the self and developed this thought in terms of tragedy or irony. The ego here is nothing but an infinite and ceaseless movement, a never-ending attempt to identify itself as authentic or self-transparent. This challenging thought cannot properly be grasped through Hegelian dialectics, but only by re-course to an aesthetics that invites and acknowledges paradox, or perhaps, as in the later phases of German Romanticism, by recourse to religion or the new kind of philosophy that eventually came to be known as 'existen-tialism.' Here we see the pre-modern principle of the tragic, originally ar-ticulated in the ancient Greek world, re-emerging in the midst of moder-nity itself. For, as Hegel again had emphasized, tragic conflict involves a collision of values that appears as inevitable as it is irresolvable, since the competing claims involved appear to be equally justified.[3] But it is true to say that Romanticism did not specifically cultivate the tragic as such, but tended rather to present 'irony' as an alternative form of art. The tragic moment appears in modernity in a less tragic form: as an *agon,* as the con-test and struggle of equally powerful elements.

All these problems also reappear in contemporary attempts to theo-rize modernity. While Habermas generally endorses Hegel's interpretation of modernity, and its characteristic principle of the subject or ego, he does not start from the Hegelian idea of a bifurcated unity, but interprets the principle in a threefold manner broadly corresponding to the structure of Kant's critical philosophy: as a relation between the dimensions of self-knowledge, of self-determination, and of what I would call, deviating from Habermas's own terminology here, self-experience. But the dimension of self-determination is fractured by an inner conflict, namely, that between autonomy and authenticity, between (deontological) morality and (eudai-monist) ethics, between self-determination in the strict sense and self-real-ization in general. 'Enlightenment' in the properly Kantian sense is direct-ed essentially toward the first alternative in each case, toward autonomy and morality, while the Romantic approach is primarily concerned with the second, with the self-realization, self-creation, and self-expression of concrete individuality.

Contemporary theorists and interpreters of modernity have reacted to this problem with a variety of different strategies that emphasize the need for an *expanded-classical,* an *agonistic,* or a *hybrid* conception of mo-dernity. The agonistic conception, along with essential elements of the hybrid one, can be regarded as versions of a generalized *Romantic* emphasis upon the ineliminable moment of *conflict,* while the expanded-classical conception can be read as a continuation of an *Enlightenment* notion of *reconciliation.* Thus Habermas transforms the basic conflict involved here with a new expanded principle of subjectivity, namely, the principle of communicative inter-subjectivity, but he can only really resolve it by granting ultimate priority to a morality oriented toward principles of justice. Rorty alleviates the conflict in an ironic, but also dogmatic, manner by appeal to the traditional liberal principle of the separation of spheres. Public morality and private self-creation are sharply distinguished and emphatically set over against one another. Taylor acknowledges the conflict and recognizes that the tensions between the different major sources of our moral tradition are characteristic of modernity itself, but he aspires to resolve the difficulty by appeal to an aesthetically redeemed form of metaphysics. For Taylor's moral ontology, and the trans-subjective value and significance of those 'hypergoods' that form the necessary background that discloses specific norms, can be justified only by recourse to the 'epiphanic' potentialities of art. A truly agonistic conception, which refuses to betray the Romantic emphasis upon dissension in a liberal or metaphysical fashion, simply leaves the conflict irresolvable in principle. It is the French theorists who furnish the clearest example of this approach, whether in its harshest form, which appeals to the experience of *rupture* (Foucault and Lyotard), or its weaker version, which invokes displacement, *différance,* or *rhizome* (Derrida and Deleuze).

To reflect upon the self in an appropriately modern way means giving much greater weight to that dimension that Habermas all too easily and quickly accommodates under the concept of the aesthetic-expressive. It means giving greater weight to the agonistic-ironic (Rorty), the agonistic-expressive (Taylor), and the hybrid-creative (Foucault, Deleuze, and Guattari), in short to the Romantic dimension. In this sense I shall be concerned here with emphasizing what I shall call the *Romantic* discourse of modernity. According to the core thesis of this discourse, modernity is the struggle of the self with and against itself.

The End of the Individual

If we now consider Adorno in relation to the context that I have just briefly sketched, we would surely have to say that he maintains an intermediate position here between the classical understanding of modernity as articulated by Hegel and the agonistic conception of modernity developed by the Romantic tradition. Adorno's achievement was to combine the theory of dialectic with an aesthetics of paradox, to present the process of thinking through a series of unavoidable contradictions, pursuing this idea not dynamically under the sign of some preordained progress, but by inscribing it emphatically within the conflictual network of a 'negative dialectic.' If we say A, we must also say B, but there is no longer any C in which both former terms could successfully be 'sublated' (*aufgehoben*). A and B continue to stand over against one another, each with an equal right, with an equal truth. And yet, although this is all too frequently overlooked, the equality here is not itself total or complete. As Adorno shows in *Minima Moralia,* perhaps his finest and most successful work from a literary perspective, which side one ultimately adopts in the case of a fundamental collision of norms or values is certainly no matter of indifference. While it is true that there is nothing absolute here, nothing absolutely good, there are indeed things that are more or less good than others. In *Minima Moralia* this thought is best expressed in a motto that derives from Francis Herbert Bradley, a famous Fellow of Merton College Oxford, where Adorno was enrolled as an 'advanced student' in the mid-1930s after he had completed his post-doctoral dissertation in Germany and eventually fled the Nazi regime. "Where everything is bad, it must be good to know the worst."[4] The good is simply knowledge of what is (more or less) bad. This moral-philosophical point is clearly shaped by the contemporary political circumstances. But it had already been theoretically anticipated by Adorno's (and Horkheimer's) original attempt to combine elements from the thought of Marx, Nietzsche, Freud, and Weber. It was this project that first produced the distinctive culturally and psychoanalytically based social theory and, ultimately, in the *Dialectic of Enlightenment,* the characteristic philosophy of history that furnished the basic premise for our chastening motto: namely, the thought that 'everything is bad.'

But the problem that this premise ascribes to the principle of society itself can also be formulated in the language of transcendental philosophy. For it was a central concern of Adorno's, and indeed of all post-Hegelian philosophy, to expose and decode the content of what Kant and the German Idealist tradition had called 'transcendental consciousness.' Marx had already contributed to this task with his concepts of 'ideology' and 'social praxis,' and twentieth-century thought would explicitly develop it further. In the field of philosophy, as in that of historiography, we can say that the twentieth century only really begins in the 1920s.[5] Wittgenstein's *Tractatus* (1921), Lukács's *History and Class Consciousness* (1923), and Heidegger's *Being and Time* (1927) are the three decisive texts in this respect. Common to them all is the attempt to penetrate behind transcendental consciousness, even if what they claim to discover there is quite different in each case: *language, society,* and *being,* respectively. The 'subject' finds itself accordingly de-centered linguistically, ideologically, and ontologically. In this respect Adorno himself clearly stands in the tradition that runs from Marx to Lukács insofar as society here reveals itself as the true transcendental subject. It is society that constitutes empirical subjects and the world-view (in the literal and extended sense) that they generally share. On the one hand, this allows us in certain rare cases of artists and thinkers to justify the genuinely universal claim that is articulated in their work and thought without appealing to the concept of genius. On the other hand, the consequences of this approach are undeniably disastrous as far as the remaining majority of subjects is concerned. The struggle of the self against itself, from this perspective, is not merely that between the moral and the aesthetic, the sensuous and the cognitive, the political and the private self, a struggle that knows no decisive victor, but merely a provisional and damaged one. (For *Minima Moralia* contains, as the subtitle explicitly tells us, "reflections from damaged life.") The struggle in question is also one between the social-transcendental and the empirical subject, and a struggle that the latter is now unambiguously losing.

Adorno, like Horkheimer, describes this defeat through his famous thesis of the end of the individual. In what follows I should like to address this issue directly in order to reveal, in an exemplary manner, the specific form that this struggle of the modern self with itself assumes in Adorno's work. In this connection Adorno draws principally on three theoretical perspectives, those of Marx, Weber, and Freud.

For Adorno 'individuality' and 'the individual' are in the first instance historical, rather than biological or ontological categories. They characterize something that has emerged in the course of history, and therefore something that can also cease to be. Historical materialism is a specific development of this governing perspective: "The individual has been crystallized in and through the forms of political economy, in particular those of urban capitalism." The individual is defined on the one hand through a certain 'independence,' and thus also a certain 'resistance' to the collectivizing tendencies of socialization, an independence on the other hand that the individual only acquires *through* that same process of socialization, namely, through the pursuit and preservation of its own 'particular interest.' The capitalist market system binds the members of society together as economic agents while simultaneously opposing them to one another. Marx proved himself a true student of Hegel in observing that in bourgeois-capitalist society each individual is an end for himself, but one who can never pursue and realize his own ends without making himself and others into mere means. The 'decline' of the individual must therefore be "derived from the overall tendency of society." But this tendency realizes itself not simply as a "mere enemy" of individuation, but precisely "by virtue of individuation."[6] To this extent the latter reveals itself as a two-sided process that is socially and economically constituted from the first.

The decline of the individual is characteristically marked by a loss of "autonomy" in the economic sense. "It is a mark of the age that, without exception, no one can now determine his own life in a relatively transparent manner, as this was once possible in relation to the market."[7] This is a thesis that is already familiar from the work of Weber and Marx (once again as an instructive student of Hegel). But Horkheimer and Adorno are willing to acknowledge the role of capitalism only in encouraging individuality in its 'liberal' phase before its eventual monopolistic development during the modern period. It is only in this earlier liberal period that some degree of distance was still possible for the individual, that is, the (small) individual employer or entrepreneur, over against the relations of the market. That is why this figure of early capitalism can also appear as a model of personal individuality in this context. Nonetheless, Adorno is also a good deal more hesitant than Horkheimer in this regard. His preferred models of individuality are to be sought in the sublimated, and therefore less determinate, realm of art and are certainly not limited to the male domain in gender terms. And there is no passage in Adorno's work that expresses this more perfectly than his 'homage' to the figure of Zerlina from Mozart's *Don Giovanni* (1787): "The rhythm of the rococo and the age of Revolution is suspended in the figure of Zerlina. She is no longer a shepherdess and not yet a *citoyenne*. She belongs to an intermediate historical moment and reveals, fleetingly, a kind of humanity neither maimed by feudal coercion nor exposed to bourgeois barbarism."[8] For it is society, historically developing capitalist society, that furnishes the condition of both the possibility and impossibility of human individuality.

But Adorno also closely combines this politico-economic analysis with a further sociological form of argument. Max Weber is the decisive theorist in this regard. Adorno's lecture "The Individual and Organization," from 1950, gathers together the various argumentative strands of his debt to Weber. There Adorno identifies the "disturbing character" of the concept of organization in the fact that it has come to assume a truly "all-embracing form that structures society through and through."[9] And this characteristic structural feature also corresponds to one equally reproduced within the subject itself, for employers and employees do not merely designate certain professions or occupations, but also "types." And as such they have come to involve certain values like "responsibility for oneself," "foresight," "commitment to duty," but also a certain "rigid self-imposition of conscience, an internalized dependency upon authorities of one kind or another."[10]

In this regard Weber exercises a particularly powerful influence in the development of Adorno's argument. Adorno's analysis of 'bourgeois anthropology' in terms of the fulfillment of duty and the coercive power of conscience points back of course to Weber's celebrated study *Protestantism and the 'Spirit' of Capitalism*. There Weber claims that the rational conduct of life based upon a vocational ethos is constitutive for modern capitalism and indeed modern culture in general, and is itself ultimately derived from the spirit of Christian, specifically puritan, asceticism. The consequence of this puritanically based ethos, which emphasizes the solitude of the individual subject who must seek God's grace, is ambivalent. On the one hand it implies the "absolutely negative attitude of puritanism in relation to all sensuous and emotional elements," while on the other hand it also represents "one of the roots" of that "illusionless and pessimistically colored" individualism that has established itself so firmly in the Anglo-American world.[11]

Horkheimer and Adorno acknowledge this ambivalence but lend it added emphasis through recourse to a Hegelian dialectic and radicalize it by reference to Marxian theory, and the subsequent cultural generalization of that theory in Lukács's *History and Class Consciousness*. They are not simply content with interpreting this ambivalence in the established moderate form that bourgeois-capitalist society liberates human beings in one respect, while simultaneously oppressing them in another. Rather, they strictly link both these respects directly with one another: each emerges only in and through the other. The birth of the individual is *only* possible *through* the concomitant mortification of that individual as a sensuous and hedonistic being. In *Dialectic of Enlightenment* this specific process is captured in pregnant formula: "self-preservation through self-destruction." "Destruction" here bears a primarily internal-psychological sense. It refers to "renunciation" and "the introversion of sacrifice,"[12] precisely that asceticism characteristic of the 'Protestant' phase of western history that Weber had analyzed and identified.

Moreover, Adorno's politico-economic and historico-sociologic argument runs parallel with a specifically psychological one. Adorno develops the latter under a title that alludes indirectly to a text by Kierkegaard: namely, "Health unto Death." The fact that "contemporary sickness consists precisely in supposed normality," that human beings are psychologically deformed without even registering the fact, thus requires a psychoanalytic explanation, or as Adorno often expresses it in a conditional form, *would* properly require just such an explanation, for Adorno can hardly suggest more than a certain "suspicion" or "supposition" in this connection. But we must here at least acknowledge his heuristic proposal for a specific etiology of neurosis that effectively goes beyond the Freudian perspective. For a psychoanalytic interpretation of the "regular guy" and the "popular girl"—the human type that is principally envisaged by Adorno here and is itself directly produced by the American culture industry—must assume that the perpetual "gaiety, openness and approachability" of such a type results from a second-order repression that is directed not merely against instinctual impulses, but also against the symptoms of first-order repression. Symptoms effectively give evidence of a sickness, but when these too are repressed, it is no longer possible to diagnose a sickness directly in the first place.

Under these conditions, which could hardly be presented or justified in purely objective scientific terms, Adorno is honest enough to admit that he requires a moral criterion for his own claims. We can only show that those who believe themselves healthy are actually sick by "revealing the disproportion between their rationalized way of life and a different possible and rational form of life."[13] How this criterion can itself be justified presents a problem for which the earlier representatives of Critical Theory were unable to provide a satisfactory solution. In *Minima Moralia,* as we have seen, and much later in *Negative Dialectics,* Adorno expounds the unsatisfactory character of solutions generally proposed by moral philosophy from the varying perspectives of universalism, particularism, contract theory, moral skepticism, and the ethics of compassion. There simply is no unconditionally right answer here. The best we can do is to discover the least bad solution. But it is impossible, at least for Adorno, to say clearly and precisely what this amounts to. In the last analysis, therefore, Adorno fails to justify or clarify philosophically the moral criterion that is required here.

It is true, in this connection, too, that Adorno upholds the central criterion of autonomy, which he interprets in accordance with Freud and the Freudian tradition. Adorno had already presented this interpretation of autonomy in relation to the figures of Zerlina and Don Giovanni: through the idea of surrender. For what surrender, or 'self-othering' as Hegel would say, properly demands, in Freudian terms, is precisely a 'strong' ego rather than a 'weak' and accommodating one. The strong ego is a psychoanalytical equivalent to the autonomous Kantian subject, the self that judges independently and acts in a universal manner. This ego also requires the equally important development of that dimension which western rationalism with its characteristically limited concept of rationality has effectively repressed: the sensuous or 'mimetic' dimension of the self.[14]

The thesis of the end of the individual can also draw further psychoanalytic support from theories of "self-identification with the aggressor" or "gratification through identification with the mass," etc. And Adorno appeals to all these theoretical approaches, deeply radicalizing them and thereby distancing them from the normal empirical procedures of scientific research, for the disadvantage of all such reliably and empirically grounded knowledge is that it readily congeals into the 'conventional.' And this is clearly a serious problem for any critic of society who sees everything unconventional threatened by historical developments, but especially for a thinker like Adorno, who emphasizes the independent character of thought and of one's own "experience" above all else.[15] In attempting to justify his thesis of the end of the individual in psychoanalytic, politico-economic, and sociological terms, Adorno's work thus deliberately operates in a kind of indeterminate and intermediate space between scientific research and unregulated, spontaneous experience. He simply hopes to formulate a general hypothesis that may prompt further investigation and independent reflection.

Heroic Nihilism and Releasement

On the one hand, therefore, the internal struggle of the modern self we have been describing culminates in Adorno in a negatively dialectical, paradoxical, or aporetic predicament. The different dimensions of the self, that is, the different dimensions of modernity, those of the universal and the particular, of (Kantian) self-determination and (Romantic) self-realization, of discursive knowledge and individual experience, cannot successfully be brought into a genuinely non-contradictory relationship with one another. On the other hand, Adorno suggests that the struggle between the individual-empirical and the social-transcendental ego in modernity has already yielded a clear victor: totalitarian society finally triumphs with the end of the individual.

In relation to this analysis Heidegger represents, in the first instance, a different kind of approach altogether. His way of thinking is paradigmatically oriented toward a philosophy of being, rather than to a philosophy of consciousness that remains within the parameters of the subject-object relation and is expressly articulated as a critical theory of society. Instead of decentering the subject through a critique of ideology, Heidegger attempts to do so ontologically. Already in *Being and Time,* the 'subject' that is recast as *Dasein* is essentially the 'there' (*Da*) of being. To this extent there is therefore a certain analogy, or identity in difference, in relation to Adorno. But there are also some specific corresponding similarities, with regard both to particular claims and to particular patterns of thought, in Heidegger and Adorno. One of the corresponding patterns of thought that particularly interests me here includes, as I shall show in more detail, the agonistic motif, that of an irreconcilable—that is to say, romantically modern—conflict within and between prevailing principles of thought. But precisely here it is also possible to identify a striking contrast between the two thinkers. Whereas *Adorno* holds a certain balance between a more *classically Hegelian* and a *Romantic-agonistic* style of thought, *Heidegger* operates in a space between an *agonistic* and what I called a *'hybrid'* style of thinking. I understand the term here not in the etymologically connected ethical or psychological sense of *hubris* as 'self-exaltation' (over-valuation of the self), but rather in the specific sense familiar from biology, namely that of 'crossing' and 'intersecting.' On this reading, the development of Heidegger's thought turns from a heroic, ethically and psychologically 'hybristic,' self to a self that is capable of affirming being, albeit a self that can no longer properly be described in the prevailing determinate modes of discourse, a self that can however be characterized as hybrid in the modern, originally biological, sense of the word.

Heidegger remained attached to the hybristic concept of the self as long as he continued to follow Nietzsche in interpreting the modern world as the culmination of European *nihilism.* In this phase of his thought he still regarded Nietzsche's provocative distinction between 'passive' and 'active' nihilism as a possible solution for the fundamental and self-generated crisis of the West. Nihilism implies that there is "no longer any end or purpose" (*Ziel*) in which "all the powers of the historical *Dasein* of peoples" could be "brought together," no end or purpose that such historical *Dasein* could project in a "unifying" fashion. And that is also to say, in Nietzsche's words, that there is no longer any God, any ground (*arche*) or purpose (*telos*) of historical development or change.[16] Every kind of super-sensible principle, and especially the Christian one, has already forfeited its historical power. Here 'active nihilism' seems at first to offer a solution. Heidegger thus proudly proclaims the need for sacrifice, adopting the maxim that "that which is falling should also be pushed"![17] 'Passive' nihilism, on the other hand, clings to the old values without recognizing that these are already dissolving through an internal logic of their own. Like many other social and cultural critics of his period, Heidegger contemptuously ascribes this passive nihilism to the mediocre type of outlook that supposedly characterizes bourgeois life, without realizing how much he was simply reproducing an established stereotype in this respect.[18] The writer Ernst Jünger belongs among such critics, too. He was also willing to draw specific social and political consequences from Nietzsche's general diagnosis of nihilism. Heidegger admiringly incorporated Jünger's essay "Total Mobilization" (1930) and his book *The Worker* (1932) into his own philosophical reflections. Rejecting the Hegelian, and in a certain sense already Kantian, view that the modern age represented a self-determining era, an epoch of freedom, Heidegger presented it rather as an age of the forgetting of being, of existential and metaphysical ignorance. Jünger's 'worker' stands for the new anti-bourgeois type of individual who finds both an aesthetic and redeeming form of creative virility in the activity of struggle, in struggle for the sake of struggle, who is prepared to serve a state that is organized throughout along principles of readiness for war. Jünger, like Nietzsche, seemed to offer Heidegger a way of escaping the European crisis. Their *heroic nihilism* wills the overcoming of prevailing nihilism through a heroic act, through actively consummating the process of decline that is immanent in European culture, through attempting a revolutionary grounding for a new culture.[19]

The total mobilization that National Socialism effectively accomplished thus initially appeared to Heidegger as a potentially successful counter-movement against nihilism. But only initially. Heidegger's reading of Nietzsche subsequently begins to pursue "a strategy of double association, of Nietzsche with the essence of modernity, and modern metaphysics with the nihilistic essence of the Western tradition."[20] While Heidegger continues to claim that Nietzsche has brought the nihilistic essence of modernity to light, he also argues that nihilism itself, together with the critique of nihilism, including therefore Nietzsche himself, is nothing but the culmination of the metaphysical tradition since Plato. This second claim is developed on the basis of a specific conception of metaphysics that Heidegger had already emphatically announced in his Inaugural Address at Freiburg in 1929. On this account metaphysics is the science of being (of the being of beings). But with the dawn of the modern age, according to Heidegger, beings are definitively identified with what is actual insofar as they submit to the calculating and rationalizing process of objectification, and thus the ongoing process of manipulation and control. The 'will' thus reveals itself as the fundamental principle here. Nietzsche had already expressed this with the formula of "the will to power" without being able himself to reflect critically in turn upon its significance. For Heidegger, nihilism has thus come to mean that the question of questions, "what is being?," can no longer be asked. If being is completely subjected to the human will, then the ungroundable super-sensible ground that religion names as God has been lost. From this perspective, the modern age represents a desperate and increasingly catastrophic attempt to find a response to the death of God, a substitute for the highest principle that once guided human action. To take leave of modernity, therefore, is to take leave of the entire tradition of metaphysics. In this respect Heidegger has found ready and eager students in Derrida and Vattimo.[21]

In the first instance, therefore, the figure of the hero represents a substitute for God, and not merely to Nietzsche and Heidegger. One could write, as I try to in *Das unverschämte Ich* (*The Impertinent Self*), the entire history of the modern age since the beginning of the nineteenth century as a profoundly ambivalent tale of heroes. Yet the hero is the very embodiment of the will, and thus remains itself a moment caught up in the history of decline that characterizes the West. It was precisely Nietzsche's achievement to reveal this, and although this was something that Heidegger himself was unwilling to appreciate, his own French followers have been more than ready to do so under the banner of post-modernism. Deleuze in particular, in his book on Nietzsche, has emphasized the overcoming of the (hybristic) self in the direction of the *Übermensch* and a corresponding kind of ontological affirmation. The Over-Man affirms a process of becoming that includes affirmation and repudiation as true being. But what Deleuze fails to recognize is that Nietzsche presents this overcoming in a *twofold* form, in terms of an infinite movement and in terms of a series of stages. The 'over' that belongs to the Over-Man refers on the one hand to something 'higher,' on the other to something 'over and above' or 'beyond.' This is not itself a contradiction, for it is only on the highest level that the infinite movement can commence. On this level, as English appropriately allows us to put it, the *superman* can become the *overman*. This level replaces the linear development from lower to higher stages with a circling movement.[22] The self no longer tries to be *better*, but to be *otherwise*. To reach this level human beings must be able to transcend and relinquish two great stages, that of the ought and that of the will, if they are to arrive at the stage of (the affirmation of) being: "Higher than 'Thou shouldst' stands: 'I wish' (the heroes); higher than 'I wish' stands: 'I am' (the Gods of the Greeks)."[23]

But in order to unfold the full sense of this ontological affirmation Nietzsche also draws upon the aesthetic tradition, and Heidegger follows him here, apparently without realizing that this is what he is effectively doing. For Nietzsche, the overman explicitly takes the place formerly occupied by the genius and the artist. The overman stands for a de-sublimated art that has been returned to life. And in this connection Nietzsche answers the relevant question concerning the nature of art in an entirely traditional way, for the overman is one who has learned to forget the 'heroic will' and thereby learned to grasp the contingent, the *Zufall,* which literally falls to our lot, as a matter of favor, fortune, or grace. But the appropriate paradigm for this, in accordance with the classical idealist tradition, is the beautiful. As Nietzsche puts it, "The beautiful eludes the vehement will."[24] It calls rather for a light and carefree effort to let it transpire, let it touch us. And when "power" becomes "gracious," as Nietzsche says, when it bestows, or appears to bestow, its "favor" (*Gunst*) upon us, as Kant and also Heidegger can say, this manifests itself for Nietzsche, as it had for Kant, precisely as "beauty." The "ultimate self-overcoming" consists therefore in shaping one's life aesthetically in the sense of permitting passivity itself to enter in all dynamic activity. This is precisely what is possible for the "overhero" (*Über-Held*) who has finally relinquished everything that marked the hero, namely: willing, struggling, fighting.[25]

It is thus the overman reconceived as overhero that furnishes a more appropriate substitute for God. Heidegger himself finds a variety of expressions for this substitute: "releasement," an "other kind of thinking," an "essential," a "commemorative," an "originary thinking," etc.[26] It would not be easy to identify the contribution of the active or passive elements, of willing and letting, in such thinking. There is much in Heidegger, however, that implies a certain priority on the part of passivity. He thus easily exposes himself to a cognitivist and political kind of critique insofar as a thinking that hearkens so faithfully to being turns to a trans-discursive realm of knowing and, from the practical and political perspective, would seem to encourage a posture of obedience.[27] But there is also something here that suggests a finely balanced relationship between activity and passivity: the way in which Heidegger characterizes the various analogous relationships explored in his thinking. He says that releasement or letting-be (*Gelassenheit*) involves a "simultaneous posture of yes and no with regard to the world of technicity."[28] Similarly, the relationship between "world" and "earth," the principle of "revealing" and "concealing," of the *dis*-closing and closing-*off* of meaning, as presented in the essay on the work of art, is marked by an agonistic parity that Heidegger calls "strife."[29] But this interdependence of activity and passivity is also particularly well-exemplified in the relationship between traditional metaphysical thought and Heidegger's own metaphysics of alterity. The latter cannot be conceived as something that is simply contrary to, or a simple contradiction of, the former. As Heidegger puts it, echoing Hegel and Freud, all "counter-movements remain entangled in what they overcome."[30] It is not as if false thought holds sway on one side, while true thought occupies the other. On the contrary, the 'other thinking,' the truly 'originary' thinking, is something that belongs to the future. It is rather, as Derrida says, something that is perpetually displaced. If this were not the case, history itself would no longer be open. There can be no end of metaphysics, and thereby of modernity, and therefore no radical post-modernity either.[31]

And yet this 'other thinking' is also supposed to be *entirely* other. Its relationship to the preceding thought of the tradition remains unclear, and certainly becomes no clearer when we are told that both kinds of thinking are "the conflictual in concordance, the concordance of the conflictual."[32] The basically *agonistic* character of this relationship, however, is quite clear. To this extent the principle of modernity, the struggle of the self with itself, appears in Heidegger on an anonymous, subjectless level of thought, as a struggle between two fundamentally different paradigms. In this sense Heidegger offers an utterly modern response to the problem of thinking. This response specifically assumes a position between the agonistic and hybrid versions of modernity, for the modern age is hybrid not only in the sense that it appeals to the principle of the creative human being as a surrogate for God and thereby tends constantly toward a certain hybris, but also insofar as it de-subjectivizes this very principle and renders it anonymous, de-sublimating the 'humanistic' form that it had assumed in the modern philosophy of subjectivity. This 'other thinking' wishes to be neither new in a revolutionary sense nor merely, so to speak, a little different from what has gone before. It wishes rather to be the one precisely through the other, to be what has never been thought precisely through the ceaseless recombination and re-articulation of what has already been thought. But it was Deleuze who expressed this emphatically hybrid understanding of thought much more uninhibitedly than Heidegger. In stressing the dynamic and radically non-circumscribable character of being, both thinkers reveal themselves as the inheritors of 'life philosophy' and the Romantic tradition. They are also indebted to the Romantic tradition to the extent that they both (like Derrida, too) make appeal to the aesthetic dimension as the appropriate *model* for thinking. To this extent Rorty is right to interpret Heidegger (and Derrida) in relation to the philosophy of Romantic self-creation. But what also leads Heidegger far beyond this kind of private philosophy of the self—and this is something for which Rorty has no appreciation whatsoever—is Heidegger's attempt to rethink metaphysics under specifically modern conditions, or to put it differently: after Hegel to reconcile modernity once again with metaphysics. And this is something, once again, that he shares with Adorno.

—*Translated by Nicholas Walker*

CHAPTER NINE

Adorno, Heidegger, and the Problem of Remembrance

Mario Wenning

The question of how thinking ought to relate itself to the past gains particular importance at a time when turning toward the past marks a radical shift from earlier modernist preoccupations with the future. Such a "culture of memory" has been in evidence since the late 1970s.[1] Adorno and Heidegger in their respective ways anticipated and helped bring about this shift. Thus if I have chosen to discuss the notions of remembrance (*Andenken*) and working through the past (*Aufarbeitung der Vergangenheit*), it is not just because they deal with a central issue of public culture, but because they mark out a specific convergence and a telling difference between Adorno's and Heidegger's responses to the question of remembrance. By contrasting the underlying assumptions of the two mnemonic practices, it will become clear that they, while being based on different assumptions, each point out important aspects of what it means to engage with the past in a critical and meaningful way. Finally, a comparison between "working through" and "remembrance" will help to elucidate Heidegger's and Adorno's responses to the philosophical problem of modernity and the challenges of living in an age of crisis, irredeemable loss, constant transition, and failed opportunities—an age in which, as Marx put it, "all that is solid melts into air." Most important, we will see how both reflect on the possibility of genuine experience (*Erfahrung*), namely, experience that engages in a responsible way with history.

Heidegger on Thoughtful Remembrance

Heidegger experiments with different forms of thinking. He borrows from Romantic models of a lack or retreat of Being, and in particular from Hölderlin's thought-figure of the *deus absconditus,* the absent or fugitive God. In *What Is Called Thinking?* he writes that the "will to action . . . has overrun and crushed thought."[2] For him, the most thought-provoking thing in our thought-provoking time is that we are still not thinking adequately. The need for thinking is not satisfied by a form of philosophy that takes an interest in things, for such interest is usually only fleeting. It relegates the thing of interest to what will soon be merely boring. What calls us into thinking is not an object but an event of absence. How can we talk about something that at the same time both withdraws and is always already under way? By pointing toward that which withdraws, Heidegger claims, we enter a state of preparation (*Vorbereitung*). Because that which withdraws from us "keeps and develops its own, incomparable nearness,"[3] we have to find a way of thinking that is attentive to the event of withdrawal, a way of comportment that addresses what is absent as something present in thinking. This leads Heidegger to develop a conception of poetic thinking as thoughtful remembrance or recollective thinking (*Andenken*).[4]

We need to think back, Heidegger claims, in order first to understand the absence of that which has been lost as an absence. Thinking back is an act of memory, "the gathering of recollection."[5] Indeed, Heidegger finds himself increasingly drawn to the past in order to recover the possibility of a genuinely new future, a true beginning: an "unspoken gathering of the whole of Western fate, the gathering from which alone the Occident can go forth to meet the coming decisions—to become, perhaps and in a wholly other mode, a land of dawn, an Orient."[6] The problematic present, the moment of loss and crisis, can be overcome by turning to the past, by an act of recollecting thinking.

It has often been assumed that Heidegger is merely reiterating a stereotypical model of modern time consciousness insofar as he takes an interest in the past only to overcome the present crisis in view of a radically new future.[7] This interpretation is misguided, however, since Heidegger is neither turning naïvely to the past nor expecting a radically new future. Instead of regarding the past as a mere prehistory to the present, to which one needs to attend in order to create new possibilities, Heidegger is experimenting with a form of thinking that hardly squares with the usual conception of a past as clearly distinguishable from the present and the future. This form of thinking does not just acknowledge that it has a history, but aims to relate authentically to its historicity. Heidegger's notion of remembrance is for him a going back, a *Zurückgehen* to the origin. This going back is an act of refinding. Yet it does not preserve something through a mere presencing of something past. Much more than that:

> This thinking-to (*Hindenken*) moves to what has been and leaves the present. But at the same time within the thinking-to what has been moves from the opposite direction to him who remembers (*den Hindenkenden*). . . . If we fully leave what is remembered in its essence and do not disturb its activity at all, then we experience that what is remembered in its return does not stop in the present. . . . [It] raises itself above our present and suddenly stands in the future. It moves toward us, still unfulfilled, a treasure not yet unearthed.[8]

Remembrance opens up a space in which the repository of meaning buried in past experiences reveals itself. The modern subject is decentered within a horizon of historical experience. Through remembrance, the repository of meaning is elevated such that we are reconnected to a world that is not of our own making. Even though remembrance is a "turning inward" (*Er-innerung*), it is the means by which a subject is opened up to an unfolding or event.

Heidegger states that "perhaps 'thinking' is essentially always 'remembrance.'"[9] On a superficial level, the mere use of words and concepts, which are necessary for thinking, presupposes a form of remembrance. This is to say that previously acquired knowledge (definitions of words, grammar rules) needs to be actualized in a productive, that is, meaningful, way. On a deeper level, however, the level Heidegger has in mind, thinking does not just have a history; it is its history. Words gain their meaning through a framework of reference. They are at the same time dependent upon and take part in constituting this framework in a given context. They take part in and contribute to the continuing unfolding of this context. In drawing on the etymological affinity between *Denken* and *Andenken*,

Heidegger concludes that thinking and remembrance are interwoven. A thinking that stands in an *andenkende* relationship to history has the ability to transform or elevate a historical event to the level of existential bearing. In this elevation the resources are gained for overcoming the present dominance of calculative thinking (*rechnendes Denken*), a mode of thought that, assuming autonomy and independence with regard to its history, neglects the fact that thinking is its history and stands within a tradition that discloses itself in and through this history. Remembrance offers itself as the kind of thinking that is attentive to that which withdraws itself and yet is incomparably near. While not ignoring the fundamental modern experience of loss, it provides a point of orientation. In contrast to the conscious life of ordinary cognition, remembrance resounds with feeling. It points beyond reflective comprehension, although it need not be opposed to it.

Thus Heidegger aims to recover meaningful experience despite the present crisis. In Hölderlin's poem "Andenken," which motivates Heidegger's interest in remembrance, the poet, who remembers his visit to southern France, lets himself, from a distance and by the movement of the wind, be moved (*bewegt*) through the greetings, since he understands that although it is he himself who has these memories, it is not *up to him* to recollect them. In *De memoria et reminiscentia*, Aristotle captures this essential feature of remembrance as a moment of passivity, of letting be and acceptance: "The reason why the effort of recollection is not under the control of their will is that, as those who throw a stone cannot stop it at their will when thrown, so he who tries to recollect and 'hunts' [after an idea] sets up a process in a material part, [that] in which resides the affection."[10] This characterization of remembrance as a passive letting-be anticipates Heidegger's conception of releasement, *Gelassenheit*. In addition to the affective dimension of remembrance, Heidegger stresses that even the ability to forget is an essential feature of remembrance. This kind of forgetting, however, is not the same as the specifically modern form of forgetfulness, which characterizes calculative thinking and conceives of history as "standing reserve." While the former allows for historical meaning, the latter is an abstraction that denies the embeddedness of thinking in history.

Adorno and the Need to Work Through the Past

Adorno also wants to direct thinking to the past, but within the medium of critical reflection only. Already in a number of radio addresses from the 1950s and 1960s,[11] Adorno warned of the danger of the emergence of our contemporary form of memory discourse—a form that emphasizes the immediacy of experience. Many of the proponents of a "culture of feeling" believe that one should respond to the growing danger of forgetfulness by mobilizing emotive responses such as empathy. For example, the "Holocaust industry" (Norman Finkelstein) instrumentalizes the collective unconscious to arouse feelings of personal dismay and guilt without providing for open and critical investigation or a cultivation of critical judgment. The film *Schindler's List,* to take a more recent example, employs means structurally analogous to Leni Riefenstahl's propaganda movies of the thirties by deploying the standard tropes of aestheticizing heroism and sympathy so as to appeal to subconscious feelings. Although the content has shifted, the medium is still one of unreflected immediacy. This appeal to feeling, without any attempt to stimulate our critical reflective capacities, is as problematic as the reaction, recounted by Adorno, of a woman who commented on a staging of the *Diary of Anne Frank* by saying, "Yes, but at least that girl should have been allowed to live."[12] Mere confrontation with images and testimonies of survivors, without at the same time presenting an analysis of the causes and working mechanisms of totalitarian ideologies, is deeply problematic. It engages in what Jay Bernstein has called a "pornography of horror." By focusing on individual cases of suffering and torture, this form of memorializing leaves the appropriation up to the immediacy of feelings and leaves open the question of understanding phenomena within a larger context (e.g., the operating logic of totalitarianism and propaganda, mechanisms of collective psychology, xenophobia, etc.). Adorno's alternative to a shallow and superficial culture of memory is *philosophical criticism*, the *raison d'être* of philosophy.

Clearly Adorno's reflections on the question of how to engage with the past cannot be separated from the totalitarian conditions that his writings and reflections on mnemonic practices attempt to counter. The centrality of Auschwitz as the epitaph of modernity is present in almost every word he wrote after 1945. Auschwitz figures as a watershed, after which all

previous history is only a prehistory and in the light of which any succes-
sive developments bear the emptiness of what is later called *posthistoire*. In
his writings one can observe a stigmatization of temporality and history
in which Auschwitz, which, at the same time, the ultimate limit situation
and culmination point, defines the whole as the false and thus every act of
unbroken remembrance as a necessary failure and a moment of revisionist
ideology. The pivotal point of modernity is depicted as a wound that cannot be healed by time, but continually perpetuates its own permanence.
Adorno anticipates later French accounts of the collapse of reason through
totalitarianism, which in an almost obsessive fashion describes the world
in its entirety as *le monde concentrationnaire*, the "concentration camp universe," as the culmination of a universal history of negativity. Radical rupture negates the possibility of reconciliation and transforms those who "by
law" should have been killed, into "spared survivors." Troubled by survivors' guilt, their existence is robbed of any positive meaning. Moreover,
any attempt even to discuss the ultimate failure of culture is condemned
as revisionist.

Instead of a superficial, reified, and immediate culture of memory,
Adorno recommends that "thoughts that are true must incessantly renew
themselves in the experience of the subject matter, which nonetheless first
determines itself in those thoughts. The strength to do that, and not the
measuring-out and marking-off of conclusions, is the essence of philosophical rigor."[13] Philosophical thinking worthy of its name allows for neither factual summary nor the distinction of process and result. It is constructive, and yet, by simultaneously focusing on its object, it is a form of
Nachvollzug. *Nachvollzug* refers to an act of comprehension that tries to
trace and understand an event in its (historical) genesis. Yet, by being self-
reflective, *Nachvollzug* does not generate a mere rhapsodic repetition or
restoration of a historic event. The task of working through the past cannot aim at restitution, because the dead are forever silent and past injustic-
es cannot be undone. Life cannot be reawakened; once striped of its voice,
life cannot be restored.

The importance of the traumatic consequences of the crimes of the
twentieth century to Adorno's view cannot be overestimated. Yet, it is
greatly misleading to read Adorno as only or even primarily investigating
the conditions of the dark sides of modernity of which Auschwitz is the

quasi-necessary teleological point of culmination.[14] He repeatedly warns us against any philosophy of history that constructs a linear account of progress or regress. How could he conceive of a *dialectic* of enlightenment, that is, an account of enlightenment modernity as ambiguous, according to which a dimension rupture always conditions its other (the promise of reconciliation), if he were merely interested in its *Verfallsgeschichte* (the history of its decline)?

Confrontation

Let us now turn to Adorno's critique of Heidegger, before revealing the limits and blind spots of Adorno's approach as seen from a Heideggerian perspective. Adorno's critique of Heidegger's "ontological impulse" is twofold. First, Adorno stresses the danger of reviving and thus naïvely accepting the modern predicament of an impotence of the subject. Heidegger's call to attentiveness and remembrance figures as a kind of evasion and silent acceptance of the death of the subject and the withdrawal of meaning under conditions of modernity. One exemplary moment where such a giving in to passivity becomes explicit is when Heidegger denounces the conception of the subjective will in favor of his alternative: "will is the knowing willingness (*Bereitschaft*) to belong to fate (*Geschick*)."[15] If one has no idea of that to which one is subjecting oneself because subjectivity is dissolved in the process of remembrance, then, as one commentator aptly puts it, "remembrance is condemned to hopelessness and impotence. It simply becomes a formula for the incessant evocation of the fate of being."[16] Contrary to Heidegger, Adorno's plea for an active engagement on the part of the subject presupposes that under conditions of an antagonistic totality we cannot seek refuge in some higher preserving power. The attempt to create a space in which the impossibility of experience is understood as just that—an impossibility—entails a form of active engagement on the part of the subject, not a passive letting-be. Letting-be would result either in subjecting oneself to the past or in "mastering the past" (*die Vergangenheit zu bewältigen*), which would amount to nothing less than a loss of history.[17] Awareness that a focus on working through the rubble of terror and brutality is required by the bleak situation of Western culture is the only form of comportment that is neither self-forgetful nor self-obsessed.

Second, Adorno sees in Heidegger a general lack of mediation. This lack blurs the genre distinction between poetry and philosophical thinking. While the first criticism amounts to a charge of fatalism, the second is an objection to unreflective poeticizing, which in turn, following Adorno, involves accepting the status quo. Contrary to Heidegger, Adorno argues that the modern division of labor between poetry and conceptual thinking wants to be reflected, not ignored. To reflect the historically generated split between philosophy and poetry also means to transcend it in an attempt to understand its limitations. This transcending is possible only, Adorno argues, if we stick to the requirements of conceptual thinking. What philosophical thinking needs to hold on to, Adorno emphasizes, is a strong genre distinction between philosophy and poetry or the arts more generally, each of which points to that which the other possesses—and which it lacks. Art and philosophy are two sides of a coin that would only be united in a state of reconciliation, which is far from achieved.

Adorno's new categorical imperative, "never again Auschwitz," directly translates into a pedagogical program according to which "the only education that has any sense at all is an education toward critical self-reflection."[18] Contrary to Heidegger's notion of thoughtful remembrance, self-reflective criticism, understood as a strategy of resistance, is supposed to break with the established conformism and by extension the present false culture of memory. It is supposed to burst open the mythic spell that an unmastered past casts over the present. Self-reflection, Adorno argues, keeps open a space that, in drawing on the failure of culture and rationality, allows us to confront the barbarism committed in the name of culture so that it does not rise again. However, although it might be a first and important step to bring to consciousness that which has made barbarism possible, more is required for building a self-critical community that would possess the reflective and conceptual resources for guarding itself against barbarism and allow for a better and more meaningful lived experience. Moreover, because the new categorical imperative is negative in orientation ("never again"), it does not just fail to specify what should be done, but dismisses history *tout court* and relegates historical time to the status of being "empty" and nihilistic. Adorno's criticism of Heidegger as being fatalistic in accepting the status quo applies to Adorno's own conception of history as one of increasing decay as well.

In distancing himself from what he calls "one-track thinking," a form of thinking that provides opinions about anything and everything, Heidegger does not distance himself from philosophy as a practice of careful and "thoughtful" evaluation. The fact that the philosophical poet has the last word in Hölderlin's poem "Remembrance" ("the poets establish what remains") shows that an insight is gained through following the path of remembrance.[19] Contrary to Adorno's criticism, reflective insight and poetic thinking do not exclude each other for Heidegger and Hölderlin. Hölderlin's writings circle around the question of the possibility of metaphysical experience under conditions of an internally divided modernity. Similarly, Heidegger's interest in Hölderlin's poetry is motivated by a concern for the recovery of experience through reconciling what is lost with what is present without forcefully appropriating it or losing oneself in it. What the overcoming of distance through remembrance aims to preserve is a lasting experience of orientation. Adorno, of course, criticizes this line of argument: "the consciousness suffering from the fissured state of the world and conjuring up a past unity out of its own deprivation contradicts the very contents it aspires to win for itself. Therefore it must autocratically promote its own primordial language. Restoration is as futile in philosophy as it is anywhere else."[20] Adorno's objections amount to the claim that Heidegger is unable to live up to the only form that philosophy can have, that is, the form of a self-reflective critique aiming to break through the mythic spell of history.

On the other hand, Heidegger's appropriation of thoughtful remembrance provides a good lens through which one can see the limits, or at least misleading temptations, of Adorno's rallying cry to work through the past. If done naïvely, concentrating on what is bad easily "create[s] the impression of being in the right."[21] Heidegger warns against the temptation to play the advocate of virtues, to practice a moralizing critique that, by always pointing to what is wrong, creates the impression of being in the right or at least suggests that the form of critique is categorically distinct from the object of criticism. Adorno's emphasis on criticism leaves open the question of how one should guard oneself against a distancing in which one pretends to set up a tribunal of history unencumbered by that very history. Second—and this problem is acknowledged by Adorno himself—working through the past can easily lead to doing away with, overcoming, or finishing up with the past (*Bewältigung*) for a new and perhaps better future. This would, however, falsely presuppose that having critically scrutinized the past, we have also distanced ourselves from its persisting influence. The etymological root of *Bewältigung* in *Gewalt*, violence, shows that an end to the guilt of being the heirs of a past buried in ruins could be achieved only through violent means, through covering up something that we want to forget, rather than critically engaging with it. By ignoring this nexus, the past might reappear as not truly forgotten but preserved on a subconscious level. The violent act of *Bewältigung* easily turns into repression. Although Adorno acknowledges this danger, he holds on to the primacy of critical reflection to the point of not allowing for any other forms of not primarily "critical" and scrutinizing comportment to the past. Hence his commitment to criticism as the only form of engaging with the past takes on paternalistic forms, e.g., in his remark about "reflective" individuals: "it is certainly not at all superfluous to fortify this group with enlightened instruction against the non-public opinion."[22] Distrusting any forms of "passive" experience, he believes that although the notion of working through is not a sufficient condition for a better state of affairs, it is the only way left open to guard against what he fears as the most pressing contemporary dangers, such as the survival of fascist tendencies within democracy.[23]

The problem with the Adornian appeal to self-reflection is that it tends to lead to paternalism and reaches only an already self-reflective audience. Even in these cases, it is questionable how much good self-reflection can accomplish. If it is not coupled with an education that leads to a capacity to feel and to remember authentically, then the most self-reflective person might turn out to be a technocrat following questionable goals. The old, troubling question returns: "What would be the upshot of transforming the unconscious into conscious life?" As Adorno admits, the authoritarian personality lacks the capacity for any experience whatsoever. Yet it seems that the very notion of having a past to work through possesses an authoritarian element in that it denigrates historical experience and locates the subject at the center of all cognitive action.

Conclusion

Both Heidegger and Adorno argue for a turn toward historical experience. Yet Adorno's demand to work through the past and Heidegger's appropriation of thoughtful remembrance reveal important differences. While the practice of critical working through runs the danger of losing its constitutive dependency upon the world, remembrance relinquishes the constitutive role of the subject and thus faces the difficulty of evaluating what counts as good and what counts as a bad form of inheritance and dependence.

What are we to hope for by engaging in a form of Adornian criticism that postpones reconciliation and perhaps forgiveness *ad infinitum,* thereby precluding genuine experience, an experience that is hinted at in Heidegger's commitment to following the course of remembrance? Within critical theory it has been assumed that the method of criticism is itself part of the redemption of a past buried in ruins. In discussing the concept of romantic criticism, Walter Benjamin writes: "criticism is far less the judgment of a work than the method of its consummation (*Vollendung*)."[24] By being criticized, however, a world in ruins does not become any more complete than it was in its state of catastrophe. The connection between the past as an object of critical reflection is essentially an aporetic interplay of debt and guilt.[25] Like the most tragic of heroes, we continually reinforce the power of a fate whose hold we seek to break. Particularly when dealing with history, the critic does not stand in a neutral framework set over against the object of critique, but stands on the very ground she is criticizing. By denying her constitutive dependency upon what she wants to replace in order to erect her own authority as critical consciousness, she at the same time transforms indebtedness into guilt. Critique is aporetic because, if it is carried through to its end, it eventually has to turn against its own contingent foundations, thereby undermining its own possibility. As a form of second-order discourse it tries to delegitimize a world that, as Heidegger teaches, is always already disclosed in pre-reflective praxis. Critique, in order to be mature, has to face the abyss of the meaninglessness of everything on which it does not bestow meaning. Its commitment to the ultimate authority of an autonomous subject as the motor of criticism does not allow for any form of dependence that has not been legitimized by this very autonomy. The practice of thoughtful remembrance, on the other hand, does allow for forms of already standing in relationships of being historically determined. While remembrance can acknowledge guilt,[26] working through the past objectifies guilt as something external. Remembrance acknowledges that our reflections are from the outset embedded in a world of complex structures of inheritance and dependence.

As useful as the method of critique might appear, it deserves a second thought in light of a Heideggerian critique. Adorno is well aware of the problem of justifying critique in light of the developments he so aptly analyzed. In this context, his holding on to rationality often appears to be a decision of faith rather than to be warranted by his own critique of the various forms of one-sided rationality. Yet, Adorno adopts the Kantian principle of critique without much reservation. He holds firm to an ethos of absolute criticism and the ideal of complete self-consciousness. One is tempted to ask the question why we should expect more from enlightening enlightenment about itself, than from mere enlightenment; that is, why should the act of putting reified categories back into motion make us less amenable to the subterranean forces that, according to Adorno, led to catastrophe and identity thinking in the first place? If Adorno is right to claim that Auschwitz demonstrated irrefutably that culture has failed, then how can a claim to critical engagement, presumably a cultural phenomenon, seem a viable form of comportment in a world that "radiates disaster triumphant"?[27] To believe that the old appeal to self-reflective autonomous action would yield better results, if applied a second time, is tantamount to believing that when taking prescription medication, taking it again would suddenly revive a patient killed by its side effects: two negatives do not make a positive, as Adorno was acutely aware. To continue traveling the path of self-criticism, we would have to be certain that we are moving forward and that generally this path leads toward true reconciliation. One could easily entertain doubts about both of these assumptions. What the encounter of Adorno and Heidegger has shown is that a viable conception of historical experience must be careful not to fall into the traps of either a blind fatalism or a naïve commitment to the enlightenment heritage. That this conclusion is negative in character perhaps indicates why a genuine dialogue between Adorno and Heidegger could not have taken place.[28]

CHAPTER TEN

Adorno and Heidegger on Modernity

Fred Dallmayr

Theories or ideas, no matter how lofty, are not immune from historical circumstance: the latter often discloses what otherwise is left unsaid. Far
from being an assortment of random data, history from this angle remains
a great taskmaster—by teaching us about the complex ambivalences and
unintended consequences of rational designs. The ideas of 'modernity' and
'enlightenment' are a prominent case in point. No one can doubt the lofti-
ness and even the intrinsic nobility of these labels. Basically, modernity (as
understood in the West) was meant to inaugurate a new age of human freedom and self-determination, as contrasted with previous eras marked by political, clerical, and intellectual tutelage. In turn, enlightenment—in Kant's
memorable phrase—was meant to awaken humankind from the "slumber
of self-induced immaturity" and ignorance, thereby paving the way for the
undiluted reign of scientific knowledge and moral self-legislation.

As history teaches, these and related ideas did indeed generate some
of the desired results—but often in unforeseen ways and saddled with dubious or less noble implications. Like a deep shadow, these implications ac-
companied from the beginning the modern spreading of 'light.' At the very
onset of the new age, Francis Bacon proclaimed the equation of knowledge
with power—thereby vindicating the prospect of human mastery over nature (as well as over less knowledgeable people). In the domain of politics
and ethics, the modern maxim of freedom exacerbated a formula that Ar-

istotle already had used against non-Greeks: "meet it is that barbarous peoples should be governed by the Greeks."[1]

The merits and demerits of modernity have been widely discussed in recent decades from a variety of angles (anti-modern, modernist, postmodern)—but often in a purely academic vein. Here again, historical circumstance demands its due. It was during the past (twentieth) century that some of the most disturbing and hideous connotations of the modern project of unlimited mastery came out into the open, and it was in response to these implications—manifest in fascism and Stalinist communism—that some of the most penetrating analyses of this project were formulated. In view of the hundredth anniversary of Theodor Adorno's birth (1903), it is fitting that close attention should be given again to his critical work—particularly to the magisterial *Dialectic of Enlightenment* (written in collaboration with Max Horkheimer) and the *magnum opus* of his later years, *Negative Dialectics*. Roughly in the same historical context, another leading German thinker—Martin Heidegger—launched an equally devastating attack on the totalizing machinations of modern technology and modern politics (in writings that only recently have became available). The following pages start out by reviewing the arguments of these two thinkers, with an emphasis on both their similarities and their differences. With the demise of fascism and Stalinist communism, these arguments seem to have lost their contextual force; this, however, is far from being the case. Under the aegis of globalization, the totalizing ambitions of Western modernity are revealed today on a planetary scale: in the opposition between the hegemonic 'North' and the dominated 'South.'

Adorno and Modernity's 'Dialectic'

Adorno's life reflects the entire drama of his period. Like many of his colleagues, Adorno was forced into exile by the rise of fascism in Germany. Under the impact of fascist policies, and especially the unfolding specter of the Jewish holocaust, Adorno came to realize the darkly sinister undertow of Western modernity—an awareness prompting him to temper the confident progressivism of his earlier years (inspired by Left-Hegelian ideas). To be sure, history had always been punctuated by grim episodes of persecution and oppression; however, what rendered contemporary politics distinctive was the totalizing or 'totalitarian' reach of political control—a reach indebted in no small measure to the triumphant sway of modern rationality wedded to the Baconian motto of knowledge/power. Some of the dangers lurking in this motto were clearly exposed by Max Horkheimer, Adorno's friend, in a study written during the war years and entitled *Eclipse of Reason*. Without simply abandoning modernity or the promises of enlightenment, Horkheimer's text severely castigated the ongoing shrinkage of critical reason and self-reflection into a mere instrument of calculation and managerial control. To a large extent, this shrinkage in his view could be traced to the Baconian (and Cartesian) split between subject and object, between rational knowledge and external matter or nature. The end result of this division, he noted, was on the one hand an "abstract ego emptied of all substance" except its will for self-preservation, and on the other, "an empty nature degraded to mere material, mere stuff to be dominated, without any other purpose than that of this very domination."[2]

Themes of this kind were further explored and deepened by Horkheimer and Adorno during the same wartime period—an exploration that culminated in their epochal work *Dialectic of Enlightenment*. Here, as in Horkheimer's text, the animus was not directed against reason and enlightenment as such—provided these labels preserved the connotation of critical understanding and self-reflection. As it happened, however, the unfolding scenario of modernity led to a steady curtailment of the latter in favor of a progressive congealment or 'reification' of both rational knowledge and the empirical target of knowledge (the two poles of the subject-object split). According to the authors, the advancement of modern scientific knowledge basically heralded an exit or exodus—a largely welcome exodus—from primitive myth or an unreflective and oppressive 'naturalism' (utterly opaque to human understanding); yet, precisely by virtue of this exodus and the resulting subjugation of nature, modern reason is in danger of being 're-mythologized' by being turned into an instrument of unreflective power. Although the program of rational inquiry always entails in some way "the disenchantment of the world, the dissolution of myths, and the substitution of knowledge for fancy," the process begins to boomerang when reason loses its critical edge by blending into 'positivist' formulas. At this point, enlightenment reveals its own dark undercurrent, and social progress its complicity with regress. Here is a passage that eloquently expresses the authors' concerns:

We are wholly convinced—and therein lies our *petitio principii*—that social freedom is inseparable from enlightened thought. Nevertheless, we believe just as clearly to have recognized that this very way of thinking—no less than the actual historical forms (the social institutions) with which it is interwoven—already contains the seed of the reversal universally apparent today. If enlightenment does not allow reflection on this regressive element, it seals its own fate.[3]

In terms of the text, the regressive counterpoint of enlightenment—its dialectical underside—derives from the streamlining of rational thought into a calculating, instrumental form of rationality, a process that underscores the growing division between human beings and nature, between cognitive power and its external targets. Ever since the time of Bacon, Horkheimer and Adorno assert, cognitive rationality has shown a 'patriarchal' face: by conquering superstition, human reason is meant to "hold sway over disenchanted nature." In the course of modernity or modernization, this patriarchal legacy has led to a steady widening of the rift between *res cogitans* (thinking subject) and *res extensa* (extended matter)—which coincides with the gulf between inside and outside, between logical form and substantive content. On the internal or 'subjective' side, the *cogito* in modernity tends to be stylized into a sovereign selfhood, a self-contained 'identity' that ejects from itself all forms of otherness as modes of alienation and reification; in large measure, modern freedom or 'emancipation' has this connotation of self-recovery or self-possession. It is only through this retreat into inwardness, the text states, that individuals gain "self-identity," a selfhood that cannot be "dissipated through identification with others" but "takes possession of itself once and for all behind an impenetrable mask." The upshot of this development is the radical subordination of matter to mind, of nature—both internal and external nature—to the dictates of a rationally emancipated humankind. As the authors add intriguingly in a foray into political theology: "Systematizing reason and the creator-God resemble each other as rulers of nature. Man's likeness to God consists in the sovereignty over the world, in the countenance of mastery, and in the ability to command."[4]

In the modern era, the streamlining effect of cognitive rationality was first evident in the sequence of grand philosophical 'systems'—all intent on grasping the universe as a whole. Later, the same tendency surfaced in social-scientific systems, especially in functional-sociological models pretending to capture the totality of social life. In the authors' words: "From the start, enlightenment recognizes as real occurrence only what can be apprehended in rational unity; its ideal is the 'system' from which all and everything follows." The primary means for accomplishing this unity—a means extolled especially by positivism and the 'unified science' movement—is number, that is, the reduction of all qualitative differences to quantitative measurement. "Number," we read, "became the canon of enlightenment: the same equations govern bourgeois [abstract] justice and economic commodity exchange." In expelling or cleansing itself of qualitative differences, cognitive rationality inevitably prepared the ground for the 'systematization' or homogenization of social life and thus for the establishment of increasingly effective social controls and disciplines. At the same time, the priority of number or formal calculus promoted a distinctive kind of social and intellectual hierarchy (or patriarchy). By defining knowledge or 'truth' as the primacy of universal form over particular content, of rational system over non-rational experience, modern rationality exacted a price: namely, the alienation of reason from the target of knowledge or, more precisely, the isolation of reason from possible learning experiences induced by its targets. Among these learning experiences are the lessons provided by human sensuality and affectivity (that is, the realm of 'inner' nature). From the vantage of modern rationality, Horkheimer and Adorno state, sensuality and instinct are "as mythical as religious superstitions" (and hence subject to the same exorcism), while the idea of serving a God not constructed by the rational self is considered "as irrational as drunkenness."[5]

As in Horkheimer's text, exposing the 'dialectic of enlightenment' was not meant as a plea for primitivism or nostalgic regression. Some help in avoiding the twin dangers of regression and rational triumphalism could be found in Hegelian dialectics, and particularly in his notion of 'determinate negation.' With that notion, Horkheimer and Adorno affirm, Hegel "revealed an element that separates [genuine] enlightenment from the positivist decay with which he lumps it together." Yet, this endorsement is qualified: by ultimately "absolutizing" the outcome of dialectics—namely, his own system of totalizing synthesis—Hegel himself "contravened the prohibition (of images) and lapsed into mythology." As a result, the authors recommend a more subdued, post-Hegelian dialectics—but one clearly geared toward the healing or reconciliation of modern divisions. To be sure, hope cannot be pinned on magical formulas or instant solutions. Only through critical reflection—one mindful of its tendentious complicity with power—is reason able to break the spell of (ancient or modern) mythology and reification. Only in this manner is reason capable of regaining its liberating élan: an élan whereby enlightenment transcends domineering rationality by regaining access to a nature "which becomes perceptible in its otherness or alienation." Thus, a healing of modern divisions is at least initiated (if not completed) through radical self-reflection pushing beyond instrumentalism—more boldly phrased: through a "recollection of nature in the rational subject," a remembrance that holds the key to the "truth of all culture." As the authors conclude, enlightenment fulfills and "sublates" itself when the means-ends nexus is suspended—at the point where the "nearest practical ends" reveal themselves as the "most distant goal" and where repressed nature is remembered as the "land of origin" as well as the portent of an "unmanageable" hope.[6]

Qualified endorsement of Hegelian dialectics is the hallmark also of Adorno's later writings, particularly his sprawling *Negative Dialectics*. 'Qualified' here means acceptance of healing mediations *minus* resort to the 'absolute' or to any kind of comprehensive or totalizing synthesis. It is this minus feature that renders genuine dialectics 'negative': namely, by confining itself to the determinate negation of existing ills and divisions while radically refusing to portray and conceptually define a fully reconciled utopia. One of Adorno's main complaints here is directed at Hegel's relentless rationalism or 'conceptualism': his effort to bring all experience under the domineering sway of concepts (culminating in the 'absolute' concept or idea). Although recognizing experiential 'otherness,' he remonstrates, Hegel's system tended to 'pre-think' and conceptually pre-arrange every concrete particularity, with the result that the diversity of phenomena was streamlined into a grand, holistic synthesis governed by reason. Proceeding in this manner, Hegelian dialectics ultimately reduced concrete phenomena to mere 'exemplars of concepts' while confining reason to the rehearsal of its own categories. In Adorno's view, the only way to rupture this self-enclosure is through thought's attentiveness to non-thought or reason's turn toward the (conceptually) 'non-identical'—which precludes any premature synthesis. Only in this manner is reason able to regain (in Hegel's own terms) its "freedom toward the object," a freedom lost under the spell of the subject's "meaning-constituting" or meaning-imposing autonomy. Basically, philosophy's genuine concern in our times, he adds, is with those matters in which Hegel (following a long philosophical or metaphysical tradition) expressed little or no interest: namely, "non-conceptuality, singularity, and particularity"— things that ever since Plato have been dismissed as "transitory and insignificant," as a "*qualité negligeable.*"[7]

According to Adorno's text, the corrective to Hegel's conceptual system is the rigorous insistence on non-totality, that is, on the inescapable 'non-identity' between reason and its targets, between concepts and the world (or the stubborn excess of the latter over the former). "To change the direction of conceptuality, to turn it toward non-identity," we read, "is the hinge or emblem of negative dialectics." Tied to traditional metaphysics, idealist philosophy offered only a truncated dialectics, which ultimately was unable to come to grips with modern social dilemmas and divisions. Basically, in its idealist version, dialectics was tied to the 'sovereign subject' as the source of rational conceptualization—an outlook that now has become 'historically obsolete,' given that none of the idealist formulas have stood the test of time. Under present circumstances, Adorno argues, only a negative dialectics holds out both intellectual and social promise: by being attentive to the 'otherness' or underside of reason as well as to the social-political underside of modernity, the legions of marginalized and oppressed peoples at its fringes. In his stark formulation, traditional idealism, by privileging the *cogito* (or subjectivity), only 'spiritualized' the Darwinian struggle for survival, thus reinstating or confirming a repressive naturalism. By proclaiming itself the Baconian master and even idealist 'maker' of all things, the modern epistemological *cogito* inevitably entangled itself in the nexus of power/knowledge: "In exerting mastery it becomes part of what it believes to master, succumbing like the lord" (in the Hegelian master-slave relationship).[8]

In departing from the idealist legacy, negative dialectics counters not only speculative illusions but also the nexus of domination prevailing in modernity with regard to both nature and society. In relinquishing the primacy of the *cogito* (or subjectivity), such a dialectics is able to confront the power/knowledge nexus that, in modernity, pits against each other reason and experience, humanity and nature, privileged or dominant and oppressed populations. As Adorno writes, dialectical thinking "respects that which is to be thought—the object or target of knowledge—even where the latter exceeds or does not heed the rules of formal logic." Differently phrased: such a thinking is able "to think against itself without self-cancellation or self-erasure." Proceeding along these lines, negative dialectics extricates itself from the modified Darwinism of traditional idealist thought, by allowing things 'to be' and by giving a hearing to voices otherwise excluded by modern reason. In Adorno's words, attention to the underside of reason means a willingness to "heed a potential slumbering in things" and thereby "make amends" to them for its own incursions. This "potential slumbering in things" is the domain of otherness or difference—a domain captured in Joseph Eichendorff's phrase of "beautiful strangeness" (*schöne Fremde*). As he concludes:

The hoped-for state of reconciliation would not annex the alien through an act of philosophical imperialism. Instead, its happiness would consist in allowing it to remain distant and different even in proximate surroundings, beyond the pale of both heterogeneity and sameness or identity.[9]

Heidegger and Modern 'Machinations'

The relation between Adorno and Heidegger is complex and hard to disentangle; probably for this very reason it is discussed in the literature infrequently.[10] Some of the differences between the two thinkers are relatively easy to pinpoint, having to do mainly with their respective life stories and intellectual backgrounds. As indicated, Adorno's life was relatively turbulent, leading him from Weimar Germany into the New World (New York and California) and finally back to Frankfurt after the war. By comparison, Heidegger's personal life was relatively sheltered, being spent for the most part in and around Freiburg and the Black Forest region. In terms of intellectual background, Adorno drew his inspiration chiefly from Left-Hegelianism and aspects of humanist Marxism; by contrast, Heidegger's intellectual pedigree is of *longue durée*, stretching from the Pre-Socratics via Aristotle to Husserlian phenomenology and hermeneutics. The most obvious difference, of course—and the one most widely debated—has to do with their respective responses to 1933 and its aftermath. Yet, it is precisely in this regard that initial impressions and popular assessments may be thoroughly misleading and hence in need of revision. During recent years, several writings that Heidegger wrote in the decade following 1933, that is, during the apogee of the Nazi regime, have become available. Far from showing a continued attachment to this regime, these writings on the contrary reveal Heidegger's steady estrangement—or what one may call his 'inner emigration'—from the hegemonic powers of his time. With growing intensity, his opposition is directed at the totalizing or totalitarian features of the regime, features that in no small part derive from modernity's infatuation with 'making' and domineering fabrication—what Heidegger calls "*Machenschaft*."

The texts from the Nazi period that recently became available are mainly three: *Beiträge zur Philosophie* (Contributions to Philosophy) of 1936; *Besinnung* (Meditative Thinking) of 1938–39; and *Die Geschichte des Seyns* (The History of Being) of 1939–40. Taken together, these texts give evidence of a profound intellectual drama that Heidegger underwent during this period—a drama that is customarily described as his '*Kehre*' or 'turning' (labels that should not be taken as synonyms for a reversal or simple 'turning away,' but rather as signposts of a deepening and more intensive 'turning toward' primary philosophical concerns). Of the three texts, the first is the most voluminous and also the dramatically most ambitious, setting forth an entire, detailed trajectory of intellectual and existential transformation and reorientation. This trajectory basically leads from the condition of modernity anchored in knowledge/power and the domineering designs of the *cogito* in the direction of a freer and more generously open mode of co-being among humans and between humans and the world (guided by 'letting-be'). The text is challenging and provocative not only philosophically, but also on a more mundane, political level. Taking direct aim at National Socialism and its motto of "total mobilization," Heidegger comments that such a "total (or totalizing) worldview" must "close itself off against the probing of its own ground and the premises of its actions," and it must do so because otherwise "total ideology would put itself into question." It is in connection with this critique that the term "*Machenschaft*" surfaces prominently—and with starkly pejorative connotations. The rise of worldviews to predominance, Heidegger notes, is a result of modern metaphysics, and in that context "worldview basically means *Machenschaft*," that is, a mode of contrived "machination" where creative praxis is replaced by organized "business" (*Betrieb*) and managerial control.[11]

Elaborating on this point, the text links the term with the modern prevalence of "making (*Machen, poiesis, techne*)," a making seen not solely as a form of human conduct, but as a distinct type of ontological disclosure. In modernity, Heidegger points out, *Machenschaft* is promoted by the sway of science and technology that renders everything "makeable" (*machbar*). Under these auspices, the instrumental cause-effect nexus becomes all-dominant, though in varying guises: "Both the mechanistic and the biologistic worldviews are only consequences of the underlying *machenschaftlich* interpretation of being." Preceded by biblical accounts of creation (construed as fabrication), the modern rise of *Machenschaft* was decisively inaugurated by the Cartesian *cogito*, especially by Descartes's equation of *ens creatum* with *ens certum* (fixed, determined being). Subsequently, this approach was further solidified by the advances of mathematical physics and technology (*Technik*), a process leading to the progressive technical-calculating management of the world and its resources. Against this background, Heidegger asks "What is *Machenschaft*?" and responds: "It is the system of complete explanatory calculability whereby every being is streamlined and uniformly equated with every other being—and thereby alienated, and more than alienated, from itself" (or its own distinctive potential). As he further elaborates, calculability and anonymous sameness are curiously allied in *Machenschaft* with something seemingly very different: namely, subjective feeling or emotion (*Erlebnis*). But the contrast is apparent only because anonymity and subjectivism are but two sides of the same coin: the cognitive and the emotive sides of the ego. Both reveal the subject's incapacity for self-transformation and its "oblivion of being."[12]

Jointly with the critique of *Machenschaft*, *Beiträge* also offers intriguing reflections on the meaning of 'power,' 'violence,' and related terms. Departing from an earlier ambivalent usage, the text stipulates a series of definitions with clearly demarcated contours. Closely associated with *Machenschaft* are the two terms 'power' (*Macht*) and 'violence' (*Gewalt*). In Heidegger's formulation, violence (*Gewalt*) signifies the willful but impo-

tent attempt to change things or conditions without deeper insight or ontological attunement: "Wherever change is sought by 'ontic' means alone
(*Seiendes durch Seiendes*), violence is needed." Power (*Macht*) stands purely
in the service of willful machination and signifies "the ability to secure the
control of possibilities of violence." In sharp contrast to these terms, *Beiträge* mentions "authoritative rule" (*Herrschaft*) as a mode of ontological
potency or capability deriving its authority from its liberating openness to
"being." "*Herrschaft*," Heidegger writes, "is the need of freedom for freedom" and happens only "in the realm of freedom"; its greatness consists in
the fact "that it has no need of power or violence and yet is more potent
(*wirksamer*) than they." Such liberating and non-manipulative *Herrschaft*
is impossible under the reign of modern worldviews, especially totalizing
worldview-ideologies, which have no room for human freedom and level
everything into the uniform system of *Machenschaft*. Under the auspices
of this system, human beings individually and people at large are reduced
to mere resources of power, and the only issue is the preservation and en-
hancement of their utility. The only way for *Dasein* and people to live genuinely and freely, *Beiträge* insists, is through an act of self-transcendence
or self-transformation (*ek-stasis*) that is simultaneously an act of self-find-
ing, highlighted by the term '*Ereignis*.' *Ereignis* means basically the chiasm
or entwinement between humans and the openness of 'being' (or the divine), a differentiated and needful encounter that opens up the prospect
of the arrival of "the godhead of the other God" (*die Gottheit des anderen
Gottes*).[13]

The critique of totalizing and domineering *Machenschaft* was further
sharpened in the book titled *Besinnung*. As in the case of *Beiträge*, the text
can be read both on a recessed, philosophical and a more mundane, political level—although the two levels are closely interlaced. Philosophically,
Besinnung urges a more reflective rethinking of human being-in-the-world,
a rethinking opening human hearts and minds again to the 'call of being'
(which guides them into a more careful and caring mode of living). As before, Heidegger dwells on the meaning of *Machenschaft* and its relation to
Macht and *Gewalt*. "*Machenschaft*," he reiterates, "means the all-pervasive
and totalizing 'makeability' of everything" and the general routine acceptance of this process in such a way that "the unconditional calculability of
everything is assured." In pursuing its leveling and domineering path, *Ma-*

chenschaft employs violence (*Gewalt*), and the latter is stabilized through the "secure possession of power (*Macht*)" aiming at universal or total subjugation. In modernity, the text continues, the aims of *Machenschaft* are promoted and abetted by technology (*Technik*) that reduces human beings to mere empirical resources whose value is assessed purely in terms of utility or productivity. It is in this context that Heidegger launches an attack on the *Führer* himself, who, in an address to the Reichstag in 1939 had made this statement: "There is no stance or attitude (*Haltung*) which would not receive its ultimate justification from its utility for the totality (of the nation)." Reacting angrily to this statement, Heidegger raises a number of acerbic questions, such as the following: What is the 'totality' that is postulated here? What is the 'utility' of an attitude or outlook, and by what standard is it to be judged? Does the entire statement not signify "the denial of the basic questionability (*Fraglichkeit*) of human *Dasein* with regard to its hidden relation to being" (and its care)?[14]

Moving beyond the critique of *Machenschaft*, *Besinnung* offers glimpses of a radically 'other' possibility: namely, the reflective recovery of the question of and care for being, a care completely immune to managerial manipulation. As before, Heidegger distinguishes between power and violence, on the one hand, and genuine 'authority' (*Herrschaft*), on the other. "Apart from exuding intrinsic dignity or worth," he writes, "*Herrschaft* means the free potency or capacity for an original respect for being" (rather than merely empirical things). To characterize this dignity, *Besinnung* introduces a new vocabulary, presenting being (*Seyn*) as a basically "power-free domain (*das Machtlose*) beyond power and non-power or impotence (*jenseits von Macht und Unmacht*)." As Heidegger emphasizes, 'power-free' does not mean powerless or impotent, because the latter remains fixated on power, now experienced as a lack. From an everyday 'realist' angle, being's realm may appear powerless or impotent, but this is only a semblance or illusion resulting from its reticent unobtrusiveness. Due to its reticence, being's realm can never be dragged into human machinations, into the struggles between the powerful and the powerless (as long as the latter merely seek power); but precisely in this manner it reveals its *Herrschaft*, a reign that "cannot be matched by any power or superpower because they necessarily ignore the nature of the *basically* power-free possibility." To be sure, access to this reign is difficult and radically obstructed by the *Machenschaft* of our age. Yet, an important pathway through and beyond these obstructions is offered by meditative thinking (*Besinnung*), which opens a glimpse into the 'time-space-play' (*Zeit-Spiel-Raum*) of be-ing as *Ereignis*, that is, into the interplay and differential entwinement of being and beings, of humans, nature, and the divine.[15]

Themes and insights of this kind are carried forward in *Die Geschich-te des Seyns*, a series of texts dating from the onset of World War II. Politi-cally, the texts are still more nonconformist and rebellious than his preced-ing writings—an aspect largely attributable to their grim context. Central to the volume is again the critique of *Machenschaft* defined as a mode of being that "pushes everything into the mold of 'makeability.'" As before, *Machenschaft* is intimately linked with the glorification of power (*Macht*), and the latter is anchored ultimately in 'will' to power and in 'unconditional subjectivity' (a chief trait of modern metaphysics). To effectuate its rule, power relies on violence (*Gewalt*) as its chief instrument. When violence or brutality becomes predominant, matters are starkly simplified: everything is geared toward the "unconditional annihilation (*Vernichtung*) of oppos-ing forces by unconditional means." The unleashing of brutal violence car-ries in its train the "devastation" (*Verwüstung*) of everything, with the result that a "desert" (*Wüste*) spreads where nothing can grow any longer—espe-cially not thoughtfulness and care for being. A particularly vivid and har-rowing sign of this devastation is the hankering for warfare—a warfare that, due to the totalizing ambitions of *Machenschaft*, now turns into "to-tal war" (*totaler Krieg*). Given the steadily widening range of modern tech-nology and weaponry, Heidegger adds somberly, the relentless struggle for power and more power necessarily leads to "unbounded or limitless wars (*grenzenlose Kriege*) furthering the empowerment of power." Not surpris-ingly, such wars ultimately take the form of "world wars" in the service of a globally unleashed *Machenschaft*.[16]

As an antidote or counterpoise to these trends, the texts refer again to the possibility of "authoritative rule" (*Herrschaft*). However, in view of its lingering proximity to power, the term now appears sufficiently suspect to Heidegger that he is willing to drop it (in favor of an unmitigated 'pow-er-free' realm). The sharpened denunciation or distantiation from *Macht* is paralleled by an intensification of political polemics. *Die Geschichte des Seyns* openly ridicules fascist leaders for their self-glorification as "mighty rulers" (*Machthaber*) whose great achievement resides in their "seizure of power" (*Machtergreifung*). Leaders, Heidegger states, are never "possessors of power" (*Machthaber*) but rather puppets in the grip of *Macht* and *Machenschaft*; they cannot "seize" or "possess" power, because they are "possessed by it" (in the manner of an obsession). The texts also critique National Socialism directly by debunking its chosen terminology. Drawing on his argument that modernity is marked by 'unconditional subjectivity,' Heidegger comments that "the consequence of this subjectivity is the 'nationalism' of nations and the 'socialism' of the people [*Volk*]." Proceeding even more boldly, the texts raise the issue of political and moral responsibility. Despite the fact that power cannot be 'possessed' but operates obsessively, the book does not hesitate to link power and violence with "criminality" (*Verbrechen*). Given the unleashing of *Machenschaft* and unconditional global warfare, Heidegger asserts, our age also produces "the great criminals" (*die grossen Verbrecher*)—criminals whose misdeeds far exceed ordinary human guilt and who, in fact, can be described as "global master criminals" (*planetarische Hauptverbrecher*). As he adds: "There is no punishment which would be sufficiently great to punish these criminals."[17]

Conclusion

Roughly half a century has passed since the time of Adorno's and Heidegger's major writings. In the meantime, the world has changed dramatically. With the destruction of the Nazi regime, fascism—at least in its overt totalitarian guise—has passed from the scene. With the demise of the Soviet Union, Soviet-style totalitarianism likewise has disappeared. However, appearances are deceiving. In new guises and under new labels *Macht* and *Machenschaft* continue to haunt the world. Under the aegis of globalization, totalizing ambitions are no longer limited to intra-societal domination but have acquired global or planetary dimensions. As a result, social and political divisions are no longer confined to domestic class conflicts but assume the character of a global divide: that between developed and developing societies, between North and South, between center and periphery. Given the enormous accumulation of technological, military, and economic power in the 'developed' hemisphere, the divide readily translates into the hegemonic domination of the North over the South or—in

Samuel Huntington's phrase—of the "West" over the "Rest." In this situation, the dialectic of enlightenment and modernity is bound to be most intensely experienced by its victims or 'subaltern' targets: ordinary people and intellectuals living at the borders or margins of development.

In our present context, marked by Western hegemony and global imperialism, nothing can be more important and salutary than the cultivation of global critical awareness, of critical counter-discourses willing and able to call into question the presumptions of global imperial rule. The dangers of such totalizing domination are becoming more evident every day. With the growing technological sophistication of weaponry we are relentlessly instructed about the underside of modernity, about the fateful collusion of power and knowledge in the unfolding of modern enlightenment (as analyzed by Adorno and Horkheimer). Coupled with the globalizing momentum, military sophistication greatly enhances the prospect of global warfare—indeed of global 'total' warfare (as envisaged by Heidegger in the 1930s). In this situation, the goal of global warfare is bound to be the 'total' subjugation of less developed or subaltern societies—a subjugation accomplished through long-distance military offensives capable of inflicting maximum casualties on enemies while minimizing the attackers' costs.[18]

Given the intoxicating effects of global rule, must one not also anticipate corresponding levels of total depravity and corruption among the rulers? In fact, must one not fear the upsurge of a new breed of "global master criminals" (*planetarische Hauptverbrecher*), whose actions are likely to match those of their twentieth-century predecessors, and perhaps even surpass them (behind a new shield of immunity)? Armed with unparalleled nuclear devices and unheard-of strategic doctrines, global masters today can not only control and subjugate populations, but in fact destroy and incinerate them (from high above). In the words of the Indian novelist Arundhati Roy, addressed to the world's imperial rulers:

To slow a beast, you break its limbs. To slow a nation, you break its people; you rob them of volition. You demonstrate your absolute command over their destiny. You make it clear that ultimately it falls to you to decide who lives, who dies, who prospers, who doesn't. To exhibit your capability you show off all that you can do, and how easily you can do it—how easily you could press a button and annihilate the earth.[19]

Notes

INTRODUCTION

1. Max Horkheimer, *Gesammelte Schriften*, ed. Gunzelin Schmid Noerr, 19 vols. (Frankfurt am Main: S. Fischer Verlag, 1996), XVIII:795.

2. Hermann Mörchen, *Adorno und Heidegger. Untersuchung einer philosophisch-en Kommunikationsverweigerung* (Stuttgart: Klett-Cotta, 1981). See also Hermann Mörchen, *Macht und Herrschaft im Denken von Heidegger und Adorno* (Stuttgart: Klett-Cotta, 1980).

3. "It's not formal laws of knowledge, which are basically completely unimportant, but material evidence about our life and its meaning that we have to look for. I know that Heidegger is one of the most significant personalities ever to have spoken to me. Do I agree with him? How could I, when all I know about him for certain is that for him the motive to philosophize does not spring from intellectual ambition or a preconceived theory, but every day afresh out of his own experience" (Horkheimer to Rose Riekher, November 30, 1921). Cited in Rolf Wiggershaus, *The Frankfurt School* (Cambridge: Polity Press, 1994), 45. At the very least, this letter reveals an early interest in Heidegger that Horkheimer keeps from Mörchen in 1972. See Horkheimer, *Gesammelte Schriften*, XVIII:794.

4. Theodor W. Adorno, "The Actuality of Philosophy," in *The Adorno Reader*, ed. Brian O'Connor, trans. Benjamin Snow (Oxford: Blackwell, 2000); Theodor W. Adorno, *Gesammelte Schriften*, ed. Rolf Tiedemann, 20 vols. (Frankfurt am Main: Suhrkamp Verlag, 1997), vol. I.

5. Theodor W. Adorno, *Negative Dialectics*, trans. E. B. Ashton (London: Routledge & Kegan Paul, 1973), 63; Adorno, *GS*, VI:71.

6. Adorno, *Negative Dialectics*, 61; Adorno, *GS*, VI:69.

7. Adorno, *Negative Dialectics*, 63; Adorno, *GS*, VI:71.

8. "The doctrine of invariants [e.g., the existentiales of *Being and Time*] perpetuates how little has changed; its positivity perpetuates what is wrong. To this extent, the ontological need is false [*Insofern ist das ontologische Bedürfnis falsch*]." Adorno, *Negative Dialectics*, 96; Adorno, *GS*, VI:103. Translation modified.

9. Adorno, *Negative Dialectics*, 72; Adorno, *GS*, VI:79.

10. Cited in Wiggershaus, *The Frankfurt School*, 593. Translation modified.

11. Martin Heidegger, *Contributions to Philosophy: From Enowning*, trans. Parvis Emad and Kenneth Maly (Bloomington: Indiana University Press, 1999); Martin Heidegger, *Beiträge zur Philosophie (Vom Ereignis)*, ed. Friedrich-Wilhelm von Herrmann II, revised ed., vol. 65, *Gesamtausgabe* (Frankfurt am Main: Vittorio Klostermann, 1989, 1994); Martin Heidegger, *Besinnung*, ed. Friedrich-Wilhelm von Herrmann II, vol. 66, *Gesamtausgabe* (Frankfurt am Main: Vittorio Klostermann, 1997); Martin Heidegger, *Die Geschichte des Seyns*, ed. Peter Trawny, vol. 69, *Gesamtausgabe* (Frankfurt am Main: Vittorio Klostermann, 1998). See also Martin Heidegger, *Hegel*, ed. Ingrid Schüßler, vol. 68, *Gesamtausgabe* (Frankfurt am Main: Vittorio Klostermann, 1993).

12. Theodor W. Adorno, *Ontologie und Dialektik*, ed. Rolf Tiedemann (Frankfurt am Main: Suhrkamp Verlag, 2002). Theodor W. Adorno, *Philosophische Terminologie*, 2 vols. (Frankfurt am Main: Suhrkamp Verlag, 1973).

CHAPTER I

1. Theodor W. Adorno, *Negative Dialectics*, trans. E. B. Ashton (London: Routledge & Kegan Paul, 1973), 104; *Gesammelte Schriften*, ed. Rolf Tiedemann, 20 vols. (Frankfurt am Main: Suhrkamp Verlag, 1997), VI:110. Translation modified.

2. Theodor W. Adorno, "The Actuality of Philosophy," in *The Adorno Reader*, ed. Brian O'Connor, trans. Benjamin Snow (Oxford: Blackwell, 2000), 35; Adorno, *GS*, I:339–40.

3. Theodor W. Adorno, "The Idea of Natural History," *Telos*, no. 60 (Summer 1984), 117; *GS*, I:354.

4. Adorno, "The Idea of Natural History," 117; *GS*, I:354. Translation modified.

5. It is also essential to mention here that early on, Adorno *credits* "neo-ontology" with having "radically demonstrated the insuperable interwovenness of natural and historical elements," while nevertheless ruthlessly criticizing Heidegger for dealing with history too formally. See Adorno, "The Idea of Natural History," 117; *GS*, I:354.

6. Adorno, *Negative Dialectics*, 114; *GS*, VI:120. Translation modified.

7. Martin Heidegger, *Being and Time*, trans. John Macquarrie and Edward Robinson (Oxford: Basil Blackwell, 1962), §3, 12. Page references are to the German edition reproduced in the margins of the English translation. The German edition used is Martin Heidegger, *Sein und Zeit*, 17th ed. (Tübingen: Max Niemeyer Verlag, 1927, 1993).

8. Adorno, "The Idea of Natural History," 116; *GS*, I:355.

9. Adorno, "The Idea of Natural History," 116; *GS*, I:353. Translation modified.

10. Heidegger, *Being and Time*, §54, 268.

11. Heidegger, *Being and Time*, §54, 269.

12. Heidegger, *Being and Time*, §54, 270.

13. Heidegger, *Being and Time*, §55, 270.

14. Heidegger, *Being and Time*, §55, 271.

15. " . . . das Moment des Stoßes, des abgesetzten Aufrüttelns." Heidegger, *Being and Time*, §55, 271.

16. Heidegger, *Being and Time*, §56, 273.

17. Heidegger, *Being and Time*, §56, 273.

18. Heidegger, *Being and Time*, §57, 275.

19. Heidegger, *Being and Time*, §57, 277.

20. "Es existiert als Seiendes, das, wie es ist und sein kann, zu sein hat." Heidegger, *Being and Time*, §57, 276. Emphasis added.

21. *Cf.* Heidegger, *Being and Time*, §57, 277.

22. See Heidegger, *Being and Time*, §58, 282–83, 286.

23. Heidegger, *Being and Time*, §58, 284.

24. Heidegger, *Being and Time*, §58, 284.

25. Heidegger, *Being and Time*, §58, 285.

26. Heidegger, *Being and Time*, §58, 283.

27. In his contribution to this volume, Lambert Zuidervaart criticizes my interpretation of these passages, citing three objections: (1) the operative difference is between 'is' and 'can be,' not between 'is' and 'ought'; (2) the responsibility discussed here has little to do with social ethics or moral duties; and (3) responsibility is the condition of guilt, not the other way around.

I get the feeling from Zuidervaart's comments that he actually expects moral discourse to attain knowledge of what is right, believing that what is 'right' is 'out there,' independent of us. More specifically, Zuidervaart seems to be critical of my reading of Heidegger for the usual anti-Heideggerian reasons: there is nothing recognizably moral about what Heidegger says. Basically, I think this critique rests on a huge misunderstanding of what is going on in this phenomenology of normativity. Heidegger's starting point is simply the idea that having done the right thing depends upon my *having chosen it as the right thing* from a range of possibilities. To have done the 'right' thing, I must have taken it upon myself to push an actual state of affairs toward a possible 'right' state of affairs. As the locus of reflection on any distinction between 'wrong' and 'right' as special kinds of possibilities, it is up to *me* and me alone to differentiate them and pursue them. (I can, of course, ask for help, but the decision as such must be mine for it to count as moral.) This specific kind of differential responsibility is called 'guilt' by Heidegger; that it has existential priority over 'real' guilt is merely Heidegger's way of saying that so-called 'real' guilt would make no sense if I could not 'first' distinguish between things as they are now and things as they might or should be. That this primordial differentiation necessarily has a social dimension is made clear in the claim that Dasein's guilt is grounded in its thrownness.

But what of the specifically moral character of certain possibilities? What if the possibility I choose is to become an ax-murderer? Have I not appropriated a possibility as mine? Is this possibility not only arbitrary but wrong and therefore most assuredly not an 'ought'? Well, there are doubtless circumstances in which becoming an ax-murderer would be the right thing to do. (If only I were an analytic moral philosopher, then I could come up with a series of complex thought experiments to illustrate this point.) But for Heidegger, what we first need to get clear on is the issue of *how*, in general, we frame possibilities in order to appropriate them. The answer is that Dasein is itself divided into an 'as it is' and an 'as it can be,' the content of which it is Dasein's specific responsibility to develop. This is what I have chosen to call an 'ought.' Why? Precisely because it involves Dasein's obligation to consider and weigh possibilities. (I could have said 'existential ought' in order to distinguish it from the usual 'ought' that Zuidervaart defends.) In any case, this 'ought' is admittedly formal and general, as Zuidervaart says, but it is only at this level of generality that we can even approach the issue of how possibility and the possibility of morality and moral error are structurally related to each other, that is, in a dynamic of responsibility, guilt, and choice. According to Heidegger, this dynamic needs to be explained if we are ever to make sense of specifically moral choices.

In short, understanding the difference between right and wrong actions depends upon a general capacity to distinguish and sort through possibilities, circumstances, and conditions, appropriating some and discarding others—none of which guarantees that the outcome will be the 'right' one or that there even is a 'right' or 'good' outcome. Now, it is true that Heidegger is only concerned with describing this general capacity, not with the issues of 'right' and 'wrong' as such; for him, these are 'downstream' issues. Consequently, we might well want him to have said more about this deferral of morality 'as such' or 'as it is commonly understood.' Be that as it may, the point is that none of Zuidervaart's objections have any traction unless such a capacity is presupposed; but precisely to the extent that it is presupposed, the objections miss the point. Moreover, I take it that the Kantian approach that Zuidervaart tries to deploy against Heidegger in fact submits to the very same demand as Heidegger's own approach: that we understand morality in terms of an individualized general capacity to assume responsibility—for otherwise, morality would merely be a matter of learning arbitrary 'rules of good conduct.' Of course, it may seem troubling that the contents of my choices have no *necessary* relation to whether I misjudge things or end up intentionally or unintentionally doing wrong—or right. But to paraphrase David Mamet: "that's why they call it *morality*."

28. In full the passage reads: "Die existenziale Interpretation dessen, wozu der

Ruf aufruft, kann daher, sofern sie sich in ihren methodischen Möglichkeiten und Aufgaben recht versteht, keine konkrete einzelne Existenzmöglichkeit umgrenzen wollen. Nicht das je existenziell im jeweiligen Dasein in dieses Gerufene kann und will fixiert werden, sondern das, was zur *existenzialen Bedingung der Möglichkeit* des je faktisch-existenziellen Seinkönnens *gehört*." Heidegger, *Being and Time*, §58, 280. Macquarrie and Robinson omit the *je* in the last clause.

29. Of course, it is important to note that this moment of non-identity is purely formal in Heidegger, and so not the 'real' or contentful non-identity that Adorno exhorts us to respect. But then we should remember that the non-identity of which Adorno speaks in *Negative Dialectics* is also treated rather formally.

30. Heidegger, *Being and Time*, §58, 286.

31. G. W. F. Hegel, *Hegel's Phenomenology of Spirit*, trans. A. V. Miller (Oxford: Clarendon Press, 1977), 282; *Gesammelte Werke*, ed. Nordrhein-Westfälischen Akademie der Wissenschaften & Deutsche Forschungsgemeinschaft (Hamburg: Felix Meiner Verlag, 1981), IX:254.

32. Hegel, *Phenomenology*, 282; *Gesammelte Werke*, IX:254. Translation modified, emphasis added.

33. I am aware that Hegel criticizes the language of 'ought' and 'should,' but the central issue here is merely the capacity to distinguish between actuality and the immanent criteria by which actuality is judged.

34. Hegel, *Phenomenology*, 53; *Gesammelte Werke*, IX:59. Translation modified.

35. Adorno, *Negative Dialectics*, 120; *GS*, VI:126.

36. On rescuing Hegel, see Theodor W. Adorno, *Hegel: Three Studies*, trans. Shierry Weber Nicholsen (Cambridge, Mass.: MIT Press, 1993), 83; Adorno, *GS*, V:320.

37. Hegel, *Phenomenology*, 65; *Gesammelte Werke*, IX:69.

38. Adorno, *Negative Dialectics*, 149; *GS*, VI:152. Translation modified.

39. Adorno, *Negative Dialectics*, 179; *GS*, VI:181.

40. Adorno, *Negative Dialectics*, 5; *GS*, VI:17. Translation modified.

41. Adorno, *Negative Dialectics*, 120; *GS*, VI:126. Emphasis added.

CHAPTER 2

This chapter is reprinted, with the permission of Cambridge University Press, from Lambert Zuidervaart, *Social Philosophy After Adorno*. The author has made slight changes to the text in this version.

The author wishes to thank Matt Klaassen for his research assistance, as well as the participants in his graduate seminar "Truth and Authenticity," held at the Institute for Christian Studies and the University of Toronto, for their responses to an earlier draft of the chapter.

1. Passages in translation are taken from Martin Heidegger, *Being and Time*,

trans. Joan Stambaugh (Albany: State University of New York Press, 1996). Page numbers refer to the pagination in *Sein und Zeit* as found in the margins of the English translation. The German edition I have used is Martin Heidegger, *Sein und Zeit*, 15th ed. (Tübingen: Max Niemeyer, 1979). I have also consulted Martin Heidegger, *Being and Time*, trans. John Macquarrie and Edward Robinson (Oxford: Basil Blackwell, 1962). I give preference to the Macquarrie-Robinson translation in retaining "Being" (capital "B") for "Sein" and in not hyphenating Dasein. These modifications are made without comment in the citations and in my own text. Other relevant modifications to citations from the Stambaugh translation are marked by square brackets.

2. Theodor W. Adorno, *Negative Dialectics*, trans. E. B. Ashton (London: Routledge & Kegan Paul, 1973); Theodor W. Adorno, *Gesammelte Schriften*, ed. Rolf Tiedemann, 20 vols. (Frankfurt am Main: Suhrkamp Verlag, 1997), vol. VI. Internal citations give page numbers from the Ashton translation, followed by the pagination in *Gesammelte Schriften* VI. Often I silently modify the translation.

3. Heidegger, *Sein und Zeit*, 220–21.

4. Ernst Tugendhat, "Heidegger's Idea of Truth," in *The Heidegger Controversy: A Critical Reader*, ed. Richard Wolin, trans. Richard Wolin (New York: Columbia University Press, 1991), 245–63; Ernst Tugendhat, "Heideggers Idee von Wahrheit," in *Heidegger: Perspektiven zur Deutung seines Werks*, ed. Otto Pöggeler (Cologne and Berlin: Kiepenheuer & Witsch, 1970), 286–97. A longer version of this critique occurs in Ernst Tugendhat, *Der Wahrheitsbegriff bei Husserl und Heidegger*, 2d ed. (Berlin: Walter de Gruyter, 1970).

5. Tugendhat, "Heidegger's Idea of Truth," 258–59; Tugendhat, "Heideggers Idee von Wahrheit," 294.

6. Tugendhat, "Heidegger's Idea of Truth," 261; Tugendhat, "Heideggers Idee von Wahrheit," 296.

7. See Lambert Zuidervaart, *Artistic Truth: Aesthetics, Discourse, and Imaginative Disclosure* (Cambridge: Cambridge University Press, 2004), chapter 4, 77–100.

8. See Heidegger, *Sein und Zeit*, §44, especially 220–23.

9. According to Daniel O. Dahlstrom, Tugendhat tries to retain the "logical prejudice" that Heidegger's conception of truth aims to expose and dismantle. See Daniel O. Dahlstrom, *Heidegger's Concept of Truth* (Cambridge: Cambridge University Press, 2001), 392.

10. Heidegger, *Sein und Zeit*, 228.

11. Heidegger, *Sein und Zeit*, 221.

12. Heidegger, *Sein und Zeit*, §§45–83.

13. Heidegger, *Sein und Zeit*, 297. As Dahlstrom points out, the pragmatic readings of Heidegger proposed by Richard Rorty and Mark Okrent overlook the centrality of authenticity and temporality or timeliness (*Zeitlichkeit*) to Hei-

degger's conception of truth. This limits their usefulness as readings of Heidegger, even though they do provide an important counterweight to Tugendhat's criticisms of Heidegger's conception. See Dahlstrom, *Heidegger's Concept of Truth*, 423–33.

14. It is worth quoting Heidegger's own summary of "authentic being-toward-death." The italics are Heidegger's: "*Anticipation reveals to Dasein its lostness in the they-self, and brings it face to face with the possibility to be itself, primarily unsupported by concern taking care of things, but to be itself in passionate anxious freedom toward death which is free of the illusions of the they, factical, and certain of itself.*" See Heidegger, *Sein und Zeit*, §53, 266.

15. Heidegger, *Sein und Zeit*, 267–68.
16. Heidegger, *Sein und Zeit*, 279.
17. Heidegger, *Sein und Zeit*, 269, 287–88.
18. Heidegger, *Sein und Zeit*, 275–77.
19. Heidegger, *Sein und Zeit*, 283–88.
20. Heidegger, *Sein und Zeit*, 295–97. Heidegger summarizes the threefold existential structure of Dasein's authentic potentiality-of-being as follows: "The disclosedness of Dasein in wanting-to-have-a-conscience is thus constituted by the attunement of *Angst*, by understanding as projecting oneself upon one's ownmost being-guilty, and by [talk] as reticence. We shall call the eminent, authentic disclosedness attested in Dasein itself by its conscience—the *reticent projecting oneself upon one's ownmost being-guilty which is ready for* Angst—*resoluteness.*" See Heidegger, *Sein und Zeit*, 296–97.

21. Heidegger, *Sein und Zeit*, 297.
22. Heidegger, *Sein und Zeit*, 297–98.
23. Heidegger, *Sein und Zeit*, 299.
24. Heidegger, *Sein und Zeit*, 307–8. Heidegger describes this "being-certain" as a "holding-for-true" (*Für-wahr-halten*) in which Dasein both gives itself to the situation and holds itself free for the possibility of taking itself back. In contrast with irresoluteness, "this holding-for-true, as a resolute holding oneself free for taking back, is the *authentic resoluteness to retrieve itself.*" The ultimate certainty here is that resoluteness is constantly certain of death, which resoluteness anticipates. At the same time, anticipatory resoluteness gives Dasein "the primordial certainty of its being closed off," of its being constantly lost "in the irresoluteness of the they." See Heidegger, *Sein und Zeit*, 308.

25. Heidegger, *Sein und Zeit*, 309.
26. Heidegger, *Sein und Zeit*, 309. In calling this an "existentiell potentiality" (rather than simply a potentiality that is "existentielly attested"), I follow Macquarrie and Robinson's translation. Heidegger's German text reads: "das Vorlaufen ist . . . der *Modus* eines im Dasein bezeugten existenziellen Seinkönnens. . . . " Macquarrie and Robinson translate: "anticipation is . . . a *mode* of an existenti-

ell potentiality-for-Being that is attested in Dasein. . . . " See Heidegger, *Sein und Zeit*, 308. Stambaugh translates: "anticipation is . . . a *mode* of a potentiality-of-being existentielly attested in Dasein. . . . "

27. Heidegger, *Sein und Zeit*, 310.

28. Zuidervaart, *Artistic Truth*, 96.

29. Adorno was especially allergic to the aura created by Heidegger's "authenticity" talk and the emptiness of what such talk commends. He objected that Heidegger turns the individual's decision to possess itself into the criterion of authenticity. This allows philosophy to ignore the real social conditions that make individuality possible, to avoid asking whether contemporary society allows people to be or become themselves, and to forget that "the old evil" (i.e., reification) might be concentrated in the Heideggerian concept of "selfness" (*Selbstheit*): "The societal relation that encapsulates itself in the subject's identity is de-societalized into something in-itself." Theodor W. Adorno, *The Jargon of Authenticity*, trans. Knut Tarnowski and Frederic Will (London: Routledge & Kegan Paul, 1973), 115, translation modified; Theodor W. Adorno, *Jargon der Eigentlichkeit. Zur deutschen Ideologie*, vol. VI, *Gesammelte Schriften* (Frankfurt am Main: Suhrkamp Verlag, 1973), 489–90.

30. Heidegger, *Sein und Zeit*, 298.

31. Heidegger, *Sein und Zeit*, 299.

32. Kevin Aho seems to miss the worrisome proximity of Heidegger's account of authenticity to Nazi ideology. Although I agree that Heidegger's account can be read in a more communalist and less individualist way, as Aho claims, I do not think such a reading removes the most problematic aspects of Heidegger's account. See Kevin Aho, "Why Heidegger Is Not an Existentialist: Interpreting Authenticity and Historicity in *Being and Time*," *Florida Philosophical Review* 3, no. 2 (2003). Julian Young suggests that by the mid-1930s Heidegger's site of authenticity shifts from individual Dasein to "great art," whose task is to secure an authentic "people" that actively appropriates its cultural heritage. See Julian Young, *Heidegger's Philosophy of Art* (Cambridge: Cambridge University Press, 2001), 52–60.

33. Michael E. Zimmerman, *Eclipse of the Self: The Development of Heidegger's Concept of Authenticity*, revised ed. (Athens: Ohio University Press, 1986). See especially the appendix, 277–300.

34. Heidegger, *Sein und Zeit*, 276–77.

35. Compare in this connection Heidegger's description of Dasein's everydayness as involving idle talk, curiosity, and ambiguity, in Heidegger, *Sein und Zeit*, §§ 35–38. Together, these make up the "entanglement" of Dasein, its "character of being lost in the publicness of the they" (175). Shortly thereafter, he uncovers anxiety as the attunement that throws Dasein back upon its own "authentic potentiality-for-being-in-the-world" (187). In anxiety, one feels the "uncanniness" of "not-being-at-home" in the world. Anxiety individualizes by calling up Dasein's

fundamental alienation from all that absorbs Dasein in its everydayness. See Heidegger, *Sein und Zeit*, §40, 184–91.

36. Heidegger, *Sein und Zeit*, 284.

37. Heidegger, *Sein und Zeit*, 287.

38. See Charles Taylor, *Sources of the Self: The Making of the Modern Identity* (Cambridge, Mass.: Harvard University Press, 1989). Theodor W. Adorno's *Habilitationsschrift* on Kierkegaard, written partly in response to *Sein und Zeit* and published as a book in 1933, yields important sociocritical insights into Heidegger's emphasis on Dasein's *Innerlichkeit*. See Theodor W. Adorno, *Kierkegaard. Konstruktion des Ästhetischen*, vol. II, *Gesammelte Schriften* (Frankfurt am Main: Suhrkamp Verlag, 1979); Theodor W. Adorno, *Kierkegaard: Construction of the Aesthetic*, trans. Robert Hullot-Kentor (Minneapolis: University of Minnesota Press, 1989).

39. Iain Macdonald, "Ethics and Authenticity: Conscience and Non-Identity in Heidegger and Adorno, with a Glance at Hegel," published as Chapter 1 of the present volume, 9.

40. Macdonald, "Ethics and Authenticity," 13–14.

41. Macdonald, "Ethics and Authenticity," 15.

42. Macdonald, "Ethics and Authenticity," 17.

43. Macdonald, "Ethics and Authenticity," 13.

44. Heidegger, *Sein und Zeit*, 221.

45. Heidegger, *Sein und Zeit*, 223.

46. Heidegger, *Sein und Zeit*, 299.

47. Heidegger, *Sein und Zeit*, 299–300.

48. Heidegger, *Sein und Zeit*, 300.

49. See especially Charles Guignon, "Philosophy and Authenticity: Heidegger's Search for a Ground for Philosophizing," in *Heidegger, Authenticity, and Modernity: Essays in Honor of Hubert L. Dreyfus*, ed. Mark A. Wrathall and Jeff Malpas (Cambridge, Mass.: MIT Press, 2000), vol. 1, 79–101; Hubert L. Dreyfus, *Being-in-the-World: A Commentary on Heidegger's Being and Time, Division I* (Cambridge, Mass.: MIT Press, 1991), 299–340.

50. Taylor Carman, *Heidegger's Analytic: Interpretation, Discourse, and Authenticity in "Being and Time"* (Cambridge: Cambridge University Press, 2003), 139.

51. Carman, *Heidegger's Analytic*, 143.

52. Carman, *Heidegger's Analytic*, 7.

53. Carman, *Heidegger's Analytic*, 268.

54. Carman, *Heidegger's Analytic*, 268–71.

55. Carman, *Heidegger's Analytic*, 293.

56. Adorno, *Negative Dialectics*, 59–131/67–136.

57. In the preface, Adorno suggests that the entire Introduction to *Negative Dialectics* "expounds the concept of philosophical experience." See Adorno, *Negative Dialectics*, xx/10.

58. J. M. Bernstein, *Adorno: Disenchantment and Ethics* (Cambridge: Cambridge University Press, 2001), 115. For a discussion of the multifaceted character of "experience" in Adorno's writings, see Martin Jay, "Is Experience Still in Crisis? Reflections on a Frankfurt School Lament," *Kriterion* 100 (1999): 9–25.

59. The need to reconnect rationality with emphatic experience is also central to Adorno's insistence on the possibility and necessity of what he calls "metaphysical experience." See Bernstein, *Adorno*, 415–56. My review of Bernstein's *Adorno*, in *Constellations* 10, no. 2 (2003): 280–83, raises questions about the ethical implications to be drawn from Adorno's negative dialectic.

60. Adorno, *Negative Dialectics*, 40–42/50–53.

61. Adorno, *Negative Dialectics*, 41/51.

62. Adorno, *Negative Dialectics*, 41/51.

63. Adorno, *Negative Dialectics*, 42/52.

64. Adorno, *Negative Dialectics*, 41/51–52.

65. Adorno, *Negative Dialectics*, 42/52.

66. Adorno, *Negative Dialectics*, 42/52.

67. Lambert Zuidervaart, "Metaphysics After Auschwitz: Suffering and Hope in Adorno's *Negative Dialectics*," forthcoming.

68. Adorno, *Negative Dialectics*, 41/51–52.

69. Adorno, *Negative Dialectics*, 42/52.

70. Zuidervaart, *Artistic Truth*, 96–100.

CHAPTER 3

1. A quite different ancestor of this chapter was given at the Adorno/Heidegger conference held at the Université de Montréal in April 2004. I am grateful to the participants of the conference, whose comments helped me clarify my thinking and pushed me to present my argument in a less tendentious manner. I am particularly grateful to one of the organizers of the conference, Iain Macdonald, for many illuminating discussions on the topic of this chapter.

2. One could, I suppose, block the whole argument just given by refusing the first premise. But to assert that the universe did not have a determinate structure at a given time would be an extremely strong metaphysical thesis, itself in need of motivation. Intuitively, it is hard to see how the universe would not have a determinate structure at any one given time. Perhaps another way to block the argument would be to assert that the determinate state of the universe at any one time depended on what was in our minds (so that its determinacy was *not* independent of our minds). But that seems a far more bizarre metaphysical thesis to uphold than the first premise of the above argument.

3. Heidegger always points to the fact that the Greek word *eidos* connotes not only that ideas are cognitive entities in the mind, but also that they provide the 'forms' or 'blueprints' for entities.

4. Martin Heidegger, *Being and Time*, trans. John Macquarrie and Edward Robinson (Oxford: Basil Blackwell, 1962).

5. The meta-practices or *existentialia* 'structure,' at the transcendental level, the actual practices a given culture has. Or, to put the point the other way round, the actual practices of a given culture 'fill out' the 'structure' that the *existentialia* provide. Whether such meta-practices are the same across all cultures or timeless is a good question, and not one that Heidegger really considers. In what follows I will leave that question aside and just assume for the sake of argument that the early Heidegger's transcendental project is tenable.

6. When objects are not so encountered, they may appear as 'present-at-hand' (*vorhanden*), that is, as 'merely extant' because they appear not to play any identifiable role in human practices. However, Heidegger shows that such extantness is dependent for its conceptualization on the suspension or interruption of the *zuhanden* mode of relating to objects.

7. Martin Heidegger, *The Basic Problems of Phenomenology*, trans. Albert Hofstadter, revised ed. (Bloomington and Indianapolis: Indiana University Press, 1988), 84.

8. The phrase 'understanding of Being' has two senses for the early Heidegger. First, it refers to the transcendental structures of intelligibility (the *existentialia*) given in *Being and Time*. Second, it refers to how those structures are *interpreted* in a particular epoch. As it is transcendentally necessary that the *existentialia* be interpreted in *some* way (this is what Heidegger calls the 'factical'—*faktisch*—nature of human existence), it is easy to see why the two senses are often used interchangeably.

9. See for example Martin Heidegger, *Contributions to Philosophy: From Enowning*, trans. Parvis Emad and Kenneth Maly (Bloomington: Indiana University Press, 1999), 322–23. Heidegger writes: "*Receiving* being is not determined in terms of the grasping of beingness in the sense of the *koinon* of *idea* but rather from within the essential sway of be-ing itself. This swaying must originally and inceptually arise in order, as it were, to decide by itself what must '*be*' ownmost to thinking . . . and to the thinker."

10. Martin Heidegger, *On Time and Being*, trans. J. Stambaugh (New York: Harper & Row, 1972), 22.

11. Heidegger, *On Time and Being*, 71.

12. See Jay M. Bernstein, *Adorno: Disenchantment and Ethics* (Cambridge: Cambridge University Press, 2001); "Negative Dialectics as Fate," in *The Cambridge Companion to Adorno*, ed. Tom Huhn (Cambridge: Cambridge University Press, 2004).

13. This inference is 'contextually sensitive' in two senses. First, it presupposes the human practice of taking the color of a fruit to indicate the progress of the biological process of ripening. Second, one might think that if the inference 'this

tomato is red, therefore it is ripe for eating' is a good one, then the inference 'this tomato is green, therefore it is ripe for eating' would be false. But this is not the case. In Tennessee, for example, people eat green tomatoes. See Bernstein, "Negative Dialectics as Fate," 42.

14. Bernstein, "Negative Dialectics as Fate."

15. Max Horkheimer and Theodor W. Adorno, *Dialectic of Enlightenment: Philosophical Fragments*, trans. Edmund Jephcott (Stanford: Stanford University Press, 2002).

16. Bernstein, "Negative Dialectics as Fate," 27.

17. Adorno's generic moniker for all forms of semantic idealism is 'identity thinking.'

18. Cf. Bernstein, *Adorno*, chapter 6.

19. Ludwig Wittgenstein, *Philosophical Investigations*, trans. G.E.M. Anscombe, 3rd revised bilingual ed. (Oxford: Blackwell, 2003), §284. Quoted in Bernstein, *Adorno*, 301.

20. Cf. Bernstein, *Adorno*, 275.

21. Cf. Bernstein, *Adorno*, chapters 6, 7 and 9.

22. "The cognitive utopia would be to use concepts to unseal the non-conceptual with concepts, without making it their equal." And also: "Regarding the concrete utopian possibility, dialectics is the ontology of the wrong state of things. The right state of things would be free of it: neither a system nor a contradiction." See Theodor W. Adorno, *Negative Dialectics*, trans. E. B. Ashton (London: Routledge & Kegan Paul, 1973), 10–11.

23. Bernstein, *Adorno*, 264.

24. For Bernstein's analysis of Adorno's relation to the metaphysical tradition, see Bernstein, *Adorno*, chapter 9.

CHAPTER 4

1. This remark is translated from volume V of Adorno's complete works, in which there is a reprint of the 1956 *Zur Metakritik der Erkenntnistheorie*. See Theodor W. Adorno, *Gesammelte Schriften*, ed. Rolf Tiedemann, 20 vols. (Frankfurt am Main: Suhrkamp Verlag, 1997), V:196, for the epigraph. I am indebted to the librarians of the Taylorian Library in Oxford, who preside over an invaluable book stack full of these various collected works.

2. This return is indicated in the exploration of the origins of negative dialectics in Adorno's lectures on Kant, first published in 1995. See Theodor W. Adorno, *Kant's Critique of Pure Reason*, trans. Rodney Livingstone (Cambridge: Polity Press, 2001).

3. In his reading of Husserl, Jacques Derrida draws attention to the question of formalism in Husserl's phenomenology. I am indebted here to conversations

with Joaquim Siles Borras and with Gary Banham, both of Manchester Metropolitan University, about Derrida's reading of Husserl's formalism as unable to do justice to genesis. See Jacques Derrida, *The Problem of Genesis in Husserl's Philosophy*, trans. Marian Hobson (Chicago and London: University of Chicago Press, 2003).

4. Volume I of the *Logical Investigations* appeared in 1900, volume II in 1901; the second edition was published in 1913. *Ideas I* appeared in 1913; the second and third volumes of this study were posthumously published in 1952. See Edmund Husserl, *Logical Investigations*, trans. J. N. Findlay, 2 vols. (London: Routledge and Kegan Paul, 1970); Edmund Husserl, *Ideas I: General Introduction to Pure Phenomenology*, trans. W. R. Boyce Gibson (London: George Allen and Unwin, 1931), known as *Ideas I*.

5. See Adorno, *GS*, I.

6. For an indication of how I set up this relation, see Joanna Hodge, "Adorno and Heidegger: Between Aesthetics and Politics," in *The New Aestheticism*, ed. John J. Joughin and Simon Malpas (Manchester: Manchester University Press, 2003).

7. Martin Heidegger, *Being and Time*, trans. John Macquarrie and Edward Robinson (Oxford: Basil Blackwell, 1962).

8. An important volume of Husserl's works in which this is explored is *Phantasie, Bildbewußtsein, Erinnerung. Zur Phänomenologie der anschaulichen Vergegenwärtigungen. Texte aus dem Nachlass (1898-1925)*; see Edmund Husserl, *Husserliana* (Dordrecht: Kluwer Academic Publishers, 1950ff.), XXIII. This volume is due to appear in English translation by John Barnet Brough. These present previously unpublished parts of Husserl's lectures from 1904–5, *"Hauptstücke aus der Phänomenologie und Theorie der Erkenntnis."* See the remarks on this in Rudolf Bernet's introduction to Edmund Husserl, *Texte zur Phänomenologie des inneren Zeitbewußtseins (1893–1917)* (Hamburg: Felix Meiner Verlag, 1985), xxiv. 'HUA' is the standard abbreviation for the volume numbers of Husserl's works as published posthumously as a result of the activities of workers in the Husserl Archive in Leuven. There are now also HUE numbers for the works as published in the new standard edition in English; see Edmund Husserl, *Husserliana: Collected Works* (Dordrecht: Kluwer Academic Publishers, 1980ff.).

9. Adorno, *GS*, VI.

10. Adorno, *GS*, VI:1.

11. These were published under the title *Analysen zur passiven Synthesis. Aus Vorlesungs- und Forschungsmanuskripten (1918–1926)* only in 1966, thus becoming contemporaneous with Adorno's *Negative Dialectics*. See Husserl, *HUA*, XI. They are now translated as part of Husserl, *HUE*, IX.

12. Husserl, *HUA*, VII–VIII. The first of these is contemporaneous with Adorno's *Zur Metakritik der Erkenntnistheorie*.

13. See Iso Kern, "Three Ways to the Transcendental Phenomenological Reduction in the Philosophy of Edmund Husserl," in *Husserl: Expositions and Appraisals*, ed. Frederick A. Elliston and Peter McCormick (Notre Dame: University of Notre Dame Press, 1977).

14. For the Husserl text, see Peter McCormick and Frederick A. Elliston, eds., *Husserl: Shorter Works* (Notre Dame: University of Notre Dame Press/Harvester Press, 1981). The sub-section in question is edited by David Carr, who introduces it, and indicates that it appeared in vol. I, no. 2, of that journal.

15. For details of this see Ronald Bruzina, *Edmund Husserl and Eugen Fink; Beginnings and Ends in Phenomenology: 1928–1938* (New Haven: Yale University Press, 2004), chapter 10.

16. A recasting of transcendental aesthetics is intimated by Husserl in both *Formal and Transcendental Logic* (1929), *HUA* XVII, trans. Dorion Cairns (The Hague: Martinus Nijhoff, 1969); and *Cartesian Meditations* (1931), *HUA* I, trans. Dorion Cairns (The Hague: Martinus Nijhoff, 1960). For Kant, see Immanuel Kant, *Critique of Pure Reason* (1781, 1787), trans. Norman Kemp Smith (London: Macmillan, 1929).

17. Jan Patočka draws attention to the fragile nature of Adorno's critique here, in his paper "The Husserlian Doctrine of Eidetic Intuition and Its Recent Critics" (1965), in English in Frederick Elliston and Peter McCormick (eds.), *Husserl Expositions and Appraisals* (Notre Dame: University of Notre Dame Press, 1977), 150–59; and also in passing in a footnote to chapter 3, "Pure Logic: The 'Logical Investigations,'" of his study *An Introduction to Husserl's Phenomenology*, trans. Erazim Kohal, ed. with an introduction by James Dodd (Chicago and La Salle, Ill.: Open Court, 1996), 43.

18. See Walter Benjamin and Theodor W. Adorno, *The Complete Correspondence 1928–1940*, trans. Nicholas Walker (Cambridge: Polity Press, 1999).

19. In France, by contrast, Merleau-Ponty was already responding to *Ideas II*, having consulted it pre-publication in the archive. In 1953–54, Jacques Derrida was drafting his dissertation, subsequently published as *The Problem of Genesis in Husserl's Philosophy* (1990), part four of which responds to the manuscripts of Husserl's *Crisis* texts. For Fink's formative texts, see Eugen Fink, "The Problem of the Phenomenology of Edmund Husserl" (1939) and "Operative Concepts in Husserl's Phenomenology" (1957), both translated in William McKenna, Robert M. Harlan, and Laurence E. Winters (eds.), *Apriori and World; European Contributions to Husserlian Phenomenology* (The Hague: Martinus Nijhoff, 1981).

20. Hans Cornelius, *Transzendentale Systematik. Untersuchungen zur Begründung der Erkenntnistheorie* (Munich: Alber Verlag, 1916).

21. For Husserl's side of this disagreement, see Thomas Sheehan and Richard Palmer (eds.), *Psychological and Transcendental Phenomenology and the Confron-*

tation with Heidegger (1927–1931), trans. from *HUA* IX (Dordrecht: Kluwer Academic Publishers, 1997).

22. See Husserl, *HUA,* XVII: 351–378; and Husserl *HUE,* IX:1–38.

23. See Martin Heidegger, *Phaenomenologie des religioesen Lebens,* ed. M. Jung, T. Regehly, and C. Strube (Frankfurt am Main: Vittorio Klostermann, 1995), *GA* 60, in Martin Heidegger, *Gesamtausgabe* (Frankfurt am Main: Vittorio Klostermann, 1975ff.), translated as *Phenomenology of Religious Life,* trans. Matthias Fritsch and Jennifer Anna Gosetti (Bloomington: Indiana University Press, 2004).

24. This distinction emerges in Husserl's *The Idea of Phenomenology, HUA* II and *HUE* VIII, trans. Lee Hardy (Dordrecht: Kluwer Academic Publishers, 1999) which formed the introduction to his lectures on *Thing and Space,* from 1907, but which was published only in 1950 (2nd edition 1973).

25. Adorno, *GS,* I:55.

26. Adorno, *GS,* I:55–56.

27. Edmund Husserl: *The Crisis of the European Sciences and Transcendental Philosophy* (*HUA,* VI, 1954), ed. Walter Biemel, trans. David Carr (Evanston, Ill.: Northwestern University Press, 1970).

28. For details of Fink's incisive intervention here, see Leonard Lawlor, *Derrida and Husserl: The Basic Problem of Phenomenology* (Bloomington: Indiana University Press, 2002), especially chapter 1.

29. See Martin Heidegger: *Introduction to Metaphysics* (1953), trans. Gregory Fried and Richard Polt (New Haven: Yale University Press, 2000).

30. Adorno, *Kant's Critique of Pure Reason* (1995), ed. Rolf Tiedemann, trans. Rodney Livingstone (Cambridge: Polity Press, 2001).

31. Adorno, *Kant's Critique of Pure Reason,* 11.

32. Immanuel Kant, *The Conflict of the Faculties,* trans. Mary J. Gregor (Lincoln: University of Nebraska Press, 1979), 139–71. For further thoughts on this see Joanna Hodge, "Ethics and Time: Levinas Between Kant and Husserl," *Diacritics: Journal of Contemporary Criticism* vol. 32, no. 3 (Spring 2002): 277–321.

33. Immanuel Kant, *Critique of Judgment,* trans. Werner Pluhar (Indiana, Ind.: Hackett, 1987), §28.

34. Husserl, *HUA,* III:43–44.

35. Martin Heidegger, *History of the Concept of Time: Prolegomena* (*GA* 20), trans. Theodore Kisiel (Bloomington: Indiana University Press, 1985, 1992), §§5–7.

36. This intimation that Benjamin is closer to the later Husserl than to Adorno is the suspicion motivating my essay "The Timing of Elective Affinity: Walter Benjamin's Strong Aesthetics," in *Walter Benjamin and Art,* ed. Andrew Benjamin, 14–31 (London: Continuum, 2005).

CHAPTER 5

1. Günther Neske, ed., *Erinnerung an Martin Heidegger* (Pfullingen: Neske, 1977), 283f.

2. Although there is much debate about the reliability of the posthumously edited versions of the transcripts of Hegel's lectures on aesthetics, I shall cite mainly from the historically influential text first published in Hegel's *Werke* (1832–45), as reproduced in G. W. F. Hegel, *Werke*, 20 vols. (Frankfurt am Main: Suhrkamp Verlag, 1970).

3. Hegel, *Werke*, VIII, §18. [Ed.: All translations from the German are the author's.]

4. Hegel, *Werke*, IX:23.

5. Hegel, *Werke*, X, §377, Zusatz.

6. Hegel, *Werke*, IX, §251, Zusatz. For Hegel, as for Kant, reality would be a 'desert' without a final end embodied in the self-conscious existence of the rational animal. Human being thus appears as the 'for the sake of which' or destination of the world, as the site of its own self-manifestation. For a particularly blunt Aristotelian formulation, consider the following: "*nous* and, in a profounder sense, spirit is the [*sc.* final] cause of the world." See Hegel, *Werke*, VIII, §8.

7. Hegel, *Werke*, XIII:50.

8. Hegel, *Werke*, XIII:51.

9. Hegel, *Werke*, XIII:51.

10. Hegel, *Werke*, XIII:52.

11. Hegel, *Werke*, XIII:102.

12. Hegel, *Werke*, VIII:24.

13. Benedetto Croce, *Saggio sullo Hegel* (Bari: Laterza & Figli, 1913), 89.

14. Hegel, *Werke*, XIV:237–38.

15. Hegel, *Werke*, XIII:142.

16. In some respects it must be admitted that Adorno's interpretation of Hegel's system in terms of a remorseless and deterministic teleology, which has long been and largely remains the standard view of his philosophy, is often more asserted than rigorously shown. Even Hegel's later texts display no 'triumphalist' tone in celebration of the rationality of the actual or the definitive accomplishment of reconciliation and not infrequently sound a sober note. Hegel speaks at the end of the lectures on the philosophy of religion of philosophers as a "caste" withdrawn from the immediate way of the world, and at the end of the philosophy of history of a certain "dissonance" (*Mißton*) in actuality and a "conflict" (*Kollision*) of elements and forces in the contemporary world that the future will have to resolve. Be that as it may, Adorno understandably asks why, as Hegel claims, the aim *must* be the 'affirmative' one of deciphering the present as the "hieroglyph of reason," rather than that of keeping open a space for the critical negativity of thought or,

not least, of art. (On the "hieroglyph of reason," see Hegel, *Werke*, VII:449.)

17. Georg Lukács, *Die Eigenart des Ästhetischen*, 2 vols. (Berlin: Neuwied, 1963), I:382–83. If science "attempts to represent objects and their relations as they are in themselves, independently of consciousness," then the 'anthropomorphic' character of "aesthetic reflection, on the other hand, proceeds from the human world and is directed to this world." Lukács, *Die Eigenart des Ästhetischen*, I:25.

18. Hegel, *Werke*, III:17.

19. See Martin Heidegger, *Sein und Zeit*, 17th ed. (Tübingen: Max Niemeyer Verlag, 1927, 1993), 131, 183. See, too, Martin Heidegger, *Kant und das Problem der Metaphysik*, ed. Friedrich-Wilhelm von Herrmann II, vol. 3, *Gesamtausgabe* (Frankfurt am Main: Vittorio Klostermann, 1991), §36.

20. From a letter to Isaak von Sinclair, dated December 24, 1798. In Friedrich Hölderlin, *Sämtliche Werke, Briefe und Dokumente*, ed. D. E. Sattler (München: Luchterhand Literaturverlag, 2004), VI:186–87.

21. See Hölderlin's letters of December 24 and 31, 1798, and that of June 14, 1799, in Hölderlin, *Sämtliche Werke*, VI:185–88 and VII:84–90.

22. Hegel, *Werke*, X:25.

CHAPTER 6

1. Theodor W. Adorno, *Aesthetic Theory*, trans. Robert Hullot-Kentor (Minneapolis: University of Minnesota Press, 1997), 230.

2. Adorno, *Aesthetic Theory*, 5.

3. Adorno, *Aesthetic Theory*, 79.

4. Adorno, *Aesthetic Theory*, 241.

5. Art appears to be less than praxis because it is not 'action' and seems ineffectual from the perspective of pragmatic action. "Art, however, is more than praxis because by its aversion to praxis it simultaneously denounces the narrow untruth of the practical world." See Adorno, *Aesthetic Theory*, 241.

6. Adorno, *Aesthetic Theory*, 241.

7. Theodor W. Adorno, *Ontologie und Dialektik*, ed. Rolf Tiedemann (Frankfurt am Main: Suhrkamp Verlag, 2002).

8. Adorno, *Ontologie und Dialektik*, 116.

9. Adorno, *Ontologie und Dialektik*, 117.

10. "*Das Nichts* der Ab-grund: Versagung des Grundes, jeder Stütze unde jedes Schutzes im Seienden; doch diese Versagung ist die höchste Gewährung der Not der Entscheidung und Unterscheidung." See Martin Heidegger, *Hegel*, ed. Ingrid Schüßler, vol. 68, *Gesamtausgabe* (Frankfurt am Main: Vittorio Klostermann, 1993), 47.

11. In *Besinnung*, Heidegger remarks that Hegel knew negativity only in terms of beingness (*Seiendheit*) and did not think it from being and the nothing in be-

ing: " . . . die Negativität nicht aus dem *Grunde* des Nichts und des Seyns entsprungen, sondern bei der Seiendheit als *Vorgestelltheit* stecken bleiben musste." Martin Heidegger, *Besinnung*, ed. Friedrich-Wilhelm von Herrmann II, vol. 66, *Gesamtausgabe* (Frankfurt am Main: Vittorio Klostermann, 1997), 293.

12. Heidegger, *Besinnung*, 67.

13. Martin Heidegger, *Die Geschichte des Seyns*, ed. Peter Trawny, vol. 69, *Gesamtausgabe* (Frankfurt am Main: Vittorio Klostermann, 1998), 50.

14. Martin Heidegger, "The Question Concerning Technology," in *Basic Writings*, ed. David Farrel Krell (New York: HarperCollins, 1993), 324–26.

15. Martin Heidegger, "The Origin of the Work of Art," in *Basic Writings*, ed. David Farrell Krell (New York: HarperCollins, 1993), 171–73.

16. Heidegger, *Besinnung*, 192–93.

17. Heidegger, *Besinnung*, 312.

18. Heidegger, *Besinnung*, 294–95.

19. Martin Heidegger, "Letter on Humanism," in *Basic Writings*, ed. David Farrel Krell (New York: HarperCollins, 1993), 220.

20. Heidegger, *Die Geschichte des Seyns*, 140.

21. "Als nichthaftes wesend ermöglicht und erzwingt es zugleich Andersheit." Martin Heidegger, *Beiträge zur Philosophie (Vom Ereignis)*, ed. Friedrich-Wilhelm von Herrmann II, vol. 65, *Gesamtausgabe* (Frankfurt am Main: Vittorio Klostermann, 1989), 267. For an English translation see Martin Heidegger, *Contributions to Philosophy: From Enowning*, trans. Parvis Emad and Kenneth Maly (Bloomington: Indiana University Press, 1999), 188.

22. This freedom, however, is never, despite frequent misunderstandings, simply anonymous or neutral, because release from power translates into the power-free disposition of relations, and into the freedom of beings involved in these relations. In other words, the freedom of *being* from power becomes coextensive with the release of *beings* from the workings of power. Freedom here refers to the power-free happening of being and is conceived in Heidegger, as Fred Dallmayr has shown, ontologically. It is thus seen more broadly than human freedom from injustice or oppression—without in any way depreciating their significance.

23. "Wie aber, wenn diese Verlassenheit des Seienden vom Sein der Anfang wäre einer ursprünglichen Geschichte, in der das Sein Seyn ist, so dass das immer wirklichere Wirkliche immer aussichtsloser vom Sein verstossen würde, vom Seyn als Verweigerung, der keine Macht und Übermacht gewachsen sein könnte, weil sie notwendig das Wesen des *von Grund aus* Macht-losen für immer verkennen müssen." See Heidegger, *Besinnung*, 190–91.

24. See Heidegger's discussion of power as essentially "constructive" and the non-productive doing as a lack in Heidegger, *Die Geschichte des Seyns*, 64.

CHAPTER 7

1. Theodor W. Adorno, *Gesammelte Schriften*, ed. Rolf Tiedemann, 20 vols. (Frankfurt am Main: Suhrkamp Verlag, 1997), VI:345. [Ed.: All translations from the German are the author's.]

2. Adorno, *GS*, VI:15.
3. Adorno, *GS*, X:743.
4. Adorno, *GS*, X:742.
5. Adorno, *GS*, X:746.
6. Adorno, *GS*, X:742.
7. Adorno, *GS*, VI:191.
8. Adorno, *GS*, VI:16.
9. Adorno, *GS*, VI:17.
10. Adorno, *GS*, VI:192.
11. Adorno, *GS*, VI:164f.
12. Adorno, *GS*, VI:164.
13. Adorno, *GS*, X:749.
14. Adorno, *GS*, X:602.
15. Adorno, *GS*, VI:38.
16. Adorno, *GS*, X:602.
17. Adorno, *GS*, X:604.
18. Adorno, *GS*, VI:191.
19. Adorno, *GS*, IV:47.
20. Adorno, *GS*, XVIII:495.
21. Adorno, *GS*, XVI:92.
22. Adorno, *GS*, IV:53f.
23. Adorno, *GS*, IV:46f.
24. Adorno, *GS*, X:602f.
25. Adorno, *GS*, IV:112.
26. Adorno, *GS*, VI:191.
27. Adorno, *GS*, IV:240.
28. Adorno, *GS*, VI:192.
29. Adorno, *GS*, VI:174.

30. Martin Heidegger, "Überwindung der Metaphysik," in *Vorträge und Aufsätze* (Pfullingen: Neske, 1954), 92.

31. Martin Heidegger, "Das Ding," in *Vorträge und Aufsätze* (Pfullingen: Neske, 1954), 171.

32. Heidegger, "Das Ding," 164, 169.

33. Heidegger, "Das Ding," 163f.

34. Martin Heidegger, "Bauen Wohnen Denken," in *Vorträge und Aufsätze* (Pfullingen: Neske, 1954), 154.

35. Heidegger, "Das Ding," 176.

36. Heidegger, "Das Ding," 164.

37. Martin Heidegger, "Zur Erörterung der Gelassenheit. Aus einem Feldweggespräch über das Denken," in *Gelassenheit* (Pfullingen: Neske, 1959), 69.

38. Heidegger, "Das Ding," 180.

39. Heidegger, "Bauen Wohnen Denken," 149.

40. Heidegger, "Bauen Wohnen Denken," 151.

41. Heidegger, "Bauen Wohnen Denken."

42. Heidegger, "Das Ding," 180.

43. Heidegger, "Bauen Wohnen Denken," 162.

44. Martin Heidegger, *Gesamtausgabe* (Frankfurt am Main: Vittorio Klostermann, 1975ff.), LXXVII:196.

45. Martin Heidegger, *Bemerkungen zu Kunst - Plastik - Raum*, ed. Hermann Heidegger (St. Gallen: Erker Verlag, 1996), 15.

46. Martin Heidegger, "Gelassenheit," in *Gelassenheit* (Pfullingen: Neske, 1959), 25.

47. Heidegger, *GA*, XLV:2.   49. Adorno, *GS*, VI:133.
48. Adorno, *GS*, X:604.   50. Adorno, *GS*, VI:192.

CHAPTER 8

1. This article draws on Josef Früchtl, *Das unverschämte Ich. Eine Heldenge-schichte der Moderne* (Frankfurt am Main: Suhrkamp Verlag, 2004). The part on Heidegger is completely new.

2. See Herbert Schnädelbach, *Hegel zur Einführung* (Hamburg: Junius, 1999), 14, 42.

3. See Martha Nussbaum, *The Fragility of Goodness: Luck and Ethics in Greek Tragedy and Philosophy* (Cambridge: Cambridge University Press, 1986). See also Christoph Menke, *Tragödie im Sittlichen. Gerechtigkeit und Freiheit nach Hegel* (Frankfurt am Main: Suhrkamp Verlag, 1996).

4. [Ed.: The celebrated phrase of F. H. Bradley, which serves as the epigraph to part two of *Minima Moralia*.]

5. See Herbert Schnädelbach, "Philosophieren nach Heidegger und Ador-no," in *Zur Rehabilitierung des animal rationale. Vorträge und Abhandlungen II* (Frankfurt am Main: Suhrkamp Verlag, 1992), 309. For the 'short' twentieth century from the First World War to the breakdown of the Soviet Union, see Eric Hobsbawm, *Age of Extremes: The Short Twentieth Century 1914–1991* (London: Michael Joseph, 1994).

6. Theodor W. Adorno, *Minima Moralia. Reflexionen aus dem beschädigten Leben* (Frankfurt am Main: Suhrkamp Verlag, 1979), §97, 195. [Ed.: All translations from the German are the author's.]

7. Adorno, *Minima Moralia*, §17, 39.

8. Theodor W. Adorno, *Gesammelte Schriften*, ed. Rolf Tiedemann, 20 vols. (Frankfurt am Main: Suhrkamp Verlag, 1997), XVII:34. See Markus Schroer, *Das Individuum der Gesellschaft. Synchrone und diachrone Theorieperspektiven* (Frankfurt am Main: Suhrkamp Verlag, 2001), 58.

9. Adorno, *GS*, VIII:443.

10. Adorno, *GS*, VIII:450.

11. Max Weber, "Die protestantische Ethik und der 'Geist' des Kapitalismus," in *Gesammelte Aufsätze zur Religionssoziologie I* (Tübingen: Mohr-Siebeck, 1983), 95.

12. Max Horkheimer and Theodor W. Adorno, *Dialektik der Aufklärung. Philosophische Fragmente* (Amsterdam: de Munter, 1968), 71.

13. Adorno, *Minima Moralia*, §36, 69.

14. See Josef Früchtl, "Adorno and Mimesis," in *Encyclopedia of Aesthetics*, ed. Michael Kelly (Oxford: Oxford University Press, 1998), 23–25.

15. Adorno, *Minima Moralia*, §40, 78.

16. Martin Heidegger, *Gesamtausgabe* (Frankfurt am Main: Vittorio Klostermann, 1975ff.), XLIII:194.

17. Friedrich Nietzsche, *Kritische Studienausgabe*, ed. Giorgio Colli and Mazzino Montinari, 15 vols. (München/Berlin/New York: dtv/de Gruyter, 1988), IV:261.

18. See Jürgen Habermas, *Der philosophische Diskurs der Moderne. Zwölf Vorlesungen* (Frankfurt am Main: Suhrkamp Verlag, 1985), 167. Cf. F. K. Ringer, *The Decline of the German Mandarins* (Cambridge, Mass.: Harvard University Press, 1969). See also Steven E. Aschheim, *Nietzsche und die Deutschen, Karriere eines Kults* (Stuttgart/Weimar: Metzler, 1996), 164; Richard Wolin, *The Politics of Being: The Political Thought of Martin Heidegger* (New York: Columbia University Press, 1990), 81.

19. See Aschheim, *Nietzsche und die Deutschen*, 161; Wolin, *The Politics of Being*, 78, 81.

20. Robert B. Pippin, *Modernism as a Philosophical Problem: On the Dissatisfactions of European High Culture* (Oxford: Blackwell, 1991), 133. See also Otto Pöggeler, *Der Denkweg Martin Heideggers* (Pfullingen: Neske, 1963), 104.

21. See Wolfgang Welsch, *Unsere postmoderne Moderne* (Weinheim: VCH, 1988), 143.

22. See Annemarie Pieper, "Zarathustra als Verkünder des Übermenschen und als Fürsprecher des Kreises," in *Friedrich Nietzsche. Also sprach Zarathustra*, ed. Volker Gerhardt (Berlin: Akademie Verlag, 2000), 111.

23. Nietzsche, *KSA*, XI:105.

24. Nietzsche, *KSA*, IV:152.

25. Nietzsche, *KSA*, IV:152. See also Nietzsche, *KSA*, X:503; Immanuel Kant, *Kritik der Urteilskraft, Gesammelte Schriften* (Berlin: Akademie der Wissenschaften in Göttingen, 1900ff.), V, §5; Martin Heidegger, *Was ist Metaphysik?* (Frankfurt am Main: Klostermann, 1969), 49.

26. Heidegger, *Was ist Metaphysik?*, 13, 21, 22, 49; Martin Heidegger, *Gelassenheit* (Pfullingen: Neske, 1959).

27. See Habermas, *Der philosophische Diskurs der Moderne*, 163, 168.

28. Heidegger, *Gelassenheit*, 23.

29. Martin Heidegger, "Der Ursprung des Kunstwerks," in *Holzwege* (Frankfurt am Main: Klostermann, 1950), 37.

30. Martin Heidegger, *Beiträge zur Philosophie (Vom Ereignis)*, ed. Friedrich-Wilhelm von Herrmann II, vol. 65, *Gesamtausgabe* (Frankfurt am Main: Vittorio Klostermann, 1989), 186.

31. See Welsch, *Unsere postmoderne Moderne*, 147, 157; Günter Figal, *Heidegger zur Einführung* (Hamburg: Junius, 1996), 162.

32. Figal, *Heidegger zur Einführung*, 161.

CHAPTER 9

1. Andreas Huyssen, *Present Pasts* (Stanford: Stanford University Press, 2003).

2. Martin Heidegger, *What Is Called Thinking?*, trans. J. Glenn Gray (New York: Harper & Row, 1968), 25.

3. Heidegger, *What Is Called Thinking?*, 17.

4. See Martin Heidegger, *Hölderlins Hymne "Andenken"* (Frankfurt am Main: Vittorio Klostermann, 1982).

5. Heidegger, *What Is Called Thinking?*, 11.

6. Heidegger, *What Is Called Thinking?*, 69f.

7. See for example Jürgen Habermas, *The Philosophical Discourse of Modernity*, trans. Frederick G. Lawrence (Cambridge, Mass.: MIT Press, 1987), 134.

8. Heidegger, *Hölderlins Hymne "Andenken,"* 54.

9. Heidegger, *Hölderlins Hymne "Andenken,"* 55.

10. Richard McKean, ed., *The Basic Works of Aristotle* (New York: Random House, 1941), 616, 453a.

11. The most prominent are "The Meaning of Working Through the Past" (1959) and "Education After Auschwitz" (1966), both of which were broadcast by Hessischer Rundfunk and are included in Theodor W. Adorno, *Critical Models: Interventions and Catchwords*, trans. Henry W. Pickford (New York: Columbia University Press, 1998).

12. Adorno, *Critical Models*, 101.

13. Adorno, *Critical Models*, 131.

14. This is not to claim that there are no passages that suggest such a reading. What I do want to argue is that a more convincing, thoroughly dialectical reading takes seriously Adorno's claim that any form of linear construction of a universal history is problematic. It is important to read the "dark" passages in the context of Adorno's methodological conviction that "only exaggeration per se today can be the medium of truth . . . to delineate a tendency concealed behind the smooth façade of everyday life before it overflows the institutional dams that, for the time being, are erected against it." *Critical Models*, 99.

15. Martin Heidegger, *Erläuterungen zu Hölderlins Dichtung* (Frankfurt am Main: Vittorio Klostermann, 1981), 87.

16. Alexander García Düttmann, *The Memory of Thought: An Essay on Heidegger and Adorno*, trans. Nicholas Walker (New York/London: Continuum, 2002), 261.

17. Adorno, *Critical Models*, 91.

18. Adorno, *Critical Models*, 193.

19. See Dieter Henrich, *The Course of Remembrance and Other Essays on Hölderlin* (Stanford: Stanford University Press, 1997), 213.

20. Adorno, *Critical Models*, 6.

21. Heidegger, *What Is Called Thinking?*, 38.

22. Adorno, *Critical Models*, 100.

23. Adorno, *Critical Models*, 90.

24. Walter Benjamin, "The Concept of Criticism in German Romanticism," in *Selected Writings, Volume 1* (Cambridge, Mass.: Harvard University Press, 1996), 153.

25. Both 'debt' and 'guilt' are possible translations of the German *Schuld*. See also Martin Jay, *Force Fields* (London: Routledge, 1993), 171.

26. Jan Assmann has argued that it has been the concept of guilt, which allows for a form of remembrance of a meaningful past. See: Jan Assmann, *Das kulturelle Gedächtnis. Schrift, Erinnerung und politische Identität in frühen Hochkulturen* (München: C. H. Beck, 1999).

27. Max Horkheimer and Theodor W. Adorno, *Dialectic of Enlightenment*, trans. John Cumming (New York: Seabury Press, 1972), 3; Theodor W. Adorno, *Gesammelte Schriften*, ed. Rolf Tiedemann, 20 vols. (Frankfurt am Main: Suhrkamp Verlag, 1997), III:19.

28. I would like to thank Lydia Goehr for stylistic improvements.

CHAPTER 10

1. Aristotle, *Politics*, ed. Jonathan Barnes, 2 vols., *The Complete Works of Aristotle* (Princeton: Princeton University Press), 1252b. (Aristotle ascribes the saying to "our poets.") Regarding Kant, see Immanuel Kant, "An Answer to the Question: What Is Enlightenment?," in *Kant's Political Writings*, ed. Hans Reiss, trans. H. B. Nisbet (Cambridge: Cambridge University Press, 1970), 54–60.

2. Max Horkheimer, *Eclipse of Reason* (New York: Seabury Press, 1974), 97. With regard to fascism, Horkheimer added this important further qualification: "In modern fascism, rationality has reached a point at which it is no longer satisfied with simply repressing nature; rationality now exploits nature by incorporating into its own system the rebellious potentialities of nature. The Nazis manipulated the repressed desires of the German people." With proper modification, something similar could be said about contemporary forms of 'fundamentalism.' See Horkheimer, *Eclipse of Reason*, 121.

3. Max Horkheimer and Theodor W. Adorno, *Dialectic of Enlightenment*, trans. John Cumming (New York: Seabury Press, 1972), xiii, 3; *Dialektik der Aufklärung* (Frankfurt am Main: Fischer, 1969), 3, 9. (In the above and subsequent citations I have slightly altered the translation for purposes of clarity.)

4. Horkheimer and Adorno, *Dialectic of Enlightenment*, 4, 8–10. "Enlightenment," the text continues, "behaves toward things like a dictator toward men: he knows them only insofar as he can manipulate them." Revealingly, the authors

draw a parallel between 'commanding' and the modern infatuation with 'making' or instrumental fabrication—an infatuation that needs to be sharply distinguished from the realm of doing or 'praxis,' especially political praxis.

5. Horkheimer and Adorno, *Dialectic of Enlightenment*, 7, 14, 29. The insight that modernity, while ostensibly promoting human freedom or emancipation, at the same time tightens the network of social disciplines was later developed in greater detail by Michel Foucault; see especially Michel Foucault, *Discipline and Punish: The Birth of the Prison*, trans. Alan Sheridan (New York: Vintage Books, 1979).

6. Horkheimer and Adorno, *Dialectic of Enlightenment*, 24, 39–42. Compare also their comment on the sense of remembrance: "The issue is not the conservation of the past but the redemption of the hopes of the past" (xv). The idea of an "unmanageable" or incalculable future resonates with the title of one of Jean-Luc Nancy's writings: see Jean-Luc Nancy, *The Inoperative Community*, trans. Peter Connor et al. (Minneapolis: University of Minnesota Press, 1991); *La communauté désœuvrée* (Paris: Bourgeois, 1986). Compare in this context also a text of mine: Fred Dallmayr, "An 'Inoperative' Global Community? Reflections on Nancy," in *Alternative Visions: Paths in the Global Village* (Landham, Md.: Rowman & Littlefield, 1998), 277–97.

7. Theodor W. Adorno, *Negative Dialectics*, trans. E. B. Ashton (London: Routledge & Kegan Paul, 1973), 8, 27–28; *Gesammelte Schriften*, ed. Rolf Tiedemann, 20 vols. (Frankfurt am Main: Suhrkamp Verlag, 1997), VI:17–18, 36. (In the above and subsequent citations I have slightly altered the translation for purposes of clarity.)

8. Adorno, *Negative Dialectics*, 6–7, 12, 19. As one should note, the above critique does not simply mean a substitution of multiplicity for unity and of particularity for universality. As Adorno adds soberly, "Like Kant and the entire philosophical tradition including Plato, Hegel is a partisan of unity. Yet, an abstract denial of the latter would not befit thinking either. The illusion of grasping the manifold directly would mean mimetic regression and a lapse into myth, into the horrors of diffuseness—just as unitary thinking, imitating blind nature through its repression, ends in mythical dominion at the opposite pole. Self-reflection of enlightenment is not its revocation." See Adorno, *Negative Dialectics*, 160.

9. Adorno, *Negative Dialectics*, 141, 179–80, 191.

10. Compare in this regard my "Adorno and Heidegger," in Fred R. Dallmayr, *Between Freiburg and Frankfurt: Toward a Critical Ontology* (Amherst: University of Massachusetts Press, 1991), 44–71. See also Hermann Mörchen, *Adorno und Heidegger. Untersuchung einer philosophischen Kommunikationsverweigerung* (Stuttgart: Klett-Cotta, 1981).

11. Martin Heidegger, *Beiträge zur Philosophie (Vom Ereignis)*, ed. Friedrich-

Wilhelm von Herrmann II, vol. 65, *Gesamtausgabe* (Frankfurt am Main: Vittorio Klostermann, 1989), 38–40, 42. For an English translation (not followed here) see Martin Heidegger, *Contributions to Philosophy: From Enowning*, trans. Parvis Emad and Kenneth Maly (Bloomington: Indiana University Press, 1999). The critique of worldviews/ideologies was continued and deepened in "Die Zeit des Weltbildes" (1938), where Heidegger denounced the increasingly virulent "contest of world-views" (*Kampf der Weltanschauungen*). See Martin Heidegger, *Holzwege* (Frankfurt am Main: Kostermann, 1950), 69–104, especially 87. For an English translation see Martin Heidegger, "The Age of the World Picture," in *The Question Concerning Technology*, trans. W. Lovitt (New York: Harper & Row, 1977), 115–54.

12. Heidegger, *Beiträge*, 126–32. As one should note, Heidegger always differentiates carefully between *Erlebnis* (emotive feeling) and *Erfahrung* (which Dasein has to shoulder or undergo).

13. Heidegger, *Beiträge*, 50–51, 140, 282. In Heidegger's words: "Ereignis hands over (*übereignet*) God to humans while dedicating/consecrating (*zueignet*) humans to God." See Heidegger, *Beiträge*, 26.

14. Martin Heidegger, *Besinnung*, ed. Friedrich-Wilhelm von Herrmann II, vol. 66, *Gesamtausgabe* (Frankfurt am Main: Vittorio Klostermann, 1997), 16–17, 122–23. As he adds, "Are humans here not definitively fixated as oriented toward the control and mastery of beings (while abandoning and being abandoned by being, *Seinsverlassenheit*)." See Heidegger, *Besinnung*, 123.

15. Heidegger, *Besinnung*, 16–17, 22, 187–88, 191. According to the text, our time finds itself at a crossroads or parting of ways: a parting that determines "whether *Machenschaft* finally overwhelms humans, unleashing them into limitless power-seekers, or whether being discloses its truth as a need—a need through which the encounter/counterpoint (*Entgegnung*) of God and humans intersects with the chiasm between earth and world." See Heidegger, *Besinnung*, 15. I am indebted to Krzysztof Ziarek for the felicitous rendering of *machtlos* as "power-free."

16. Martin Heidegger, *Die Geschichte des Seyns*, ed. Peter Trawny, vol. 69, *Gesamtausgabe* (Frankfurt am Main: Vittorio Klostermann, 1998), 46–48, 50, 64, 69, 76–78.

17. Heidegger, *Die Geschichte des Seyns*, 44, 63, 70, 77–78, 180, 209. For a critique of "leaders" (Führer) as supreme technicians, see Martin Heidegger, *The End of Philosophy*, trans. J. Stambaugh (New York: Harper & Row, 1973), 103–109; "Überwindung der Metaphysik," in *Vorträge und Aufsätze* (Pfullingen: Neske, 1954), 71–99, especially 85–88.

18. This strategy was already in place at the time of the conquest of the Americas. In the words of Tomás de Torquemada, commenting on the Spanish conquest of the Aztec empire: "Less than one hundred Castilians died, a few horses. . . . Of the Mexicans one hundred thousand died, without counting the ones who died of

hunger and plague." See his *Monarquia Indiana,* cited by Enrique Dussel, *The Underside of Modernity: Apel, Ricoeur, Rorty, Taylor, and the Philosophy of Liberation*, trans. Eduardo Mendieta (Atlantic Highlands, N.J.: Humanities Press, 1996), 52. Recent superpower wars against third-world countries reveal a similar scenario.

19. Arundhati Roy, *The Cost of Living* (New York: Modern Library, 1999), 79.

Bibliography

This specialized bibliography contains primary and secondary literature relevant to the Adorno-Heidegger debate and its history. We do not claim to have exhausted the literature, but the following will certainly give the reader an excellent idea of the state of research today. It lists the main works by Adorno that discuss Heidegger at some length, but by the same token it does not list works by Heidegger. Discussions of the Adorno-Heidegger dispute in the works listed vary in length and are sometimes oblique.

Adorno, Theodor W. "The Actuality of Philosophy." In *The Adorno Reader*, edited by Brian O'Connor. Translated by Benjamin Snow. Oxford: Blackwell, 2000. This translation first appeared in *Telos* 31 (Spring 1977): 120–33. Original: Adorno, Theodor W. *Gesammelte Schriften*. Edited by Rolf Tiedemann. 20 vols. Frankfurt am Main: Suhrkamp Verlag, 1997, vol. I.

———. "Der Begriff der Philosophie." In *Frankfurter Adorno Blätter II*, edited by the Theodor W. Adorno Archiv. München: edition text+kritik, 1993.

———. "The Idea of Natural History." *Telos* 60 (Summer 1984): 111–24. Original: Adorno, Theodor W. *Gesammelte Schriften*. Edited by Rolf Tiedemann. 20 vols. Frankfurt am Main: Suhrkamp Verlag, 1997, vol. I.

———. *The Jargon of Authenticity*. Translated by Knut Tarnowski and Frederic Will. London and Henley: Routledge & Kegan Paul, 1973. Original: *Jargon der Eigentlichkeit. Zur deutschen Ideologie*. Frankfurt am Main: Suhrkamp Verlag, 1964.

———. *Negative Dialectics*. Translated by E. B. Ashton. London: Routledge & Kegan Paul, 1973. Original: *Negative Dialektik*. Frankfurt am Main: Suhrkamp Verlag, 1966.

———. *Ontologie und Dialektik*. Edited by Rolf Tiedemann and the Theodor W. Adorno Archiv. Frankfurt am Main: Suhrkamp Verlag, 2002.

———. *Philosophische Terminologie*. 2 vols. Frankfurt am Main: Suhrkamp Verlag, 1973.

Baur, Michael. "Adorno and Heidegger on Art in the Modern World." *Philosophy Today* 40, no. 3 (Fall 1996): 357–66.

Bernstein, Jay M. *The Fate of Art: Aesthetic Alienation from Kant to Derrida and Adorno.* Cambridge: Polity Press, 1992.

Bowie, Andrew. "Adorno, Heidegger, and the Meaning of Music." In *The Cambridge Companion to Adorno*, edited by Tom Huhn. Cambridge: Cambridge University Press, 2004. First appeared as "Adorno, Heidegger, and the Meaning of Music." *Thesis Eleven* 56 (1999): 1–24.

Brunkhorst, Hauke. "Adorno, Heidegger and Postmodernity." *Philosophy and Social Criticism* 14, no. 3–4 (1989): 411–24. Original: Brunkhorst, Hauke. "Adorno, Heidegger und die Postmoderne." In *Martin Heidegger: Innen- und Außenansichten*, edited by the Forum für Philosophie Bad Homburg. Frankfurt am Main: Suhrkamp Verlag, 1989.

———. "Weder Affirmation noch Ausstieg: Adorno, Heidegger und die Hegelsche Rechte." In *Theodor W. Adorno: Dialektik der Moderne*, edited by Hauke Brunkhorst. München and Zürich: Piper, 1990.

Cascardi, Anthony J. "Heidegger, Adorno, and the Persistence of Romanticism." *Dialogue and Universalism* 13, no. 11–12 (2003): 13–22.

Dallmayr, Fred R. "Adorno and Heidegger." *Diacritics* 19, no. 3–4 (1989): 82–100.

———. *Between Freiburg and Frankfurt: Toward a Critical Ontology.* Amherst: University of Massachusetts Press, 1991.

Dews, Peter. *Logics of Disintegration.* London: Verso, 1987.

De Mul, Jos. "Hegel, Heidegger, Adorno and the Ends of Art." *Dialogue and Universalism* 13, no. 11–12 (2003): 23–41.

Eley, Lothar. "Konstruktive Phänomenologie und kritische Theorie. Adornos Kritik der transzendentalen Phänomenologie Husserls. Eine Anmerkung zu Heideggers Seinsfrage." In *Die Negative Dialektik Adornos. Einführung—Dialog*, edited by Jürgen Naeher. Opladen: Leske Verlag + Budrich, 1984.

Erjavec, Aleš. "Adorno and/with Heidegger: From Modernism to Postmodernism." *Dialogue and Universalism* 13, no. 11–12 (2003): 53–66.

Escoubas, Éliane. "Le *polemos* Adorno-Heidegger." In Theodor W. Adorno, *Jargon de l'authenticité*, translated by Éliane Escoubas. Paris: Payot, 1989.

Früchtl, Josef. "Zeit und Erfahrung: Adornos Revision der Revision Heideggers." In *Martin Heidegger: Innen- und Außenansichten*, edited by the Forum für Philosophie Bad Homburg. Frankfurt am Main: Suhrkamp Verlag, 1989.

Gandesha, Samir. "Leaving Home: On Adorno and Heidegger." In *The Cambridge Companion to Adorno*, edited by Tom Huhn. Cambridge: Cambridge University Press, 2004.

————. "Writing and Judging: Adorno, Arendt and the Chiasmus of Natural History." *Philosophy and Social Criticism* 30, no. 4 (2004): 445–475.

Garbrecht, Oliver. *Rationalitätskritik der Moderne. Adorno und Heidegger.* München: Herbert Utz Verlag, 1999.

García Düttmann, Alexander. *The Memory of Thought: An Essay on Heidegger and Adorno.* Translated by Nicholas Walker. New York/London: Continuum, 2002. Original: García Düttmann, Alexander. *Das Gedächtnis des Denkens. Versuch über Heidegger und Adorno.* Frankfurt am Main: Suhrkamp Verlag, 1991.

Geulen, Eva. *Das Ende der Kunst. Lesarten eines Gerüchts nach Hegel.* Frankfurt am Main: Suhrkamp Verlag, 2002.

Guzzoni, Ute. *Identität oder nicht. Zur kritischen Theorie der Ontologie.* Freiburg/München: Karl Alber Verlag, 1981.

————. *Sieben Stücke zu Adorno.* Freiburg/München: Karl Alber Verlag, 2003.

————. *Wendungen. Versuche zu einem nicht identifizierenden Denken.* Freiburg/München: Karl Alber Verlag, 1998.

Hodge, Joanna. "Adorno and Heidegger: Between Aesthetics and Politics." In *The New Aestheticism*, edited by John J. Joughin and Simon Malpas. Manchester: Manchester University Press, 2003.

Hohendahl, Peter Uwe. *Prismatic Thought: Theodor W. Adorno.* Lincoln and London: University of Nebraska Press, 1995.

Huhn, Tom. "Heidegger, Adorno, and Mimesis." *Dialogue and Universalism* 13, no. 11–12 (2003): 43–52.

Jarvis, Simon. *Adorno: A Critical Introduction.* Cambridge: Polity Press, 1998.

————. "Thinking-cum-Knowing. Review of Alexander García Düttmann, *The Memory of Thought: An Essay on Adorno and Heidegger.*" *Radical Philosophy* 117 (2003): 43–45.

Jay, Martin. "Is Experience Still in Crisis? Reflections on a Frankfurt School Lament." In *The Cambridge Companion to Adorno*, edited by Tom Huhn. Cambridge: Cambridge University Press, 2004.

Kompridis, Nikolas. "Heidegger's Challenge and the Future of Critical Theory." In *Habermas: A Critical Reader*, edited by Peter Dews. Oxford: Blackwell, 1999.

Macdonald, Iain. "Returning to the 'House of Oblivion': Celan Between Adorno and Heidegger." In *Adorno and Literature,* edited by David Cunningham and Nigel Mapp. New York/London: Continuum, 2006.

McCarthy, Thomas. "Heidegger and Critical Theory: The First Encounter." In *Ideals and Illusions: On Reconstruction and Deconstruction in Contemporary Critical Theory*, edited by Thomas McCarthy. Cambridge, Mass.: MIT Press, 1991.

Mörchen, Hermann. *Adorno und Heidegger. Untersuchung einer philosophischen Kommunikationsverweigerung.* Stuttgart: Klett-Cotta, 1981.

————. *Macht und Herrschaft im Denken von Heidegger und Adorno.* Stuttgart: Klett-Cotta, 1980.

Naeher, Jürgen. "Das ontologische »Bedürfnis im Denken«. Das erste Teil der *Negativen Dialektik* (67–136): Zum Verfahren der »immanenten Kritik«." In *Die Negative Dialektik Adornos. Einführung—Dialog*, edited by Jürgen Naeher. Opladen: Leske Verlag + Budrich, 1984.

O'Connor, Brian. "Adorno, Heidegger and the Critique of Epistemology." *Philosophy and Social Criticism* 24, no. 4 (1998): 43–62.

————. *Adorno's Negative Dialectic: Philosophy and the Possibility of Critical Rationality.* Cambridge, Mass.: MIT Press, 2005.

Ouattara, Bourahima. *Adorno et Heidegger: une controverse philosophique.* Paris: L'Harmattan, 1999.

Paetzold, Heinz. "Adorno and Heidegger In-/Outside Postmodern Culture." *Dialogue and Universalism* 13, no. 11–12 (2003): 67–81.

Petitdemange, Guy. "Au-delà de la philosophie par la philosophie." In Theodor W. Adorno, *Jargon de l'authenticité*, translated by Éliane Escoubas. Paris: Payot, 1989.

Polti, Adolf. "Ontologie als »Inbegriff von Negativität«. Zu Adornos Interpretation der Philosophie Heideggers." In *Martin Heidegger: Innen- und Außenansichten*, edited by the Forum für Philosophie Bad Homburg. Frankfurt am Main: Suhrkamp Verlag, 1989.

Rath, Norbert. *Adornos Kritische Theorie. Vermittlungen und Vermittlungsschwierigkeiten.* Paderborn and München: Ferdinand Schöningh, 1982.

Roberts, David. "Art and Myth: Adorno and Heidegger." *Thesis Eleven* 58 (August 1999): 19–34.

Rochlitz, Rainer. "Le *Jargon* en français." *Critique* 503 (April 1990).

Rose, Gillian. *The Melancholy Science: An Introduction to the Thought of Theodor W. Adorno.* New York: Columbia University Press, 1978.

Rosiek, Jan. *Maintaining the Sublime: Heidegger and Adorno.* New York: Peter Lang, 2000.

Scheible, Hartmut. *Theodor W. Adorno.* Reinbek bei Hamburg: Rowohlt Taschenbuch Verlag, 1989.

Schmidt, Dennis. "Adorno and Heidegger (by H. Mörchen)." *International Studies in Philosophy* 18, no. 1 (1986): 106–8.

Schnädelbach, Herbert. "Dialektik als Vernunftkritik. Zur Konstruktion des Rationalen bei Adorno." In *Adorno-Konferenz 1983*, edited by Ludwig von Friedeburg and Jürgen Habermas. Frankfurt am Main: Suhrkamp Verlag, 1983.

————. "Philosophieren nach Heidegger und Adorno." In *Zur Rehabilitierung des animal rationale. Vorträge und Abhandlungen 2*, edited by Herbert Schnädelbach. Frankfurt am Main: Suhrkamp Verlag, 1992.

Schröter, Hartmut, ed. *Technik und Kunst. Heidegger-Adorno*. Münster: Parabel/liberación, 1988.

Schwarte, Ludger. *Die Regeln der Intuition. Kunstphilosophie nach Adorno, Heidegger und Wittgenstein*. München: Wilhelm Fink Verlag, 2000.

Seubold, Günter. *Das Ende der Kunst und der Paradigmenwechsel in der Ästhetik: Philosophische Untersuchungen zu Adorno, Heidegger und Gehlen in systematischer Absicht*. Freiburg: Karl Alber Verlag, 1999.

Sherman, David. "Adorno's Kierkegaardian Debt." *Philosophy and Social Criticism* 27, no. 1 (2001): 77–106.

Tietz, Udo. *Ontologie und Dialektik. Heidegger und Adorno über das Sein, das Nichtidentische, die Synthesis und die Kopula*. Wien: Passagen Verlag, 2003.

Vorlaufer, Johannes. "Negative Dialektik und Hermeneutik des Daseins. Zur Kritik der Dialektik bei Heidegger und Adorno." In *Vielfalt und Konvergenz der Philosophie. Vorträge des 5. Kongresses der Österreichischen Gesellschaft für Philosophie*, edited by Winfried Löffler and Edmund Runggaldier. Wien: öbv & hpt, 1998.

Wenning, Mario. "Heidegger and Adorno: Opening Up Grounds for a Dialogue." *Gnosis* 6, no. 1 (September 2002).

Wiggershaus, Rolf. *The Frankfurt School*. Cambridge: Polity Press, 1994.

Wilke, Sabine. *Zur Dialektik von Exposition und Darstellung: Ansätze zu einer Kritik der Arbeiten Martin Heideggers, Theodor W. Adornos und Jacques Derridas*. New York and Frankfurt am Main: Peter Lang, 1988.

Wisser, Richard. "Das Fernseh-Interview." In *Erinnerung an Martin Heidegger*, edited by Günther Neske. Pfullingen: Verlag Günther Neske, 1977.

Wurzer, Wilhelm S. *Filming and Judgment: Between Heidegger and Adorno*. Atlantic Highlands, N.J.: Humanities Press International, 1990.

Ziarek, Krzysztof. "Radical Art: Reflections After Adorno and Heidegger." In *Adorno: A Critical Reader*, edited by Nigel Gibson and Andrew Rubin. Oxford: Blackwell, 2002.

Index